WARRIOR IN TWO CAMPS

THE Iroquois AND THEIR NEIGHBORS

Laurence M. Hauptman, Series Editor

Ely S. Parker or Do-ne-ho-ga-wa, Seneca sachem, wearing the medal he inherited from his ancestor, the Seneca orator Red Jacket. The photograph matches the description of a picture taken at Elmira, New York, in 1855. *Courtesy of the Western Reserve Historical Society, Cleveland, Ohio.*

WARRIOR
IN TWO CAMPS

ELY S. PARKER
Union General and Seneca Chief

WILLIAM H. ARMSTRONG

SYRACUSE UNIVERSITY PRESS

All Rights Reserved
First Paperback Edition, 1989
14 15 16 17 18   10 9 8 7 6

This book is published withthe assistance of a grant from the
John Ben Snow Foundation.

Winner of the 1978 John Ben Snow Manuscript Prize

∞The paper used in this publication meets the minimum requirements of the American
National Standard for Information Sciences—Permanence of Paper
for Printed Library Materials, ANSI Z39.48-1992.

For a listing of books published and distributed by Syracuse University Press,
visit our website at www.SyracuseUniversityPress.syr.edu.

ISBN: 978-0-8156-2495-0

Library of Congress Cataloging in Publication Data
The Library of Congress has cataloged the first printing of this title as follows:
Armstrong, William Howard, 1932–
Warrior in two camps.

(An Iroquois book)
Bibliography: p.
Includes index.
1. Parker, Ely Samuel, 1828–1895.   2. Seneca
Indians —Biography.   3. Generals—United States—
Biography. 4. United States.   Army—Biography.
I. Title. II. Series.
E99.S3P3253   970'.004'97   [B]   78-5719
ISBN 0-8156-0143-3
ISBN 0-8156-2495-6 (pbk.)

Manufactured in the United States of America

WILLIAM H. ARMSTRONG holds the B.A. in philosophy from Swarthmore College, M.Div. from Union Theological Seminary in New York City, and S.T.M. from the Lutheran Theological Seminary at Philadelphia. He is the author of *Organs for America: The Life and Work of David Tannenberg* (Foreword by E. Power Biggs); *Minister, Heal Thyself;* and *A Friend to God's Poor: Edward Parmelee Smith*. He served as associate director of the Peace Corps in Ethiopia and as director of the Peace Corps in Swaziland. He is presently pastor of the Burton Congregational Church (United Church of Christ) in Burton, Ohio.

Contents

Preface

THE NAME ELY SAMUEL PARKER is seldom found among famous Indian chiefs. Indeed the name seems somehow out of place in the company of men called Black Hawk or Crazy Horse or Geronimo. But the prosaic name is part of the story of an American Indian who chose to live his life in the white man's world. It is a story in which a frock coat replaces the traditional deerskin, and a surveyor's level and a soldier's orderly book take the place of the wampum belt and the war club.

Still, it is an Indian story. Ely Parker was a Seneca Indian from the Tonawanda Reservation in western New York who began his life in a cradleboard hung on the branch of a tree and who boasted that he could track a deer on the run over leaves and follow the trail of a snake. And he had not one Indian name but two; he was called Ha-sa-no-an-da, "Leading Name," as a child, and Do-ne-ho-ga-wa, "Open Door," after he became a sachem of the Iroquois Confederacy in 1851.[1]

That he had also been given an English name was not unusual. Many Senecas received English names, even when they rejected the culture of the whites. But he readily accepted that culture, and his use of the name Ely Parker was symbolic of the life he chose to live. From an early age he was determined to enter the white world, to compete with white men on their own terms, in their own society, and he succeeded in rising to a position in that society that was the envy of many white men. Well educated for the day, he was trained in the law, although he was not admitted to the New York State bar or permitted to practice because Indians were not considered citizens. He was also an accomplished civil engineer who held important engineering posts under both the New York and the federal governments. A close student of the Indians, especially the Iroquois or Six Nations of Indians of which the Senecas were a part, he collaborated in preparing one of the first scientific accounts of that or any other group of Indians. He was a skillful diplomat, representing the Tonawanda Senecas in Albany and Washington while still in his teens, conferring with presidents from Polk to Buchanan, and pursuing the rights of his people in legal cases through the New York courts and to the Supreme Court of the United States.

A chance friendship formed in Galena, Illinois, with Ulysses S. Grant led to service on Grant's personal military staff from Vicksburg to Appomattox Court House. And it was Ely S. Parker, a Seneca Indian chief acting as Grant's private secretary, who copied the terms of surrender given to General Robert E. Lee which ended the Civil War. When Grant became president, he appointed Parker commissioner of Indian affairs, the first Indian ever to hold that office. Parker later made a fortune on Wall Street, and only when that was lost did he settle down to a modest engineering post for the remainder of his days.

Racial slurs, legal barriers, and physical violence obstructed Parker's acceptance into white society, but with the help of influential friends and by virtue of his own capabilities and determination, Parker made a mark on nineteenth-century America that deserves full notice, especially to a generation now open to a reassessment of the Indian's role in American history.

Such a recital of Parker's accomplishments is more than he would have volunteered about himself. He was a private man, and few who met him suspected the breadth of his experience. To many he was simply "the Indian," a quiet curiosity at the headquarters of the army or the salons of New York society. But with pen in hand Parker was exceptionally articulate, and his many writings make his life one of the best documented of all American Indians.

A great debt is owed by any student of Ely Parker to his grandnephew, Arthur C. Parker, who was at one time archaeologist of the New York State Museum. Arthur Parker's *Life of General Ely S. Parker, Last Grand Sachem of the Iroquois and General Grant's Military Secretary* (1919) has been outdated by new material on the general's life, but much of that information was discovered by Arthur Parker himself, after the preparation of Ely Parker's biography, and the major collections of Ely Parker's papers are those painstakingly gathered over many years by his admiring grandnephew. Many additional sources have been used in the preparation of this book, but the debt owed to Arthur Parker is nonetheless immense.

Anyone who has engaged in historical research knows how much an author owes to other people: to courteous reference librarians and efficient archivists whom he has been able to thank in person, and to nameless compilers of indexes and bibliographies whom he can thank only indirectly and impersonally in a preface like this. To all who have assisted me in so many ways in this study, I owe my thanks, but especially to: John Y. Simon for sharing his knowledge of Ulysses S. Grant and his staff; Esther Blueye for introducing me to the Tonawanda Reservation; Madeline Perry, granddaughter of Ely and Minnie Parker, for the use of her family photographs; Marion M. Meyer for reading the book in manuscript and offering valuable suggestions for its improvement; and to my family for their patience and understanding during my long preoccupation with Ely Parker.

Burton, Ohio
Spring 1978

WILLIAM H. ARMSTRONG

A Visit to Tonawanda

LEWIS HENRY MORGAN had come to Albany to learn what he could about the New York Indians. In his hometown of Aurora, New York, Morgan and a group of friends had formed a club which met in a deserted Masonic hall and called itself the Grand Order of the Iroquois. For some of the members the club was simply an excuse for social gatherings, and their Indian costumes merely added color to their frivolities, but for Morgan the Grand Order was the expression of a genuine interest in the Indians as a rapidly vanishing part of America's heritage. His inquisitive lawyer's mind had led him to the few books available on the Indians, and in April 1844, he was in Albany to do some further research among the Indian treaties in the state files.

But Morgan's prize discovery took place in a bookstore entirely by chance. Browsing there among the books, he found a sturdily built sixteen-year-old youth with the straight black hair and the dark brown skin that showed his Indian ancestry, yet who was fluent in English and who showed a degree of education and culture unusual for any boy of his age. If books could not satisfy Morgan's curiosity about the Indians, perhaps here was a person who could. "To sound the war whoop and sieze the youth might have been dangerous," Morgan later told his associates, "but to let him pass without a parley would have been inexcusable"; and so Morgan struck up a conversation with the young Indian.

He learned that the boy was a Seneca from the Tonawanda Reservation in western New York, near Buffalo. His name was Ha-sa-no-an-da, which meant "Leading Name," but he also had an English name, Ely Parker, having been named after "Elder" Ely Stone, a Baptist minister associated with a mission school which adjoined the Tonawanda Reservation. He pronounced his first name to rhyme with

1

Ha-sa-no-an-da, Ely S. Parker, as a youth, dressed in traditional Seneca costume. Parker represented the Tonawanda Senecas in Albany and Washington while still in his teens. At the age of eighteen he conferred at the White House with President James K. Polk and boasted about having ridden about Washington in a carriage with Mrs. Polk. He became acquainted with Daniel Webster, Henry Clay, and many other senators and congressmen while representing the Tonawandas before the Senate Committee on Indian Affairs. *Rare Book Division, The New York Public Library, Astor, Lenox and Tilden Foundations, New York, New York.*

freely, but throughout his life he would have to contend with people who insisted on converting the unusual name to the more common Eli. Morgan learned, too, that Ely Parker was a student at Yates Academy in Orleans County, New York, near the reservation, but that the chiefs at Tonawanda had called him home to go with a delegation of Tonawanda Senecas to Albany to act as interpreter when they met with Governor William C. Bouck.

The Indian was clearly conversant with Seneca affairs and willing to answer Morgan's many questions, and before they parted Morgan made an appointment to call on the entire delegation that evening in their rooms. When he arrived, Ely introduced Morgan to his grandfather, "a fine looking old man in his 67th year," who was known both by the Seneca name Sose-ha-wa and the English name Jimmy Johnson. Johnson was not only the leader of the delegation, but great high priest of the entire Six Nations and a nephew of the celebrated Seneca orator, Red Jacket. The old man wore a large silver medal suspended from his neck which Morgan recognized from portraits of Red Jacket as the famous medal George Washington had given him in 1792, and which had been his most prized possession. Jimmy Johnson had inherited the medal when Red Jacket died, and he allowed Morgan to examine the cherished relic.

Morgan arranged to return each day while the Indians were in Albany (or "Skenectati" as they insisted on calling the city). He spoke for hours with Ely and through him with Jimmy Johnson and the two younger chiefs who made up the delegation. He listened attentively to the sound of their language and took elaborate notes for the members of the Grand Order. He learned the basic structure of the Iroquois Confederacy, or the Six Nations of Indians, which included the Mohawks, the Oneidas, the Onondagas, the Cayugas, and the Tuscaroras, in addition to the Senecas. And he came away convinced that Ely Parker should become a member of the Grand Order of the Iroquois to insure that its activities would be an accurate reflection of Indian ways.[1]

On his return from Albany, Morgan proposed that Ely be given an honorary membership in the Grand Order and that he be invited to its next annual meeting. He also began to correspond with Ely and laid plans for enrolling him in Cayuga Academy in Aurora, where Ely could continue to provide information for the Grand Order of the Iroquois, and the Order could aid him in completing his education. Spurred on by his curiosity about the Indians, Morgan arranged the

"Red Jacket, Seneca Chief," a portrait by Charles Bird King, painted about 1825. The large silver medal he received from George Washington is a prominent feature in all the portraits of Red Jacket. Ely Parker was a grandson of Red Jacket's nephew. *Yale University Art Gallery, Gift of de Lancey Kountz.*

following year to visit a condolence council—the raising up of the chiefs—of the Six Nations on the Tonawanda Reservation.

The picture of Indian life which many Americans had formed from the novels of James Fenimore Cooper was quite different from the life the Indians were living. The days when the Iroquois ruled New York and were respected and feared as far away as Illinois and Tennessee were gone. There were less than four thousand Iroquois left in New York State in 1845; two-thirds of them were Senecas living on four small reservations which stood like islands in a rising sea of white settlers. The forests were rapidly disappearing, the day of the hunter was almost gone, and the Indians' life had become in many respects little different from that of their white neighbors. "The pursuits of old Indian life are being forgotten," Ely's brother wrote a few years later, "they no longer follow the deer, or march in file along the trail, but they now follow their teams in the field, and walk in the trail of their plows."[2]

When Morgan and several other members of the Grand Order reached the Tonawanda Reservation in October 1845, they found it surprisingly small, covering only twenty square miles. Only a few months earlier, the eminent Indian authority Henry Rowe Schoolcraft had also visited Tonawanda in order to make a census of the New York Indians, and his *Notes on the Iroquois* provide a clear picture of the reservation as it was when Morgan saw it. There were, in the summer of 1845, 505 people living on the reservation, most of whom were Senecas, born in New York State, but there were also a few members of the other tribes of the Six Nations and a few Canadian-born Iroquois. The men were mostly farmers, growing corn, oats, rye, barley, wheat, beans, peas, turnips, and potatoes, and although some of them still depended in part on the hunt, cattle, hogs, and sheep were raised. There were over a thousand fruit trees on the reservation, especially apple trees, a favorite of the Iroquois. But the Indians had improved only about one-sixth of the reservation; part of the remaining land was rented to white settlers, and the rest provided timber, firewood, and hemlock bark which was sold to the whites.

The buildings, like the farms, were similar to those of the Indians' white neighbors. Ely's parents had lived in the traditional Iroquois longhouses in their youth, and Ely's father later satisfied Morgan's curiosity about them by making a model of a longhouse for him. But log cabins and a few frame buildings later took the place of the old longhouses. There was also a Baptist church on the reservation, and a small school operated by Baptist missionaries adjoined the Indian lands. Carts and wagons, and even some buggies and sleighs were scattered about the reservation.[3]

The Indians' buildings and farms may have resembled those of their white neighbors, but in their social customs the Tonawanda Senecas followed the old Iroquois ways. With Ely Parker as interpreter, the Indians spoke to their visitors about their customs, their clans and tribes, and their sachems and chiefs. Each person belonged to a clan; Ely was a Wolf, as were his mother and his brothers and sister, but his father belonged to the Turtle clan. Among the Iroquois no one could marry within his own clan, and children always belonged to the clan of their mother, not their father. Membership in one of the eight clans provided kinship with Indians in the other tribes of the confederacy, for the same clans existed in those tribes as among the Senecas. It was one of the subtle ties that kept peace in the confederacy, for an Iroquois would not willingly shed the blood of a member of his own clan.

The tribes were also bound together by a political order dating back centuries to the time of Da-ga-no-we-da and his spokesman Ha-yo-went-ha, whom Longfellow was to make famous as Hiawatha. Da-ga-no-we-da was said to have established a great peace among the tribes by uprooting a tall tree and casting all weapons of war into the cavity beneath it. Then he formed the tribes into a confederacy led by fifty civil officers called sachems or grand sachems, who represented the various tribes and who were nominated by the women of certain clans. The sachems' decisions were made only after careful deliberation, and an attempt was always made to reach unanimity, for the tribes were bound only by unanimous decisions. War chiefs were nominated by women as were the sachems, and a system of civil chiefs which had evolved alongside the sachems served as "braces in the longhouse."[4]

Morgan's purpose in visiting Tonawanda had been simply to gather information for the Grand Order of the Iroquois so that it could be modeled after authentic Indian customs, but seeing those customs first hand, he became interested in them for their own sake. He was beginning to see that everything the Indians described to him, even the festivals and the dances, had a purpose. There was a system to Indian life seldom appreciated by whites.

It was probably on this visit that Morgan first met Ely's family. Ely's father could speak a little English and was well-known for his hospitality to visitors. His name was Jo-no-es-sto-wa, "Dragon Fly," but he and his two brothers had also taken the name Parker from a British

Jo-no-es-sto-wa or William Parker (c. 1793–1864), a chief of the Tonawanda Senecas and the father of Ely S. Parker. William and his two brothers took the English name Parker from a British officer who had been adopted by the Indians. From Arthur C. Parker, *The Life of General Ely S. Parker.*

officer who had been adopted by the Indians. Ely's father adopted the name William Parker, and his brothers became Henry and Samuel Parker. William and Samuel were among the almost 700 Iroquois warriors to come to the aid of the United States in the War of 1812. They served on the Niagara frontier during the summers from 1812 to 1814, and took part in the battles of Chippewa and Fort Niagara. William was wounded during the war and later received a pension for his injury.

Like most of his neighbors, William Parker was a farmer, but he also operated one of the earliest saw mills on the Tonawanda Creek, making lumber on shares when logs were brought to the mill. He later became one of the chiefs of the Tonawanda Senecas, and he and Samuel, who was already a chief, played leading parts in the Indians' civil affairs as they had in military affairs. Ely's father was rather stout, had an olive complexion, and was accustomed to going to town wearing a black broadcloth suit and a stovepipe hat. He was "a man of large physical proportions and of fine presence, and possessed much intelligence and good sense. He was withal thoroughly honest, and bore a reputation beyond reproach."[5]

As was customary, William Parker had taken a woman six or seven years older than himself as a wife. She was Ga-ont-gwut-twus or Elizabeth Johnson, the daughter of Jimmy Johnson, the old chief Morgan had met in Albany. Elizabeth was an industrious woman, who in addition to her housework and farmwork, made baskets and sold them in the neighboring towns. In time she came to wear the "white folks' dresses" she saw there, but for many years she wore only the traditional "beaded broadcloth skirt, an overdress covered with brooches, leggins and moccasins." Lewis Morgan thought Ely's parents were two of the most noble-looking Indians he had ever seen. "Ely's mother is the very picture of goodness of heart and natural kindness . . . a very dignified, industrious and noble looking woman." And she was a good cook, too, famous for the bear and venison steaks and quail and partridge that her husband loved to bring home from the hunt.[6]

There were seven children in Ely Parker's family, six boys and one girl. Ely's oldest brother was thirty years old and had separated himself to a degree from the rest of the family. Named Ga-nos-qua after some ancient monsters mailed in stone, he had early in his life been placed in the charge of a noted Baptist clergyman, who took a special interest in his education and gave him his own name, so that Ga-nos-qua called himself Spencer Houghton Cone. The rest of the

Ga-ont-gwut-twus, Elizabeth Parker (c. 1786–1862), the mother of Ely S. Parker. Through her father Jimmy Johnson, she was a direct descendant of the prophet Handsome Lake, and a grandniece of Red Jacket, the Seneca orator. Portrait painted by Florence Roggie from a daguerreotype. *Courtesy of the Six Nations Indian Museum, Onchiota, New York.*

children used the name Parker as their father had done before them. Two other brothers were older than Ely. Levi, who was about twenty-five, had been to school but preferred the life of a farmer. Nicholson, or Nic, who was about nineteen, was better educated than anyone in the family except Ely. Their sister Caroline, or Ga-hah-no, was then about fifteen. Having already heard of her ability, Morgan was attempting to enroll her with Ely in the school at Aurora. Another brother, Newton, then twelve years old, later came to call himself Isaac Newton, or as Ely playfully called him *Sir* Isaac Newton. The youngest brother, Solomon, had died of "dropsy of the brain" a few months before Morgan's visit. Together they formed a family of extraordinary ability; Morgan later called the Parkers "the most talented Indian family of the Iroquois stock."[7]

Morgan learned later that William Parker's mother had been a white woman who was taken captive and adopted as a Seneca. Ely and his brothers and sister were therefore one-fourth white. That was a fact, however, which few people knew, and the children were usually spoken of in the nineteenth-century manner as "full-blooded Indians," since they looked Indian rather than white. In fact, one of Ely's contemporaries, when she heard it intimated that he was part white, expressed her disbelief sharply: "If this is the case, the Indian was put on the outside, and the white blood was kept for the lining."[8]

Ely Parker's family was a talented and happy household, living in relative comfort but living also under a cloud which threatened to burst and carry away their home and the entire reservation within a mere six months. Since the first white settlers had moved into western New York, there had been repeated attempts to remove the Senecas from their lands. In 1830, the federal government had adopted a policy of removing all the eastern Indians to an Indian territory west of the Mississippi, and the land speculators, who coveted the rich farmland on which the Senecas lived, pressed for a speedy application of the policy in New York State. In January 1838, a treaty had been concluded with the New York Indians which provided for the sale of the four Seneca reservations in New York to the Ogden Land Company and the removal of the Indians within five years.

There was good evidence that the treaty had been obtained by deceit. The Quakers, who had missions among the Senecas, gathered the evidence and published it in 1840. When the treaty was discussed in open council, the Quakers reported, only 16 of 81 chiefs were willing to sign it, but after the proceedings had been moved to a nearby tavern, where some new chiefs were illegally elected, whiskey distributed, and more than $20,000 and leases on land given to eight chiefs to use their influence on behalf of the treaty, the necessary signatures were readily obtained. The result was that lands worth nearly $2 million were to be sold to the Ogden Land Company for one-tenth that amount. The Quakers wrote that they were "thoroughly satisfied of the revolting fact, that, in order to drive these poor Indians from their lands, *deception and fraud* had been practiced to an extent, perhaps, without a parallel in the dark history of oppression and wrong, to which the aborigines of our country have been subjected!"

But in spite of strong appeals by the Quakers and the reservations expressed by President Van Buren, the treaty was ratified by the Senate in a close vote, decided finally by Vice-President Richard M. Johnson, who based his political career on the claim that he had fired the gun that killed Tecumseh at the Battle of the Thames. When the ratification was announced to the Indians "consternation and gloom were every where spread over their villages. . . . Their women were seen on all sides weeping in their houses, along the roads as they passed to their occupations, and in the fields whilst employed in their labors."[9]

Spencer Cone, alone among the Parker family, was in favor of the Treaty of 1838. The rest of the Parkers and almost all of the Tonawanda Senecas opposed it, as they opposed a compromise treaty made in 1842, which would have saved the Seneca reservations at Cattaraugus and Allegany at the expense of those at Buffalo Creek and Tonawanda. But that treaty, too, became law, and under its provisions the deadline for removing the Indians from Tonawanda was April 1, 1846.

The event which brought Morgan to Tonawanda in 1845, was a three-day council of the Six Nations for which five to six hundred Indians, representing all of the tribes, gathered near the council house on the reservation. The council offered an opportunity for long conversations with the Indian leaders: with John Blacksmith, the portly Seneca sachem, and Jimmy Johnson, the two leaders of the Tonawanda Senecas; with Peter Wilson, the Cayuga chief recently graduated from Geneva Medical College and a practicing physician; with Abram LaFort, the educated Onondaga sachem with his treasure of old Iroquois information; and through Ely Parker with many others, who shared freely the customs of religion and government that so fascinated the white visitors.

The council had been called to install several new sachems to serve with the rest of the fifty sachems and lead the Iroquois Confederacy. There were condolence ceremonies for two deceased sachems, which included a recital of the ancient laws of the confederacy, and still other rites which the visitors found "profoundly mysterious." At the conclusion there was a feast of boiled beef and bread and succotash, and dances; the trotting dance, the fish dance, and the corn dance, accompanied by turtle shell rattles and the sound of drums. On the last two days of the council, the teachings of the prophet Handsome Lake were recited by Ely Parker's grandfather, Jimmy Johnson.

Handsome Lake had received a revelation in a series of visions beginning in 1799, which became the basis for a new religion among the Iroquois. His Gai-wiio or "good message" spread quickly among the Indians and instilled a new pride in them, replacing the humiliation they felt at the destruction of their homes and crops by General John Sullivan's army during the Revolutionary War, the loss of much of their land after the war, and their confinement on the reservations. Jimmy Johnson, an "erect, fine looking, and energetic" man of sixty-nine years, was Handsome Lake's grandson and had been appointed his successor. Each fall he repeated the stories of Handsome Lake's life and visions and carefully recounted his teachings.

Johnson spoke, among other things, about the duty of husbands and wives to live together peacefully in ordered marriages, the evils of petty thievery and card-playing, and disrespect toward the aged. But his most vivid warnings were against drunkenness and selling Indian lands. He spoke of the prophet's journey over the great sky-road, and of Handsome Lake's vision of the Evil One dipping red hot lead from a great kettle and forcing a drunkard to drink it, "for he says, this liquid will have the same effect, as the fire waters manufactured by the whites." Fire water, Handsome Lake said, was made for the whites, not the Indians. While in the upper regions, the prophet also met his friend Farmer's Brother, who was drawing sand. "He said that from a great heap of sand, he was taking a grain of sand at a time, and although laboring continually the heap of sand did not diminish. Such, he said, would be the punishment of those continually selling lands."

Morgan was an attentive listener at the council and left Tonawanda filled with new information about the Indians. He told Henry Schoolcraft: "My head is so crammed with matters pertaining to the Iroquois that I intend for my own relief to sit down immediately and write a series of essays upon the government and institutions of the Iroquois for publication." And he appealed to Ely to join him by contributing an essay on the Iroquois' religion. There was an urgency to recording the Indian ways, for with the threatened removal of the Tonawandas, it appeared that the ceremonies Morgan had seen at Tonawanda would never be repeated there again. "They have probably beheld the light of the Grand Council fire for the last time," one of Morgan's associates wrote. "Its last glimmer was seen upon the Tonawanda Reservation. It went out when the Council dissolved."[10]

But the Tonawandas were adamant; treaty or no treaty they would not relinquish the lands where their fathers had lived and died and were buried. They chose instead, to appeal directly to the Great Father in Washington, and because few of them could read or write, they placed their hopes more and more in the abilities of the young man whom Lewis Henry Morgan had met in an Albany bookstore.

2

A White Man as Well as an Indian

SOME FOUR MONTHS before he was born, Ely Parker's mother had a dream about the child she was carrying—a dream which strangely foretold his life as "a white man as well as an Indian." Parker himself in later years would listen to nothing about the dream, since he could not accept the implication that he was a "child of fate" whose life had been determined before he was born. But the Senecas had a keen appreciation of dreams, and even if his mother's dream did not determine Ely Parker's life, it nevertheless revealed a great deal about Elizabeth Parker, whose ambitions and hopes did play a part in determining the course of her son's life.

In her dream Elizabeth Parker found herself in Buffalo, near the home of a former Indian agent, Judge Erastus Granger. It was winter and a heavy snow was falling. "Suddenly the sky opened, the clouds were swept back by an invisible hand and she beheld a rainbow that reached from the reservation to the Granger farm, when it was suddenly broken in the middle of the sky. From the lower side of the rainbow were strange pictures, which she recognized as resembling the signs over the little shops in Buffalo."

The Senecas believed that the symbolism of dreams often prevented a person from understanding his dreams himself. It was natural then that Elizabeth Parker, troubled by her dream, should go to the council house at Tonawanda to seek out the dream interpreter to explain it to her. The Senecas believed, too, that dreams were often the expression of a person's unconscious desires, and the dream interpreter showed great insight into the desires of this ambitious mother living in an Indian culture which she knew was fast giving way to the culture of the whites. He told her: "A son will be born to you who will be distinguished among his nation as a peacemaker; he will become a white man as well as an Indian, with great learning; he will be a

14

warrior for the pale faces; he will be a wise white man, but will never desert his Indian people nor 'lay down his horns as a great Iroquois chief'; his name will reach from the East to the West—the North to the South, as great among his Indian family and the pale-faces. His sun will rise on Indian land and set on the white man's land. Yet the ancient land of his ancestors will fold him in death."[1]

The Senecas believed that once a dream was interpreted and the soul's desires clarified, it was important to satisfy those desires, for to frustrate them was to invite calamity for the individual or the community.[2] It is not hard then to imagine Elizabeth Parker pondering these things in her heart, preparing herself to raise a child who would learn the white man's ways as well as the Indian's, who would make his mark in the white man's world, and who in so doing would satisfy a mother's ambition.

Elizabeth's son was born on the Tonawanda Reservation some time during the year 1828, and was named Ha-sa-no-an-da, "Leading Name." He did not know the exact day of his birth and once compared himself with Topsy in *Uncle Tom's Cabin* "who never had a birthday, never was born, and only growed up," and he said that he was therefore "neither elated or depressed on any special day of the year."[3]

His early upbringing was the responsibility of his mother, and to give her guidance in her task, Jimmy Johnson passed on to his daughter the wisdom of Handsome Lake who was "ever the lover and champion of children." A mother was to tell her children what was right and wrong and allow them to learn by experience that what she said was true. She was not to whip or strike them when they were unruly, but rather she was to discipline them with water. "Now this is the way ordained by the Creator: Talk slowly and kindly to children and never punish them unjustly. When a child will not obey let the mother say, 'Come to the water and I will immerse you.' If after this warning the child is still obstinate she must take it to the water's edge and say, 'Do you now obey?' and she must say so again and if at the third time there is no obedience then the child must be thrust in the water. But if the child cries for mercy it must have it and the woman must not throw it into the water. If she does she does evil."[4]

Raising her children in no way interfered with Elizabeth's work. She had several sugar bushes, and one of her grandchildren remembered how she would take the children along when she worked there, carrying them in a great packbasket on her back. Her husband built a bark cabin for her in each bush, and the children stayed in the cabins with her while she boiled the sap in big kettles to make maple sugar. The children were never afraid when they were with her for Elizabeth "had an ax and was a very good shot with either a gun or a bow. She always had both with her, and would shoot rabbits, coons, big birds and other game as well as any man."

The Parkers' home was a two-story log dwelling, built alongside an older log cabin which served as a kitchen. The lower floor of the house consisted of one large room with a fireplace and a number of benches for furniture. The family ate from the benches which were sometimes covered with sheets of bark as tablecloths. Their dishes were made of bark and wood, and each person had his own wooden spoon with a bird or animal carved on the top of the handle. The Iroquois are a hospitable people, and there was always a kettle of food warming by the fire to feed guests. And the visitors came—as many as twenty at a time—for William Parker and his brother Samuel were respected men and were sought out for their advice in the affairs of the community. "Many a night the men sat up until two or three o'clock in the morning talking. Then they took blankets and rolled up on the floor by the fire and slept until Grandmother arose to pound the corn meal for the breakfast porridge."[5]

Elizabeth Parker was a grandniece of the Seneca orator Red Jacket, who was a frequent visitor to the Parker home, and although Red Jacket died when Ha-sa-no-an-da was only two years old, the Parkers often discussed his exploits. William Parker had served under Red Jacket in the War of 1812, and both Red Jacket's skill as a speaker and his cowardice on the battlefield were part of the family's common memories. Ha-sa-no-an-da's grandfather, Jimmy Johnson, also visited the Parker home and shared his memories of his own grandfather, Handsome Lake, and of the Cornplanter, Handsome Lake's equally famous half-brother. Elizabeth too, added to the stories, for she was "ho-ya-neh," a member of the noble families whose women held the right to nominate the sachems of the Iroquois Confederacy. Here in his home, Ha-sa-no-an-da learned the legends and fables of his people: tales of the pygmies who dwelt within the earth; fables of the flying heads who propelled themselves through the air; and stories of the monster mosquito, the stone giants, and the huge buffalo which tore down forests in its path.

But Elizabeth Parker's children learned more than folk tales and family history. Her father had often repeated Handsome Lake's advice about learning the white man's ways, and that advice seemed even more appropriate in the 1830s than it had a generation before. "Now let the Council appoint twelve people to study, two from each nation of the six. So many white people are about you that you must study to know their ways."[6]

At an early age, Ha-sa-no-an-da was sent to a Baptist mission school adjoining the reservation. The New York State Baptist Convention had purchased a farm there and provided a missionary family to give a practical education to the children on the reservation. Ha-sa-no-an-da was one of about forty children who were entered in the school and boarded and clothed at the mission's expense. The girls were taught the art of "housewifery," while the boys were put to work on the farm, both to learn agricultural skills and to help defray the cost of their education through the crops they raised. Their academic education was provided for in a modest schoolhouse with the help of Webster's spelling book, Lindley Murray's grammar, Olney's geography, and Daboll's arithmetic. The attempt to teach the children to speak English was, however, only partially successful. The missionaries' policy was to insist that the children always speak English; they were permitted to speak Seneca on only one day of the week. But since all the students were Indian, they persisted in speaking their own language when their lessons did not require English, and when Ha-sa-no-an-da left the school the little English he had learned was nearly forgotten. Still, there was one legacy of the school. The Reverend Ely Stone passed his name on to Ha-sa-no-an-da, and the boy began to call himself Ely Parker.[7]

After his graduation from the Baptist school, Ely returned to the woods to learn to hunt and fish. When he was about ten years old he was sent to the large Iroquois settlement on the Grand River in Ontario, Canada, to perfect his knowledge of woodcraft. "Here I made good and rapid progress in gunnery and archery, in the use of the fishing spear, the science of decoying the unsuspecting fish by means of the torch-light and of the handling of the light birchbark canoe."[8]

At the age of twelve or thirteen, Ely became homesick and struck out by himself for his home in New York. At London, Ontario, he met with some English officers and traveled with them to the city of Hamilton. As they traveled the men amused themselves at Ely's expense with jokes they thought he could not understand. In fact, he knew just enough English to understand what they said, but not enough to enjoy the jokes, and he came away from the experience determined to master the English language.

Perhaps he also remembered the time, before he had gone to Canada, when he had been embarrassed by his inability to translate for the Baptist missionary. The family had gone to church one Sunday only to find that there was no one to translate the missionary's sermon. Because he had been to school, Ely was called on for the task and put in front of the congregation. As he tried unsuccessfully to put the difficult English words and thoughts into Seneca, he began to speak slower and slower, closing his eyes, and finally falling into a faint. Defeated by the language on two occasions, he was determined to master it.[9]

When he returned home from Canada, Ely obtained the blessing of his parents on his new venture—the only assistance they could afford to give him—and returned to the mission school to review his studies and qualify himself to enter a more advanced school. He succeeded, and about the fall of 1842, he was admitted as a tuition-free student at Yates Academy in Orleans County, New York, some twenty miles north of the reservation. It was a new school, begun only a year before, but it boasted an enrollment of 114 "ladies," 119 "gentlemen," and a faculty of three, including the principal, Benjamin Wilcox, who was a graduate of Williams College and, according to Ely, "a most able, competent and conscientious teacher."[10]

At Yates Ely was the only Indian student, and the constant necessity of speaking English resulted in progress that was rapid, though painful. "I have been engaged," he said in one of his early speeches there, "in translating the crooked Indian language into the English & the English back to the same, & now I should like to have the society release me for I feel myself crazy, in getting the two languages mixed into my head." But soon he was writing good compositions in the florid style of the time, and a few years later his friend Morgan told Ely's sister Caroline that if she wrote carefully she would "soon write as accurately as Ely does and he is a fine writer. He is quite as correct as any of us."[11]

Ely was also making regular addresses at the meetings of the Euglossian Society, a literary group to which he belonged and defended passionately against the claims of their rivals, the Cleosophic Society. Ely mastered his Greek and Latin studies as he had mastered English, but it was in his orations for the Euglossians that he made his mark at the Academy. "When it was announced that Parker was to address the school the house was filled to its full capacity and necks craned, eager to catch every word that came from his deep, full voice, which penetrated to the farthest corner of the spacious schoolroom."[12]

Yates Academy was a nonsectarian school and although it offered greater religious freedom than the Baptist school at Tonawanda, there was still a religious emphasis, and Ely's stay at the school impressed him with the claims of the Christian religion. In one of his earliest letters he advised his brother Nic: "If you have not yet attented to the salvation of your soul I advise you to do it immediately and the rest of the family if they too will take advice. And if you think that it would not be right for you to join the visible church of Jesus I want you to do all that is right and not say because I am not a member it is not my duty to do right."[13]

Ely's father and his sister also encouraged his interest in Christianity. His father, deeply involved in the Baptist mission, served about this time as both deacon and treasurer. And his sister, Carrie, wrote to him in October 1843 about the interest the other Indians were showing in Christianity and added, "I want you to be a Christian too. . . . I don't want my brother to go to hell." Ely seems never to have been baptized nor to have become a church member, but he was eagerly trying on the white man's religion, as he had tried on his language and his culture, and it seemed to him that the fit was good.[14]

Ely later looked back on his three years at Yates as among the happiest days of his youth. He had mastered a new environment and had won deep friendships in the process. Reuben Warren, from Alabama, New York, and Henry Flagler, a Presbyterian minister's son, were special friends. There was also a girl friend. He began to escort one of the white girls from lectures and evening meetings and became the talk of the school. It was rumored that he would take the young lady for a drive on the Fourth of July, and people wondered whether the girl, who belonged to a leading family, would allow herself to be seen publicly with an Indian. When the day came, and the curious gathered for the event, Parker did indeed appear in a fine rig, with a Negro driver, and the girl at his side. It was said that shortly thereafter the girl went abroad for a long vacation.[15]

The chiefs at Tonawanda were watching Ely's academic progress closely. Other Senecas had received an education—Cornplanter's sons had been sent to school in Philadelphia, and Maris B. Pierce, a Seneca from the Buffalo Creek Reservation, had graduated from Dartmouth College—but few of the Tonawandas had been educated at all. Some of the chiefs were suspicious that Ely's education would in some way prove harmful to them, but because of his growing facility with the English language, they nevertheless decided to put him to work as their interpreter. When he was only fourteen, he signed a memorial that the chiefs had made to President Tyler, and from that time on it was usually Ely Parker who wrote the documents and certified the signatures and marks of the chiefs in their many communica-

tions to the state and federal governments. In 1844 he went as interpreter to Albany, when he met Lewis Morgan, and again the following
year he was in Albany as interpreter for chiefs John Blacksmith and
John Bigfire, who went to meet the new governor, Silas Wright.[16]

All these activities were responses to the ratification of the compromise treaty of 1842, under which the Cattaraugus and Allegany
Reservations were to be retained by the Indians, and only the Buffalo
Creek and Tonawanda Reservations sold to the Ogden Land Company. The Senecas at Cattaraugus and Allegany had signed the
treaty under the advice of the Quakers, who told them that by doing
so they could at least save two of the four reservations they would have
lost under the former treaty. But the Tonawandas refused to sign the
treaty and said repeatedly that they could not be held to its provisions
because under the laws of the confederacy only unanimous actions of
the Indians were binding on them. But their appeals to Albany and
Washington were in vain. The Ogden Land Company was already
making plans to sell the Indian lands and had distributed maps of the
Tonawanda Reservation showing the lots available at auction at
Batavia, the county seat.

The Tonawandas finally came to the conclusion that their only
hope for forestalling the sale of the reservation lay in a provision in the
new treaty for payments to individual Indians for the improvements
they had made to their lands. The Indians' land was held in common;
an individual had the right to use the land but not to own it. Any
improvements he made to the land, however, were his and could be
sold or willed to his family. The treaty recognized these customs and
stated that each person's improvements were to be appraised so that
he could be paid for them, and the Indians were not to be removed
until two years after the appraisals had been filed in Washington. But,
the Tonawandas reasoned, what if the appraisals were not made?
Then, it seemed to them, that provision of the treaty would not have
been fulfilled, and they could not be removed.

Ira Cook and Thomas Love were appointed to make the appraisals, and they went to Tonawanda in October 1843, to begin the
work. They met with the chiefs but were told that the appraisals would
not be permitted. The next day, with Ely's help, the Indians sent a
letter to the secretary of war, whose department included the Office of
Indian Affairs, saying that they had not agreed to sell their land, and
because there was no such thing as majority rule among the Senecas,
they could not be compelled to do so. And they would not allow any
appraisals of their improvements to be made.

Cook and Love returned in December, but the Indians again refused to allow the appraisals. The Tonawandas were unanimous in their opposition to the appraisals and said that they would carry the men off the reservation if they tried to make them. To test the determination of the Indians, Cook and Love suggested that if there were any individual Indians who wanted their lands appraised, it would be done. That suggestion brought the whole assembly to its feet, and gently but firmly the Indians led the two men off the reservation.[17]

Convinced of the Indians' determination, the appraisers gathered what information they could from the white settlers in the area, arrived at an estimated value of the improvements, and sent it to Washington on April 1, 1844. Over the objections of the Indians, their report was accepted and filed, which meant that within two years, by April 1, 1846, the Tonawandas were required to leave their homes.

Their unimproved land was already being sold, and as the white purchasers began to settle on the reservation, John Martindale, one of the many white men who sympathized with the Tonawandas, offered them his aid. Martindale was a graduate of West Point who had resigned from the army and begun a law practice in Batavia. In 1842 he was appointed district attorney, and now, angered by what was happening to the Indians, he took action against the white settlers under a law passed by the New York Legislature in 1821. Under the law, none but Indians were permitted on the New York reservations, and the district attorney in each county was given authority to ask for the removal of any whites who entered their lands. Martindale tried to exercise this authority, but the courts ruled that because of irregularities in his action his efforts to remove the settlers were not binding, and the sale and settlement of the lands continued.[18]

In spite of the reliance of the Tonawandas on him as an interpreter in all these affairs, Ely Parker managed to continue his studies. In order to remain in school, he applied to the federal government for financial assistance from the Indian Civilization Fund, an annual appropriation of $10,000 which had been provided since 1819 for the education and civilization of the Indians. After an initial refusal, which he thought would mean the end of his education, he received the assistance and stayed at Yates until the fall of 1845. Since their meeting, Lewis Henry Morgan had been hoping to enroll Ely in the Cayuga Academy at Aurora, New York, and in October 1845, Parker left Yates to enter school at Aurora.

The Cayuga Academy was located in a "spacious and convenient brick edifice" in the small town of Aurora on Cayuga Lake. Here Ely prepared himself for college with the advantages of a library of several hundred volumes and a variety of scientific equipment which the school's catalogue claimed included an "Air Pump, manufactured at Paris, not surpassed by any in the country; also, a 36 inch plate Electrical Machine, of the latest and most approved model." Schoolwork at Cayuga was done in earnest, beginning at five o'clock each morning with recitations, and ending with evening lectures four days a week. Ely's lack of money proved no obstacle in Aurora; the money from the Civilization Fund was regularly paid; Morgan's Grand Order stood ready to lend assistance; and the annual catalogue of the school noted that "Little or no pocket money is necessary, as there are no places at which it may be spent for useless and injurious articles." Nevertheless, Ely, who had learned that among the whites "the coat makes the man," found a shop from which he purchased a "fine frock coat" with money from the Civilization Fund to complete his transition to the Cayuga Academy.[19]

Ely's room overlooked the beautiful waters of Cayuga Lake, and he was especially pleased that he was living on the old hunting grounds of his forefathers. He liked to roam the hills looking for relics of the ancient inhabitants of the land and to go hunting as his ancestors had. He had no difficulty with the Greek and Latin lessons or the debates that he was accustomed to at Yates, but he did encounter some hostility as a newcomer and as an Indian. "Since I have been here, I have generally been used well. Much better than I expected, coming here an entire stranger. Once or twice I have been severely abused. But I returned blow for blow with savage ferocity. Whether I gained the upper hand of my antagonist I leave the public to decide. For mind you, these quarrels were public. Bad business, but it could not be helped."[20]

He was also challenged in the school debates. He argued in one of his speeches that those who were called "savages" were happier in their lives in the forest than those who were said to be "civilized," and he was asked, why then had he abandoned that life and come to the Academy. "The door is open for him, why does he not go back?"

Ely replied that he had lived among the Indians and had closely studied their lives. The Indian *was* happy; his wants were few and easily satisfied; he took pains to cultivate good social relations and to carry out his few duties and responsibilities; and he found happiness in the contemplation of the works and the attributes of the Great Spirit. "He sees the Great Spirit in the strong hurricane—he hears His whispers in the gentle zephyrs of evening—he studies Him in the thunder cloud, and views Him as he darts through the heavens in his electrical cars and humbly bows with reverence to his loud callings from the skies."

Ely explained that he had come to the school because he had heard it rumored that the civilized life was able to produce even more happiness than the savage life, but thus far he had not found it to be true. He had heard of civilized men possessing great wealth, power, and wisdom but not real happiness. But he would continue to look for it. "If *then*, we do not find it, we shall resume the blanket, the cap & feathers, the bended bow & arrow, the tomahawk & scalping knife & resume savage life in all its wildness & then you may justly say 'do what you will an Indian will still be an Indian.' "[21]

After Ely arrived at Aurora, Morgan and some of the other members of the Grand Order of the Iroquois made plans to bring Caroline Parker and Sarah Spring, another girl from Tonawanda, to Cayuga Academy. Carrie had been studying at the Brockport Academy, but the Parkers were unable to continue her education there, and the Grand Order began a public subscription to bring the girls to Aurora. Morgan wrote enthusiastically to Henry Schoolcraft, asking for a contribution. "We have never been called to give the least trifle to the Indians. They are untouched objects of benevolence. We cannot do better than to commence in this way. . . . If any romantic character (say a bachelor) will send up $100 to instruct one of the girls; at the end of the year she shall send him a letter of thanks and a pair of moccasins. Suppose you make to someone the offer!"[22]

By the time the girls arrived at Aurora, in January 1846, Ely was once again caught up in the Tonawandas' struggle for their homes. Morgan offered the aid of the Grand Order to the Tonawandas, and Ely was called to a council at the reservation to tell them about Morgan's society. Ely testified to the sincerity of the group, and the Indians accepted the offer of help. Morgan then visited the reservation, and the result was a plan to use the Grand Order to appeal to Washington to prevent the removal of the Indians.[23]

A meeting of the Order was called at Ithaca on January 7, and a campaign begun to circulate petitions throughout the state urging the Senate to set aside the treaties of 1838 and 1842. The support of the Grand Order was reassuring; the society was established in various cities in New York and claimed three United States senators as members. "We think," one of the members wrote, "that the voice of all New York raised in tones of remonstrance will have some effect. If we fail, it will be in a noble cause, if we succeed, how good a deed shall we have the consciousness of having done."[24]

Ely spent little time in school that month. He went from the council at Tonawanda to the Grand Order's meeting at Ithaca, and from there to a festival at the Onondaga Reservation near Syracuse. He was also circulating petitions and asking for signatures. "We want the Petitions to be constantly flowing in to Washington between now & next April," he wrote, "and if the US Senate & President will then do nothing to aid the miserable & oppressed let them be d——d & go to grass." By the end of January he was back at Aurora, but his travels had allowed him no time to make any progress in his studies.[25]

In February he made his first, brief trip to Washington where late one night he confided to his diary his bitter mood: "Oh how I do long for my native woods. This place has no charms for me; the choicest wisdom of this great American republic gather here, around the great National Council fire, but what care I for that. It is from this place, the decrees have emanated, dooming my kin to the grave. They are to become extinct without even leaving a monument to remind the antiquarian that they once existed a happy race of beings. They are soon to be lost to the memory of man."[26]

When he returned from Washington, Ely found a letter from a friend urging him to attend Wilson Collegiate Institute with him in preparation for entering Williams College in the fall. But whatever his personal desires, Ely's future plans were made for him at Tonawanda when the chiefs called him to return to Washington with a delegation to appeal to the Great Father himself, President Polk, in a last effort to save their homes, and by the middle of March he was back in the capital. His stay at Cayuga Academy had been brief, but in that short time the principal had discovered him to be a "close student and an apt scholar," and another official added that "he is highly respected here for his moral and gentlemanly deportment." Those abilities were to be tested on the national scene in a task such as few eighteen-year-olds are called to undertake.[27]

3

"Hurra For Polk!!"

THE SENECA DELEGATION to Washington was composed of two chiefs, John Blacksmith and Isaac Shanks, both experienced leaders of the Tonawanda Senecas, and Ely Parker. Blacksmith was sixty years old and the leading sachem of the Senecas; they called him Do-ne-ho-ga-wa, the keeper of the western door of the Iroquois longhouse, which was the title of his office. He was a "keen, shrewd, calculating man, . . . a man of strong mental powers, just as nature fashioned him." But he could not speak a word of English, and neither Blacksmith nor Shanks could write his own name. The delegation arrived in Washington on Monday, March 16, 1846, and on the following Thursday was introduced to President Polk. "Hurra For Polk!!" Ely wrote his friend Reuben Warren. "He is a fine and pleasant gentleman. By him I was honored by being introduced to V. P. Dallas & distinguished Senators who happened to step in while we were there. He is very talkative and inclined to be merry. That's the man for me."[1]

It proved easier, however, to gain an introduction to the president than to the secretary of war, and since the president would discuss the Indians' case only in the secretary's presence, the delegation was forced to wait until Secretary William Marcy would see them. Ely was impatient with the delay and wanted to press the matter forward, going directly to the Senate if necessary, rather than through the president, and he was disgusted with Chief Blacksmith's more cautious approach. "Blacksmith is lying supinely, afraid to do or say any thing lest he be directed homeward. He is a coward. It takes all my skill to keep up his spirits." But the older man's approach prevailed, and the delegation waited.[2]

Ely used the delay to investigate the city, touring the Library of Congress and the Capitol building, visiting a session of the Senate, and attending a church service. But he was equally impressed by the brick mansion once occupied by President Washington and by Washington's clothing and military equipment in the National Gallery. The Iroquois had a high regard for Washington because of his magnanimous attitude toward them after the Revolutionary War. Most of them had sided with the British during the war, yet afterward, Washington had treated them kindly and fairly. They were convinced that he was allowed to reside at the gate of heaven—the only white man ever to leave the earth—and Ely Parker was awed to be in the presence of these reminders of the Iroquois' great benefactor.[3]

Finally, on March 25, the secretary of war and the commissioner of Indian affairs accompanied the Senecas to the White House to meet again with the president. Polk directed the secretary and the commissioner to look into the Indians' grievances and assured the delegates that after the investigation had been made he would be glad to meet with them again. After the meeting the Indians presented the secretary with a petition they had brought from the chiefs and warriors at Tonawanda in which the Tonawandas repeated their opposition to both the treaties and pleaded that if their land were sold, not only would they receive far less than what the land was worth, but they would then have nowhere to go. The other Seneca reservations were already crowded, and very few of the Indians had any desire to emigrate to the West. "We prefer to progress, as we do now, towards the customs of the whites, rather than to go into the wilderness again." They asked that the president and the Senate investigate the matter, and if necessary prepare a new treaty.[4]

The Tonawandas' petition worked its way through channels back to the president, and on April 1, Polk forwarded it to the Senate, who referred it to their Committee on Indian Affairs. That committee became the focus of the struggle, and both the Seneca delegation and the representative of the Ogden Land Company, Joseph Fellows, prepared to exert what pressure they could on the committee. Fellows presented the company's point of view that the treaties had both been ratified, were therefore the law of the land, and should be enforced, even if troops had to be called in to remove the Indians. He also deposited $15,018.36 with the government, the amount the appraisers had estimated was due the Indians for their improvements, and over the objection of the Seneca delegation, the money was accepted. According to Fellows, all the conditions had now been met for the removal of the Indians.

The Indians, countering Fellows' actions, employed attorney William Linn Brown of Philadelphia to serve as their counsel and prepared to blanket the Senate with petitions asking that the treaties of 1838 and 1842 be set aside. Petitions were arriving almost daily from all parts of New York State. One, a printed form signed by Parker's friend Reuben Warren and thirty-four of his neighbors, said the Tonawandas "are a moral, industrious, honest people, rapidly improving in their condition, possessing good farms, and are strongly attached to the homes of their fathers. The people of the State of New York do not desire their removal, and have no sympathy for their spoilers." In Genesee County a mass meeting was held at the court house in Batavia under the leadership of John Martindale and Lewis Morgan. The local newspaper saw the meeting as "indubitable evidence of the almost universal sympathy which pervades this community" in behalf of the Indians. The meeting adopted a memorial favorable to the Indians and appointed Morgan to take it to Washington.[5]

Soon after Morgan arrived in Washington, Ely Parker left for Albany to ask Governor Wright to protect the Indians while their fate was being decided by the Senate. On April 17, he saw the governor, and on the following day Wright gave him a formal reply for the chiefs. Perhaps sensing the danger of rash action in the Senecas' youthful emissary, he urged the Indians "to be cool and calm in your feelings and actions, and to do nothing in violation of the law, or to the interruption of the public peace." From Albany, Ely went on to New York City where he solicited expert testimony from Henry Schoolcraft and Albert Gallatin to present to the Senate committee. Schoolcraft, who had met Ely on his visit to Tonawanda the year before, answered his questions by saying that the Cattaraugus and Allegany Reservations were not, in his opinion, large enough to support the Senecas from Tonawanda and Buffalo Creek, and furthermore that unanimity was demanded on all important questions among the Iroquois. Coming from one who was considered an expert on the Indians, Schoolcraft's letter added prestige and credibility to what the Indians had been saying all along.[6]

A brief trip to his home left Ely no time even to visit his friends, for he was "a slave to the will of the chiefs the whole time." But in New York City he did have time for himself while waiting to meet with William Linn Brown, the Indians' counsel. For about two weeks he had "great times both day & night," attending "many theatrical & circus performances concerts, and what not" and meeting with old friends from Yates Academy, who assured him that their school was now the leading literary institution in western New York.[7]

While Ely was in New York waiting for Brown, and in the midst of the preparation of the Indians' case for the Senate Committee on Indian Affairs, Brown disappeared. Ely finally learned that he had gone to Cuba on a secret mission for the president. (It is doubtful that Ely ever knew the exact nature of Brown's mission, although his guesses were close. Brown met Santa Anna in Cuba and reported to the State Department on the Mexican leader's future plans. He also proposed to capture Santa Anna and hold him as a hostage and went so far as to take the preliminary steps to do it, but that plan appears to have been his own rather than the president's.) When Ely learned of Brown's trip, he was furious and hurried to Washington to try to prevent any action against the Senecas during their counsel's absence.[8]

Discouraged with the whole affair, Ely was inclined to go home and tell his people to "mind nothing about the Treaty, the law and the Company, but remain until driven out of their houses by force." He did go so far as to advise the Indians at Tonawanda to resist the efforts of the whites who were beginning to plant fields on the reservation. Acting on his advice, several of the Indians ordered the whites off the land and put in their own crops on the land claimed by the white men, only to find themselves arrested for trespassing on what they considered their own lands. In the midst of this confusion, Ely decided that he would have to stay in Washington to continue the Indians' appeal without Brown.[9]

Blacksmith and Shanks also left Washington to return to Tonawanda, and on May 18, 1846, Ely went by himself to see the president. He carried a recent letter from the Tonawanda chiefs telling the president that the Ogden Land Company was "crowding themselves upon our lands, and taking possession of our improvements by force & by arms." He also had a personal letter from his brother Nic telling him that armed agents of the company were coming onto the reservation, some of the men carrying as many as four pistols, and urging Ely to convince the government to protect the Indians while the matter was being decided by the Senate.

Ely reminded Polk of the Treaty of Peace and Friendship signed by the United States and the Six Nations in 1794, and said that rather than seeking revenge or retaliation against the settlers, they were bringing their grievance to his attention as they had agreed to under the treaty. Ely concluded his appeal saying:

> We have ever felt a strong friendship for the people of the United States. We love its republican institutions. We have shed our blood in common with the good citizens of the United States, in the defence of

her rights, and all we desire and ask now, is, that our love of peace and the great friendship we have for the United States may not suffer by the misconduct of individuals—of unprincipled white men; but in the spirit of that Treaty which we hold as almost sacred we desire to establish a firmer friendship which shall ever remain unbroken, by amicably adjusting our present difficulties.

Polk referred the matter to the commissioner of Indian affairs, who in turn informed Ely that, even though the treaties of 1838 and 1842 had to be recognized as the law of the land, the executive branch could be counted on to take no action against the Indians while the matter was pending in the Senate.[10]

Ely was of two minds about his stay in Washington. When he thought about the Tonawanda affair and the reluctance of government officials to act on the Indians' behalf, he was "raving mad." But when he could forget that, "there is no one, I believe, who enjoys himself half so well." He was living at the best hotels, eating well, and enjoying city life. The developing war with Mexico filled the city with political excitement, and Ely was in the crowd that gathered at the Capitol to hear the debates on the war. A national fair to exhibit American manufactures and handicrafts filled the city with visitors from all parts of the country. A huge building erected for the fair was so large that it reminded one observer of "the Dutchman's barn, which was said to have more room inside than out." Ely browsed among the exhibits— the farm utensils and the steam engines, the furniture and pianos—and wrote to his friends that it was a sight worth going hundreds of miles to see. He attended an Odd Fellows celebration, listened to the group's music and speeches, and decided to become a member. "If life is preserved to me, I expect to join them, before many full moons shall set behind the western hills." He was not as impressed with the volunteers he saw marching off to Mexico, "a hard set of miserable looking fellows," who put the whole city in commotion by their escapades outside their camp.[11]

For the first time in his life Ely encountered Indians from other parts of the country. John Ross and a delegation of Cherokees were at the White House at the same time as the Senecas, and Ely visited a delegation of Comanches, who hardly recognized Ely as an Indian because he wore no paint. Still another group of about fifty Indians from the frontiers of Texas and Mexico were in the city. They were dressed in their "native costume, . . . covered with paint, and ornamented from head to foot with all kinds of brass rings & beads &

shells." Ely had never seen anyone like them. "They look wild enough to throw any one of a delicate constitution into the fits. If I had such Indians at the north, I could whip the Ogden Company & all their accomplices in less time than you could say 'Jack Roberson.' They have as you may suppose but very little clothing to cover their bodies, which of course would make the virtuous portion of the fairer sex blush as far up as the crown of their heads, and probably a little below the ancles."[12]

By July Brown still had not returned, and the Senate Committee on Indian Affairs had made no report. Ely spent the Fourth of July in Baltimore, where he visited the Washington Monument, and the following week he went to Mount Vernon, "that almost sacred spot," and to Alexandria, where he visited the church which Washington had attended. He and a friend sat in Washington's pew and "took the privilege of imagining ourselves Generals." Back in the capital, he spent his time following the Congressional debates. Paradoxically, while fighting to save the Seneca lands, he was sympathetic to the rhetoric of the imperialists. He wanted to see the whole of Oregon annexed and as much land to the south as "the Genius of Democracy can travel with his great boots. War or no war, republicanism should extend its sway over the whole American continent. I would rejoice to see it."[13]

But as Ely continued to wait for Brown, even the excitement of the capital city began to pale, until it felt like a "dreary" place. Ely was also running out of expense money and was too proud to keep asking the chiefs for more. Nic wrote from Tonawanda that someone was agitating to send Blacksmith back to Washington, saying that Ely was "nothing but a d—— fool [, that you] don't know any thing yet as you are . . . nothing but a little boy, not old enough yet to attend to such a great business." But with the splendid assurance of youth, Ely saw himself as a David being criticized by a Goliath soon to fall. What did disturb him was the disunity among the Indians which Nic's letter revealed, a disunity which could not be afforded "in this our last struggle for the homes & graves of our honored dead."[14]

On July 14, Brown finally returned from Cuba, and he and Ely prepared to meet with the Senate committee. But debate on a tariff bill delayed matters even further, until on August 6, the committee, anticipating the adjournment of Congress, postponed the matter until their next session. The committee reported that the case had been fully presented, but that there had not been time to study the great bulk of documents received. The August 7 *Daily National Intelligencer* quoted one of the committee members as saying that the postponement was not due to any opposition to the Indian petitioners, but only to lack of time.

Almost five months after Ely Parker arrived in Washington Congress adjourned without taking any action on the Senecas' behalf. Ely was naturally disappointed, but he found some comfort in knowing that the committee had merely postponed the appeal rather than rejecting it entirely. Whatever the legalities of the matter were, the Indians were still at Tonawanda.

Ely passed through Aurora in mid-August on his way home. Morgan's Grand Order of the Iroquois was celebrating an anniversary there, and Ely shared in the festivities. The white "warriors," dressed in fringed leggings, headdresses, and frock coats, and with tomahawks in their hands, gathered in the evening for a torchlight procession through the town. During a pause in the activities, Ely Parker stepped out from the lines, dressed in Indian costume and wearing his grandfather's prized medal. A newspaperman, reporting the incident, wrote that "This was Ha-sa-no-en-da, a highly intelligent and educated Indian of the Seneca Nation. The medal which he wore was the very one which was given by Washington to [Red Jacket]. . . . Ha-sa-no-en-da now bears the medal, and his conduct as one intelligently devoted to the interests of his people, proves him an appropriate bearer of a relic so precious."[15]

Ely's return to Tonawanda raised the question of his future plans. He had been ready to enter college for more than a year, but he had not yet found the means to do so. He thought, if he could not enter college, he would like to visit the West and said, "if I could get a profitable berth any where, I dont know but I would stay." But the chiefs had other plans for him; they needed him to see their case through the Senate. Events during the summer convinced even the undecided Senecas that the reservation must not be abandoned. In May a party of between 135 and 200 New York Indians had left for the western lands that were allotted to them. Preparations for their settlement were inadequate, the season was unusually warm and unhealthy, and within four months eighty of them were dead. Fearful of a similar fate, the chiefs wanted Ely to return to Washington. They wrote to the Indian Office explaining that he was absent from his studies on their business and asked that his educational allowance not be forfeited because of his absence from school. At the chiefs' request, Ely stayed at Tonawanda until Congress reconvened, and on January 1, 1847, he returned to Washington to resume the fight.[16]

4

A Lawyer and an Engineer

IT WAS ELEVEN O'CLOCK on New Year's Day 1847, when Ely arrived in the capital, and he went immediately to the White House, which was to be open for a public reception at noon. When he arrived, he found the building so crowded with visitors that some of the men were leaving by climbing out through an open window. Making his way into the mansion, Ely wandered from room to room admiring the beautiful women in their finery, while becoming a bit annoyed by the gazes of others trying to guess who he might be. "But close inspection and my native costume soon assured them that it was a savage brave, who thus had the audacity and impudence to mingle with the nobility." President Polk was there greeting the visitors, and Ely was pleased that the president "instantly recognized me, and very familiarly and courteously offered his hand," after which the president's private secretary introduced Ely to Mrs. Polk.

When he had taken his turn at clambering out of the window, Ely made his way to the home of Dolley Madison, which was also open for the holiday. After fighting his way through another crowd, Ely was introduced to Mrs. Madison by a member of Congress and was agreeably surprised to find that, although she was nearly eighty, she was "so young looking, so healthy and so cheerful, and withal retaining strong and evident traces of her former beauty." From Dolley Madison's home, he went to Mayor William Seaton's residence and was invited to share in the food and drink prepared for the day. Failing to find Mrs. Alexander Hamilton's home, he retired to his room at the Gadship Hotel to confide the day's events to his diary, and to reflect on the beginning of another new year.

The next day was Saturday, and since he could not conduct any business, he visited the Capitol where a series of pictures of Indians set him to thinking about the injustices his people had suffered at the hands of whites. In the rotunda he happened on a painting of the landing of the Pilgrims.

> They are represented as in a starving condition, and being about to land, an Indian has come forward offering them provision of his bounty. Who now of the descendants of those illustrious pilgrims will give one morsel to the dying and starving Indian. . . . May the Great Spirit reward & keep the red man. Turning around we are met by another representation in plaster paris of William Penn & the Indians entering into an alliance. What virtue is there now in Indian Treaties. . . . Methinks Indians are right when they say that letters lie more than the head. Turning round a little more, we observe another representation, that of the young and beautiful Pocahontas saving Captain Smith at the risk of her own life. Who now among the descendants of those whom she saved will risk his or her life for an Indian. . . . How ungrateful is man to his fellow man. Turning still more around we find another and a last representation, intended no doubt as a climax to the whole scene, that of Col. Boon the hero of Kentucky in a mortal contest with an Indian. Both are struggling for life. But Boon has already killed one Indian & has trampled upon his mangled body. Such is the fate of the poor red man. His contest with the whites is hopeless yet he is not permitted to live even in peace, nor are his last moments given him by his insulting foe to make his peace with his God. Humbly we ask whether justice will always sleep and will not the oppressed go free?

His sense of injustice was not diminished when he went to church on Sunday. Seeing that the sexton did not care to seat him, he was about to find a seat himself when he was told that he would have to be seated upstairs. He said nothing, but turned and left, thinking to himself, "if such was to be my treatment in a house devoted to the worship of God, I had rather be somewhere else."

When he was finally able to visit the Senate, he found that the Indians' case had not yet been referred to the Committee on Indian Affairs, but after seeing several senators he was able to have the matter properly referred to the committee. He also met two members of Congress, John Martin of Kentucky and George Hopkins of Virginia, who listened sympathetically to him and promised to assist his work by introducing him to those senators he had not already met. It must have appeared that Ely needed their help, for once again the Indians' counsel, William Linn Brown, was absent, and the responsibility of presenting the Senecas' case to the Senate fell solely on him. But Ely wrote to the chiefs that he was quite willing to take on the

Indians' business himself. "I feel just as strong to help you and just as confident to get our case as though I had a host of Lawyers about me."[1]

The chiefs at Tonawanda, however, were concerned that Ely was in Washington alone. Before he left, Ely had said in council that he would like some of the chiefs to go with him, but at that time the council felt that he would do well enough by himself and gave him the authority to use his own judgment in all matters that might come up during this session of the Congress. Some of the Indians decided later that it would be best to send some chiefs to be with Ely, "not thinking however that they would be any use to you there," Blacksmith and Johnson wrote, "but that the blame might not rest upon you so strongly if we should happen to loose our lands." So to ward off the old argument about Ely's youth, plans were made to send Blacksmith and Shanks to Washington to give at least the appearance of older judgment.[2]

Ely, meanwhile, was taking his case to whatever senators would listen to him, and in spite of his dislike for the task—"to chase & hunt up these lazy Senators is a miserable work"—he became optimistic about the outcome. John Calhoun had taken the position that the treaty was invalid because it had not been ratified by the Indians according to their custom nor properly ratified by the Senate, and John Crittenden also supported the Indians' position. In fact, all the senators Ely had access to, except Daniel Webster, were favorable to his case. Brown had finally appeared, and he and Ely were working closely with Senator Ambrose Sevier of Arkansas on their presentation to the committee. Petitions were arriving almost daily from New York State, asking that the Senecas be exempted from the operation of the treaties; so many petitions had been received that Senator David Atchison of Missouri said he believed nearly half the state of New York had petitioned in the Indians' favor. Ely looked forward to the committee's report: "We shall have scratched at the eyes of the Ogden Company, and they will look upon us hereafter as dangerous customers."[3]

The report of the committee, on February 19, came as a shock. The committee recommended that the Tonawandas' petition not be granted, acknowledging the allegations of fraud in making the original treaty but explaining that to annul a treaty on that or any other grounds would "tend strongly to unsettle the whole of our Indian policy," and would "open a field of interminable difficulty, embarrassment, and expense." Whatever their merits or demerits, the treaties were the law of the land, and all parties were bound by them.[4]

Greatly disappointed, and believing that nothing more could be done for the Tonawandas in Washington, Ely returned home, stopping on the way in Albany to ask the governor to enforce the law of 1821 as a means of keeping the whites off the reservation and asking the state legislature for its aid and protection. Several other Indians were also in Albany on business for the various tribes, but a reporter who visited the Indian delegations gave special mention to the "delegate from the Tonawanda Senecas, a very intelligent young man named Ely S. Parker, or as the Indians would call him, Ha-sa-no-an-da," and noted that he was wearing the famous Red Jacket medal suspended from his neck on a bead chain.[5]

With Ely's return to Tonawanda, the hope of securing assistance from the Senate appeared at an end. After years of effort and the expenditure of over $5,000 for delegations, legal fees, and petitions, the Tonawandas' efforts to convince the Senate to free them from the treaties had ended in failure. But the Indians still had no intention of giving up the reservation, they simply changed their strategy: they appealed to the courts.

A year earlier, agents of the Ogden Land Company had turned John Blacksmith out of a sawmill on the reservation, claiming legal ownership under the treaty, and they had assaulted him in the process. With the help of John Martindale, in 1847 the Indians sued the whites over the matter, and the suit became a test of the legal ownership of the reservation. Blacksmith based his suit on the appraisals required under the Treaty of 1842. Until he had received the money due him for his improvements, he argued, he could not legally be forced to give them up. His argument hinged on the fact that the Indians had not allowed any appraisals of the improvements and had no plans to allow them. The case was tried in September 1847, and the court ruled in favor of the Indians, saying that because the Ogden Land Company had not made the appraisals it had not established title to the reservation. The matter immediately became involved in a series of appeals, and the Indians asked only to be left where they were until the case was finally settled in the courts.[6]

After spending an entire year on the Tonawandas' business, Ely had to think about his own future. He applied for admission to Harvard College and asked the assistance of his congressman in gaining admission, but nothing came of the application. He wrote to Henry Schoolcraft to ask what chance an Indian would have in obtaining a clerkship in the Indian Office in Washington, where he thought he could be of some service to his people, but nothing more was heard of

that either. He also asked the help of Alfred B. Street, a member of
the Grand Order of the Iroquois and a poet. Ely had helped Street by
providing him with Seneca names and terms for some poems he was
writing, and Street promised to look for a position in Albany, but
none was found.[7]

An offer of a position finally came from the sub-agent for the
New York Indians, William P. Angel. Angel was a young lawyer, who
after a career as a printer and publisher, had settled in Ellicottville in
Cattaraugus County, New York, where he was serving both as
district attorney and as the federal Indian agent. He asked Ely to come
to Ellicottville to assist him in his work with the Indians, and at the
same time proposed that Ely study law with him and his partner,
Addison G. Rice. Ely quickly accepted the offer, moved to Ellicottville, and began a new career as "student at Law," glad at last to be
free of the responsibility for the Indians' future and glad to be free of
their constant criticism. He complained to Reuben Warren that during
the planning of the Blacksmith case, the Indians "abused me, all but
to death, charging me of intriguing with the Com[pany], and the most
bare faced treachery was laid to me." He had been deeply hurt by
their accusations and left for Ellicottville with few good-byes.[8]

But he had also been drawn to Ellicottville by a real interest in
the law. Ely had seen the respect given to lawyers in Albany and
Washington, and was aware of what a knowledge of the law could
mean for the Indians. He began, therefore, with real pleasure to read
Blackstone's *Commentaries* and to learn the practical ways of the
lawyer, taking the advice then given to young lawyers to "live in your
office . . . answer all letters as soon as they are received . . . put
every law paper in its place . . . be patient with your foolish clients
. . . read, delve, meditate, study, and make the whole mine of law
your own."[9]

The budding lawyer soon found a place in Ellicottville's society.
Ellicottville was the county seat—the Senecas called it "the place for
holding courts"—and it was the center of both trade and culture for
the county. One of its prominent citizens remembered Ely as "a fine
looking man, of stalwart proportions" and said that "he mixed in
society, where he was a favorite, and was a cultured man." Ely
apparently served for a time as postmaster and later told a friend that
Ellicottville had "a great many good folks & some very queer ones. I
used to have some very pleasant times when I lived there."[10]

He was also finding satisfaction in his new status as a member
of the Masonic Lodge. Ely was fascinated by the mystery and the

pageantry of secret societies. He had not only been impressed by the Odd Fellows he had seen in Washington but had participated in the secret societies of the Indians and had grown up with some knowledge of Masonry itself. The celebrated abduction of William Morgan, who had threatened to expose the secrets of Masonry, had taken place shortly before Ely's birth, at nearby Batavia. There were stories that Morgan had been hidden on the Tonawanda Reservation, and it was true that about that time a stranger had given William Parker some Masonic books and asked him to hide them for him. Some Indians had already become Masons—Joseph Brant, the Mohawk chief, had been initiated into Masonry in England in 1776—so it was not without precedent when Ely Parker was welcomed as a member of Batavia Lodge No. 88, Free and Accepted Masons in 1847.[11]

But even though Ely's life was becoming more settled, the affairs of the Tonawandas were still unresolved. Despite their criticisms of Ely, the chiefs realized they were dependent on his skills in dealing with the white men. Early in 1848 they called on him to return to Washington with Isaac Shanks to see where they stood with the federal government, and Ely dutifully agreed to go.

The two traveled by way of New York City, where Ely visited some fellow Masons and gathered letters of recommendation to other Masons in Washington. From New York Ely and Shanks traveled to Philadelphia, where they met William Linn Brown. Brown offered to accompany them to the capital, but after waiting two days for him to get ready, the delegates went on without him. When they arrived in Washington, Henry Schoolcraft and New York Senator Daniel Dickinson informed them that their case was no longer under consideration by the Senate, all the business of the previous Senate having died with the expiration of the Twenty-ninth Congress the year before. For the new Senate to consider the case, it would have to be introduced as an entirely new item of business.

Brown finally arrived from Philadelphia, and his advice as well as Schoolcraft's and several senators' was for Ely and Shanks to return home. Nothing could be done now in the Senate; if necessary, the matter could be introduced again later in the year. Ely and Shanks concluded their business by leaving an expression of the Tonawandas' intentions with the commissioner of Indian affairs, saying that the Tonawanda Senecas would not surrender their lands, would not receive any monies provided for in the treaties, and would not permit any appraisals to be made of their improvements. They pointed out that the whole matter of the title to their land was now being investigated by the courts, and they asked that the government take no action against them until the courts had ruled in the matter. With that, the two delegates returned home, leaving word with Schoolcraft to let them know of any attempt to renew their case in the Senate.[12]

Their mission had been futile, but Ely had gained some personal satisfaction during the trip from an introduction to Henry Clay. Congressman John Botts of Virginia had introduced them, and Ely was greatly impressed by Clay's ease and informality, saying that Clay had talked with him, "as an old and familiar friend." Clay confided that he had been asked to try the validity of the Treaty of 1838 before the United States Supreme Court on behalf of the Indians but had declined because he thought its success doubtful. Clay also said that he had heard Ely was a lawyer. "He thinks," Ely wrote, "he would go a great distance to hear me plead in the U. S. Supreme Court."[13]

There was another experience, too, from his Washington visits that Ely cherished. Mrs. Polk had once stopped on the street and taken him into her carriage, and he liked to tell how he had proudly ridden about the city at the side of the first lady of the land.[14]

No sooner had Ely returned home than he became physically involved in the struggle for the reservation. One Ichabod Waldron had been going onto the reservation since the previous September and carrying off the Indians' timber. On January 29, 1848, he again went onto the reservation and, meeting Ely Parker there, assaulted him "with force and arms." John Martindale, the district attorney, promptly charged that Waldron "did then and there beat strike wound and evil treat and other wrongs to the said Ely S. Parker . . . against the Peace of the People of the State of New York and their dignity." The case was tried with Ely's four brothers serving as witnesses, and the jury, without leaving their seats, found Waldron guilty and fined him fifteen dollars. Despite the physical abuse he had suffered, it must have been encouraging to Ely to have Martindale's continued assistance and to know that a jury of Genesee County white men would treat the Indians with justice.[15]

William Angel was eager to have Ely return to his work in Ellicottville, and in March Ely returned to the study of law. Already he and his family fancied him a lawyer. Spencer addressed him as "Attorney and Counselor at Law," and Ely, writing to Washington about a claim of Spencer's, signed himself "Special Attorney for Cone." His friend, Henry Flagler, had high hopes for Ely's legal career. "I hope to hear one day," he wrote, "the name of Ely S. Parker as our most distinguished lawyer." And Ely was beginning to put his legal knowledge to work for the Indians, acting not only for the Tonawanda Senecas, but also for the Senecas at Allegany and even for the Tuscaroras.[16]

In addition to his legal work, Ely was spending more and more time researching and recording Seneca traditions and customs for his white friends. During 1847 and 1848, Henry Schoolcraft made repeated requests for information about the Senecas, and Ely replied with long descriptions of Indian dances, amusements, superstitions, festivals, crimes, language, history, legends, and religious customs. For much of the information he relied on his own observations, but he also consulted the older Indians and studied the few published works on the Iroquois, such as those of DeWitt Clinton and Baron LaHontan. He was also familiar with Schoolcraft's own *Notes on the Iroquois* and once pleaded that Schoolcraft had already collected more information than he could readily provide. But Schoolcraft continued to urge Ely to provide him with material, recognizing that he had a rare informant in Ely Parker, one who not only had access to all the ancient laws and customs of the Iroquois but who was at the same time intelligent and well-educated enough to evaluate and record them in an objective manner.[17]

Lewis Henry Morgan, too, was looking to Ely for information on the Iroquois. Morgan had begun to record what he was learning about the Indians for the Grand Order of the Iroquois, and in 1847 he published a series of "Letters on the Iroquois" in the *American Review*. He planned to expand the "Letters" into a book on Iroquois government and institutions, and he needed Ely's help as an informant. He was especially interested in the annual council of the Six Nations at Tonawanda, at which Jimmy Johnson recounted the tenets of Handsome Lake's religion. In 1848, as he had two years earlier, he asked Ely to record Johnson's speeches for him. Morgan was insistent in his requests, and well he might have been, for the old Indian order was fast passing away. In December 1848, at the urging of the Quakers, the Senecas at Cattaraugus and Allegany abolished the old forms of government and adopted a new republican government, calling themselves "the Seneca Nation of Indians." Their action left the Tonawandas the only New York Senecas continuing the old institutions, and Ely Parker, as the best educated Tonawanda Seneca, became invaluable as an informant for men like Schoolcraft and Morgan.[18]

Ely's legal career proved short-lived. In the summer of 1848, William Angel, whom Ely was assisting in his duties as the sub-agent for the New York Indians, was removed from his position. Ely, fearing

Lewis Henry Morgan (1818–81). Ely Parker collaborated with Morgan in a classic study of the Iroquois which was published in 1851 as *The League of the Ho-de-no-sau-nee, or Iroquois*. Morgan has been called "the father of American anthropology." *Courtesy of the University of Rochester Library.*

for his own position, had campaigned to have him retained in office, arguing that he was the kind of person who could work well with the Indians, who were themselves completely satisfied with his work and not impressed with the man rumored to be his replacement. He had also forwarded petitions from the other Indians supporting his arguments. But in spite of Ely's protests, Angel was removed from his office because of allegations that he was not a good Democrat.[19]

A legal obstacle also blocked Ely's way to becoming a lawyer. Under New York State law, only a natural born or a naturalized citizen of the United States could be admitted as an attorney or counselor in the courts. Ely may have been "natural born," but the Indians were not American citizens, and there was no provision for their becoming citizens. There is a persistent story that Ely applied to be admitted to the bar and was refused admission by the courts. The story may be true, for by December 1848, barely a year after he had gone to Ellicottville, Ely was once again casting about for a career.[20]

Ely thought again of going west, and he asked Morgan, who was living in Rochester, to see if the editors of the Rochester newspapers would employ him as a western correspondent. Morgan talked to the editors, but he made it clear to Ely that he disapproved of the plan. He was undoubtedly afraid that he could not finish his work on the Iroquois without Ely's help, and he made inquiries about another job which would keep Ely nearby. Morgan proposed to friends who were employed on the New York canals that Ely be given a position with one of the engineering parties working on the Genesee Valley Canal, arguing that the state had a duty to employ any Indians who had obtained an education. Then he urged Ely to accept an engineering position by telling him the advantages of working for the state and suggesting that Ely would also be able to find work for Nic and Newton, once he himself was working as an engineer.

No engineering positions were available immediately, but early in 1849 there was an opening, and Ely, convinced by Morgan that he should take the position, accepted it. He moved to Nunda, a small town in Livingston County, near the Genesee River, where he joined an engineering party engaged in extending the Genesee Valley Canal south toward the Allegheny River. Under the supervision of an assistant engineer, engineering parties of three or four men went into the field to make surveys, take levels, and plan the work to be done on the canal. The parties then returned to their office to make their computations and prepare estimates of the work. Although Ely worked only as an axeman clearing timber for the party, the job gave him the opportunity to learn the fundamentals of engineering from the other men, all of whom were well-educated. After he had been at Nunda a short time, Angel's partner, Addison Rice, offered to take Ely into the law office, where he could at least attend to the office work. But even though he had expressed a determination to return one day to the law, Ely chose to remain with the engineers.[21]

Ely's life at Nunda was not all work. One of the contractors employed on the canal took Ely along to some country dances, and the man's wife taught him to dance. Uneasy at first in the white man's dances, Ely was bashful, but once he mastered the art it seemed to the contractor that Ely wanted to dance all the time. One evening, when a dance was held at a hotel at Ischua, Ely stayed there overnight. When he looked out in the morning, he saw fresh deer tracks near the hotel. Dressing quickly, he followed the tracks, outran and killed the deer, and brought it back on his shoulders to the hotel. The skills learned in the wilds of Canada had not been forgotten, even though the hunter was in the process of becoming an engineer—and a country dancer.[22]

During his absence from the reservation, the Tonawandas kept Ely informed about their struggle with the Ogden Land Company. In December 1848, James Wadsworth, an agent of the company, took a surveying party onto the reservation to attempt to survey and appraise the Indians' improvements. When the Indians forbade them to make the surveys they left but returned the next day with a party of fifty men armed with clubs, prepared to compel the Indians to consent to the work. A fight broke out in which the surveyor's chain and compass were broken, and the whites were forced to leave. Several of the Indians were arrested and tried but were acquitted, and some of the whites were indicted for rioting.

Ely wrote to the new sub-agent, Robert Shankland, describing the incident and asking the government's protection for the Indians. Shankland transmitted Ely's letter to Washington, but the Ogden Company was also pressing its views on the capital. James Wadsworth, who had led the armed party onto the reservation, went to the Indian Office with a recommendation from his congressman, Millard Fillmore—"Mr. Wadsworth is a most respectable and wealthy gentleman of Geneseo, New York, whose statements are entitled to full credit." After hearing Wadsworth, the Indian Office refused to take any action on the Indians' behalf.[23]

John Martindale had also initiated another legal action to force the eviction of about thirty white families already settled on the reservation. Martindale asked again for enforcement of the law of 1821, forbidding white intrusion on the reservation. This time his request was granted, but the matter was appealed and a stay of execution granted while the case was under appeal. In view of these new events and the inauguration of a new president, Zachary Taylor, the Indians decided to send another delegation to Washington, but this time Nic Parker went, accompanied by Martindale as counsel.[24]

Ely was not nearly as involved in these affairs as he had once been. He continued his work at Nunda, and although he remained there for only ten months, he made a lasting impression on the local residents, who remembered him as a person who was unusually honest and high-minded, and highly regarded by his associates, although also a somewhat diffident and sensitive person.[25]

In September 1849, the chiefs at Tonawanda recommended Ely for the position of United States interpreter in the New York sub-agency, stating that he was "a young man of fine, accomplished talents, and his perfect knowledge of both languages makes him fully competent to fill that station and discharge the duties thereof," but Peter Wilson was already serving as the interpreter, and no change was made. Then early in 1850, Morgan told Ely that he thought he could arrange for another engineering job in the office of the resident engineer for the New York canals at Rochester. But Ely was again toying with the idea of going west. He wrote to Schoolcraft in Washington asking whether the Indian Office had any vacant agencies in the West or any other vacancies he might fill, but nothing came of his request. In the end, Ely decided to accept Morgan's offer, and in the spring of 1850 he moved to Rochester to continue his engineering work on the New York canals.[26]

5

Grand Sachem of the Iroquois

THE MOVE TO ROCHESTER took Ely still deeper into the mainstream of midcentury America. He was no longer living where deer tracks could be seen outside his window, but where the smoke from Rochester's mills and factories filled the air, and where the new steamboats could be heard as they came puffing along the canals. Rochester was a busy, growing, industrial city, a major port at the junction of the Genesee Valley and the Erie canals, and like most eastern cities, it had already consigned the Indian to the romantic past. The Iroquois warrior, who once claimed these lands as his own, was now reduced to a cigar store Indian gathering dust on Rochester's streets. Here Red Jacket was no longer the name of a Seneca orator and chief; in Rochester *Red Jacket* was the name of a saloon and a giant ox on exhibition in the Hay Market Lot. *Tonawanda* was more likely to make people in Rochester think of the ocean ship of that name or of a railroad, than of the Indian reservation some forty-five miles to the west. An occasional Indian appeared as a lecturer in Rochester, and the Senecas from Tonawanda sometimes came to play lacrosse or to run in footraces, but when Ely Parker took a room in a boarding house on Main Street and began his work at the canal office, it was something new for Rochester as well as for him.

Some of the Indians had difficulty in adjusting to urban life even during their brief visits. About the time Ely moved to Rochester, a chief from Tonawanda named Big Fire was killed during a visit to Batavia. He was staying on the third floor of the Eagle Tavern, and being in the habit of getting up in the night to go outside, he forgot that he was not in his own log house, climbed out a window, and fell thirty feet to his death. But Ely's previous experiences in Washington and New York had prepared him for city life, and he encountered few difficulties in his new situation. He began his work in the canal office

44

in Rochester and within a year had progressed through the positions of axeman, rodman, leveler, and transitman, to second assistant engineer, learning engineering on the job from the state engineers who had responsibility for the extensive work then being done to enlarge the Erie Canal.[1]

With Ely close at hand, Morgan continued to call on him for assistance in preparing his book on the Iroquois. Not only was Ely providing him with information, but Morgan was using some of Ely's work almost verbatim in the book. After receiving a speech Ely had recorded for him, Morgan told him that he would print it "almost word for word just as you write it." The two were also gathering Indian artifacts for the State Museum at Albany, traveling on one occasion as far as the Iroquois settlement on the Grand River in Canada to make their collections. Ely's prize acquisition was a tomahawk which had once belonged to the Seneca chief Cornplanter, and when he sold it to the State Museum, he prepared and deposited with it a concise history of Cornplanter and his tomahawk.[2]

Morgan's book, League of the Ho-de-no-sau-nee, or Iroquois, published in Rochester early in 1851, was more than a simple description of the Iroquois; it was the first scientific account ever given of any American Indians and the first attempt to interpret Indian life on its own terms. It stated in great detail a theme that Ely borrowed to use in one of his lectures on the Indians: "Notwithstanding the simplicity of Indian life, and its barrenness of those higher social enjoyments which pertain to refined communities, Indian society was bound together by permanent institutions, governed by fixed laws, and impelled and guided by well-established usages and customs." The book came to be regarded as a classic anthropological work, the first of several pioneering books by Morgan which have led some to refer to him as "the Father of American anthropology."[3]

The book was indeed Morgan's, but it also bore the stamp of the Parker family. Nic, in the traditional costume of the Senecas, had posed for the frontispiece, and Carrie, with her head characteristically tilted to one side, had posed for the picture of the Seneca Indian girl. The artifacts illustrating the book had been gathered mainly at the Parker home at Tonawanda, and Morgan acknowledged his indebtedness to Ely "for invaluable assistance during the whole progress of the research, and for a share of the materials. His intelligence, and accurate knowledge of the institutions of his forefathers, have made his friendly services a peculiar privilege." He also dedicated the book to Ely:

Nicholson Parker (c. 1820–92) and Caroline Parker (c. 1830–92), brother
and sister of Ely S. Parker. These drawings, showing Nic and Carrie in
traditional Seneca dress, were used as illustrations in Lewis Henry Morgan's
League of the Ho-de-no-sau-nee, or Iroquois, published in 1851. From
Lewis H. Morgan, *League of the Ho-de-no-sau-nee, or Iroquois. Courtesy of
the University of Rochester Library.*

Caroline Parker. Carrie studied at the Brockport and Cayuga Academies in New York, and later at the Albany State Normal School. At the Normal School she was referred to as an "accomplished, intelligent and beautiful young lady" who was in her own quiet way "outstripping all her companions." From Arthur C. Parker, *The Life of General Ely S. Parker*.

Nicholson Henry Parker as a student at the Albany State Normal School, in 1854. At that time Nic was also lecturing on the Iroquois in central New York. An advertisement for one of his lectures said that "he possesses testimonials of a thorough education, and native powers of eloquence, and will not fail to interest any intelligent audience." From Arthur C. Parker, *The Life of General Ely S. Parker*.

To
Ha-sa-no-an-da,
(Ely S. Parker,)
A Seneca Indian,
this work,
the materials of which are the
fruit of our joint researches,
is inscribed:
in acknowledgment of the obligations,
and in testimony of the friendship of
the Author.

Ely was justly proud of the book and later that year gave a copy to Daniel Webster, who as secretary of state was visiting western New York with President Fillmore, and who in thanking Ely for the book, signed himself "Your friend Danl Webster."[4]

Morgan's gratitude for the Parkers' assistance was also shown by his efforts to enroll Carrie, Nic, and Newton in the State Normal School at Albany. In March 1850, the state legislature passed a law providing for the education of a limited number of Indians at the Normal School, and with Morgan's help the three Parkers were soon entered in the school to begin their training as teachers. People were especially impressed by Carrie, whom they referred to as an "accomplished, intelligent and beautiful young lady," who was in her own quiet way "outstripping all her companions." Ely told Newton how pleased he was that he was enrolled in the school, assuring him that he would now know much more than if he had remained "wild in the Tonawanda woods."[5]

With Ely in Rochester, and Carrie, Nic, and Newton in Albany, Spencer was taking on much of the leadership that the Tonawanda Senecas had come to expect of the Parkers. In March 1851, Ely drafted a bill to be introduced in the state legislature, but it was Spencer who went to Albany as the representative of the Tonawandas and stayed there during the entire session to look out for the Indians' interests. Nevertheless, the Indians still looked to Ely for guidance, and in July 1851, Spencer wrote to him that he was confident the Indians were going to select Ely as a sachem to take the place of John Blacksmith, who had recently died. Ely returned to Tonawanda to attend the council which was to select the new sachem, or grand sachem as the office was also called, and on September 19, 1851, he was proclaimed grand sachem of the Six Nations.[6]

The Mohawks, Oneidas, Onondagas, Cayugas, Tuscaroras, and Senecas were all represented at Tonawanda for the council. A council fire was first kindled, and then the Oneidas, Cayugas, and Tuscaroras, who were "children" to the other three tribes, advanced in double file with their leaders singing the mournful Roll Call of the founders of the confederacy, expressing their grief at the death of the Seneca sachem, John Blacksmith. When the condolence ceremonies ended, the whole group moved to the council ground to hear the ancient laws of the confederacy repeated in song. A number of chiefs were installed in their offices, and then Ely Parker was installed as one of the fifty sachems of the Iroquois Confederacy. Mention was made of deer antlers, the emblem of his office, and he was given his charge as a mentor of the Six Nations. "The thickness of your skin shall be seven spans—which is to say that you shall be proof against anger, offensive actions and criticism. Your heart shall be filled with peace and good will and your mind filled with a yearning for the welfare of the people of the Confederacy. With endless patience you shall carry out your duty and your firmness shall be tempered with tenderness for your people. Neither anger nor fury shall find lodgement in your mind and all your words and actions shall be marked with calm deliberation."

The sachem was also given a new name. He would no longer be Ha-sa-no-an-da; he would be known as Do-ne-ho-ga-wa, "Open Door." It was an appropriate title. The Iroquois thought of their confederacy as a longhouse built across the state of New York. The sachem who bore the name Do-ne-ho-ga-wa had traditionally been the keeper of the western door of the Iroquois longhouse, the one through whom all approaches by other tribes were made. In the changing nineteenth century, Ely Parker had become the one through whom the Indians dealt with outsiders, and he was now in name as well as in fact their "Open Door." His title was equally impressive in English, for he began to sign his official letters "E. S. Parker, Grand Sachem of the Six Nations of Indians in New York and Canada." The man who bore that impressive title was twenty-three years old.[7]

During the council, Ely Parker was also formally invested with the Red Jacket medal. The master of ceremonies identified the medal as the one George Washington had given to Red Jacket in 1792, and he hung it from Parker's neck, counseling him to keep and wear it as a symbol of the bond of peace which was always to exist between the United States and the Six Nations. Parker had actually possessed the medal before this time. When he had visited Albany and Washington as a youth, the medal had been loaned to him by his grandfather

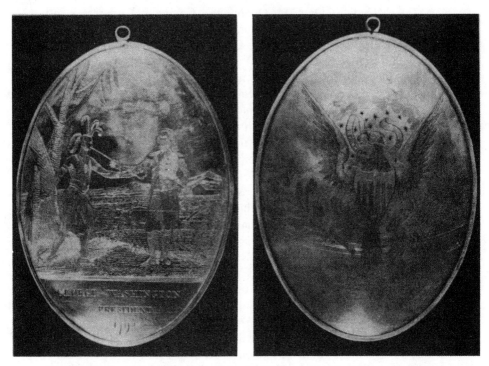

The Red Jacket Medal (front and back). George Washington presented the silver medal to the Seneca orator Red Jacket in 1792. It descended to Ely S. Parker and was his most prized possession. Parker believed that the medal was engraved by David Rittenhouse when he was director of the mint. After Parker's death the medal was purchased from his widow by the Buffalo Historical Society which still has the medal in its collections. *Courtesy of the Buffalo and Erie County Historical Society, Buffalo, New York.*

Jimmy Johnson, who had inherited the medal from Red Jacket, and Parker had worn it as a badge of his authority to speak for the Tonawanda Senecas. Later, learning that Johnson had sent the medal to Albany to be sold to the state museum, Parker intercepted it and purchased it for himself. But now he was to wear it officially as a grand sachem of the Iroquois and the successor of Red Jacket.[8]

Less than a month later, Parker was also elevated in the white man's world. On October 17, 1851, the New York State Canal Board appointed him first assistant engineer on the state canals. His family was proud of his accomplishments, but their pride was soon displaced by grief. On November 11, Ely's brother Spencer died at his home at Tonawanda after an eight-day illness. Spencer and his family had not always agreed on Indian affairs. He once favored emigration to the West and had gone to Missouri for a time, but he had recently drawn closer to the rest of the family, even to the extent of sometimes using the name Parker instead of Cone. He was becoming more and more valuable to the Tonawandas and had frequently visited Albany and Washington on their behalf, often serving as an interpreter in the courts. At the council which raised Ely to the office of sachem, Spencer had been installed as a war chief, but two months later, at the age of thirty-six, he was dead.[9]

After he was raised to the office of sachem, Ely Parker became more involved in the affairs of the whole confederacy, or at least of the Indians who maintained the old forms of government. In January 1852, he was in Albany, where he wrote a letter of introduction for some Onondagas who were going to Washington to meet with President Fillmore. He wrote a sketch of the Cayuga sachem Logan, whose famous speech Thomas Jefferson had greatly admired, and he pressed the federal government for payment of funds which had been embezzled by a former Indian agent. It became clear to the whites that Ely Parker was the man with whom they must deal in their relations with the Iroquois, and in January 1853, New York Governor Horatio Seymour formally recognized him as the "elected Chief and Representative of the ancient confederacy of the Six Nations."[10]

In theory, the Iroquois sachems were all equal, but just as the governor had recognized Parker's superior abilities, others too began to refer to him as "the Chief of the Six Nations," and the "Head Sachem" of his people. Parker found it useful in gaining recognition from the whites to refer to himself sometimes as the Indians' "principal sachem" or "head chief." And whatever the traditional theory, there was little question that many of the Indians as well as the whites regarded him as their leader.[11]

The Tonawanda Senecas continued to depend on his leadership, and called on him to return again to Washington to meet with the officials of Franklin Pierce's new administration to make sure that they understood the Indians' situation. Parker had confidence in Pierce and had even made a speech for him in the recent election. Speaking at a Democratic rally at Fairport in September 1852, Parker said that he was reluctant to express an opinion on the elections since he was not a citizen and could not vote, but that if he could vote, it would be for the Democratic candidates. The September 21, 1852, *Rochester Daily*

Advertiser noted that his speech "displayed a choiceness of language, and an imagery that would do credit to men of more oratorical pretension. Mr. Parker was repeatedly cheered, and resumed his seat amidst the applause of his audience."

The Indians were bitter about the actions of the Fillmore administration and determined to see that the new administration understood their feelings. Fillmore had served as counsel for the Ogden Land Company in their court cases against the Indians. When he became president, he had appointed Benjamin Pringle of Batavia as a special agent to pay the company's improvement money to the Indians and had kept Pringle as his agent for two years, even though the Indians consistently refused to accept the money. Parker's mission in Washington was to let the new administration know that the Indians would never accept the improvement money. As Parker explained: "They do not want it. They do not ask for it, nor would they take it even if it were left at their door, so strong is their determination not to barter away their rights and the true interests of their offspring."[12]

In July 1853, Parker conferred in Washington with George W. Manypenny, the new commissioner of Indian affairs, and perhaps with Pierce himself. He asked that Pringle's commission be recalled in order to avoid any impression that the federal government wanted the Indians to receive the money and lose their lands. He also lodged the Indians' objection to a statement made about them by New York Sub-Agent Stephen Osborne. Osborne had said in one of his reports that the Tonawanda Senecas were "surely but slowly retrograding." Parker wanted the government to know that in spite of constant harassment from the Ogden Land Company, the Tonawandas were, in fact, progressing toward the civilization of white men. They were continually adding to their improvements and were cultivating twice the acreage they had ten years before. They were raising a large surplus of grain and taking stock to the local markets. Within the last three years, fifteen to twenty new frame houses had been built, "which are neatly furnished in the American style, and the outside neatly painted with white paint." Barns had also been built, and they had three schools where five years before there had been only one.

Listening to Parker's arguments, reading his long, reasonable appeals, and seeing the man himself—articulate, knowledgeable, his great emotion deliberately restrained by legal precision—there could be no doubt about the truth of what he was saying: the Tonawanda Senecas were not savages to be forced west of the Mississippi, but reasonable men who believed they had been wronged. A few weeks

Ely S. Parker in a photograph taken in New York City, probably before the Civil War. Parker studied law, but was refused admission to the bar because he was not an American citizen. He later became a civil engineer and was employed by the New York State Canal Board and the U.S. Treasury Department. *Courtesy of the Galena Historical Society, Galena, Illinois.*

after Parker's visit, Pringle returned the improvement money that President Fillmore had placed in his hands, and the Indians rested easier.[13]

When Parker returned home in 1853, he learned that the Indians had won another victory in the courts. The year before, the crucial Blacksmith case had been decided in the Indians' favor by the New York Court of Appeals (although it had again been appealed), and now a judge had finally agreed to issue a warrant to remove the white settlers from the reservation under the law of 1821. It was seven years since the Indians were to have been removed from Tonawanda, and even though the issue was still undecided, the court cases were going well, and Tonawanda was still the Indians' home.[14]

Things were also going well for Ely Parker in his new home in Rochester. He kept in touch with his family, discussing the constant conflicts between the Indians and the white settlers, giving advice to Newton in his studies, and listening to Carrie's concern for Levi's excessive drinking. There were also occasional visits home when he could enjoy his mother's blackberry pies, bread, and green corn. But he was increasingly involving himself in the affairs of Rochester society and gaining that society's acceptance.

He had transferred his Masonic membership to Rochester, progressed into Royal Arch Masonry, and become a member of the Knights Templar, where he enjoyed wearing the knight's uniform of tunic and scarf, gauntlets, and sword. He was a popular speaker at Masonic gatherings. When he spoke at a banquet at Auburn in 1854, "the *ladies vied* with the brethren in closing up the ranks around the *valiant Batchelor Chief*, that they might hear the eloquent outpourings of his generous heart." In his speeches he often testified to the genuine brotherhood he had found in Masonry. He told a gathering of Knights Templar at Owego that "in no other organization or association of men, organized under whatever principle, does the Indian find more genuine and heartfelt sympathy than among the Masons. The Indians ever find them with their hearts in their hands, and arms outspread, ready to receive and sympathize for him; with ears ever open to hear his story of repeated wrongs and oppression, and always ready to alleviate his distresses without malice or deceit."[15]

He had also been accepted as a member of the Rochester Atheneum and Mechanics Association, an organization of over twelve hundred members devoted to enriching the cultural life of the city. Membership in the Atheneum meant access to a library of some fifty-five hundred volumes and a reading room with newspapers from most of the larger eastern cities. This was the age of the lyceum, and the Atheneum, like several other groups in Rochester, brought lecturers and artists to the city, where they performed in Corinthian Hall before as many as sixteen hundred people. During Parker's stay in Rochester the Atheneum brought men like Ralph Waldo Emerson, Oliver Wendell Holmes, and Benjamin Silliman to Corinthian Hall. There were also frequent addresses by such local citizens as Susan B. Anthony and Frederick Douglass. Jenny Lind's appearance had been especially memorable for Parker because in addition to her public concerts, she had given a private concert in one of the hotels for a small group of people which included four Indian chiefs, among whom was Ely Parker.[16]

In January 1854, Parker ran on the Military ticket for election as an associate director of the Atheneum. He was not elected, but the following year he ran again, this time for president of the Atheneum. There were four tickets entered, but the real contest was between John N. Pomeroy, running on the People's ticket, and Ely Parker on the American ticket. Parker was expected to win, and he might have if his opponents had not circulated a rumor that he would not serve if elected. Unfortunately, he was not present to defend himself, and his absence from the city probably cost him the election. He had gone to New York City to attend a meeting of the Military Association of the State of New York as a captain of engineers in the Fifty-fourth Regiment of the New York Militia.[17]

Parker's interest in the militia was not unusual. There were several uniformed military companies in Rochester—the City Dragoons, the Light Artillery, the German Grenadiers, the Union Guards, the Citizens Corps, and the Union Grays—which together comprised the Fifty-fourth Regiment of the Militia and were a major element in the social life of the city. On a national level, the militia was encouraged as a means of reducing the regular army and making the armed forces "more compatible with our republican institutions." But to the average member of the Rochester companies the frequent military excursions, balls, serenades, concerts, parades, and showy uniforms were probably more appealing than any philosophy of government. Parker had served in the militia at least since the summer of 1853, when he participated in an encampment of a thousand men near Syracuse as a captain of engineers with the Rochester regiment. Between twenty and thirty thousand people, including some of the Onondaga Indians who lived nearby, witnessed the militia's parades and sham battles, and Governor Seymour himself visited the camp to review the troops.

A year later Parker attended a camp near Rochester and because of some disagreement during the camp, offered his resignation to Colonel Henry Fairchild, the Rochester banker who commanded the Fifty-fourth Regiment. Fairchild refused to accept the resignation and assured Parker: "You have officially discharged your duty to my entire satisfaction and allow me here to say that there is not an officer in my staff who has been more prompt nor one I think more of or respect higher than yourself. . . . When I retire there is no one who will do more to have you promoted than myself."[18]

But it was promotion by the canal board rather than the militia that Parker was seeking. Although another person held the office, Parker had risen to the point where he was doing the work of the resident engineer at Rochester, the most important residency on the Erie Canal. He had about thirty-five young men working under him, was in charge of some five million dollars worth of work, and wanted to be appointed to the office itself. Early in 1854 there were rumors about a change in the position, and Parker wrote to one of the canal commissioners, Frederick Follett, to tell him that if any change was to be made he wanted the residency himself. Parker disliked the idea of a new man coming in, since that would only result in his having to do another man's work, as he had already been doing.

The following year the matter came up again. At a meeting of the canal board in June 1855, one of the members introduced a resolution to appoint Parker as the resident engineer at Rochester, but the resolution was tabled until July. On July 10, the board met again and appointed Richard Vernam, an engineer who had previously held the position, to the office Parker sought. Feeling that the appointment had been made for political purposes and not on merit, Parker promptly resigned, took a position as chief engineer for the construction of a new ship canal in the South, and on July 23, left Rochester for Norfolk, Virginia, taking with him a corps of engineers to assist in the new work. Some of Parker's young friends voiced their disappointment that he had not been appointed resident engineer but said that "his abilities are appreciated elsewhere if not at home."[19]

A month later Parker and his engineers were back in Rochester. An epidemic of yellow fever had broken out in the South, Parker himself had become quite ill, and the group returned to Rochester to wait until the epidemic subsided. Parker went home to Tonawanda to recuperate and caught up there on the changing conditions in the Parker family. Carrie was teaching at Tonawanda, and Newton had left school and traveled to Indiana, on to Pennsylvania, and finally to Hartford,

Connecticut, where he had embarrassed the family by living with a married woman. Nic had recently been appointed to the coveted position of United States Interpreter for the New York Indians. He had also been married to Martha Hoyt, a white woman and a niece of the Reverend and Mrs. Asher Wright, missionaries at Cattaraugus, for whom Nic was translating the Bible into Seneca. And the Parkers had again been assisting in the preparation of a book on the Iroquois. Anna Johnson, who wrote under the name Minnie Myrtle, had met Nic, Carrie, and later Ely, whom she had been told by the other educated Indians was "the brightest star in the constellation," and when her book on the Iroquois appeared, she included the three Parkers among the Indians who had been her "friends and helpers."[20]

After he had recovered from his illness, Parker left again for Norfolk, stopping on the way in Elmira, New York, where he received the Masonic degrees of Royal and Select Masters. From Elmira he went on to Philadelphia, for the dedication of the Masonic Temple where he "responded to the call for a sentiment with his usual eloquent and appropriate remarks." When Parker and his engineers returned to Norfolk, they began work on a new canal which they named the Chesapeake and Albemarle Ship Canal, extending south from Norfolk into the Albemarle Sound in North Carolina. The work was done for a private company and involved locating and staking out the line and beginning the actual construction of the canal. There was also time for social events. Once, to interrupt the monotony of their evenings, Parker and his men decided to attend a ball in Norfolk, but as they were about to enter the ballroom, they were met and denied admission, perhaps because there was an Indian among them. Parker silently stepped to the front of the group, seized the man in charge by the collar and seat, lifted him over a bannister, and dropped him to the landing below, settling without any further argument the question of their admittance.[21]

In September 1856, Parker returned to New York State, visited Rochester and Tonawanda, where he assisted in the division of Spencer's estate among his three children by his three marriages, and then prepared to go once again to Washington. The Ogden Company was pressing the Pierce administration to appoint another agent to pay the improvement money to the Indians and had gone so far as to offer bribes to the Indians to sign a petition requesting such an appointment. As a result, the Tonawanda chiefs gave Ely and Nic their power of attorney to go to Washington to protest the appointment. The Parkers also carried with them letters from several influential white citizens supporting their case. Frederick Follett of Batavia wrote on behalf of himself "and at least ninety-nine out of every one hundred of the inhabitants of this region" against the appointment. The treaty was a fraud, he said, and the whole matter should be left to the courts to settle. N. E. Paine wrote from Rochester that the overwhelming opinion there was in favor of the Indians, and the New York sub-agent wrote that the Indians were indeed all opposed to receiving the money.[22]

On October 21, 1856, Nic and Ely met with President Pierce. Ely had written a long letter outlining the history of the improvement money and asking that the money not be offered to the Indians again. He laid his letter, along with a petition from the Indians and the letters from their white supporters, out on a table for Pierce's information but found that the president was already well informed in the matter. Pierce told the Parkers that he had thoroughly examined all the papers on the subject twice, in order to meet the constant appeals of the Ogden Company and defend the rights of the Indians. He discussed Ely's and Nic's concerns but assured them that he and the commissioner of Indian affairs had already agreed not to appoint a special agent as Fillmore had done, and that they had no intention of forcing the improvement money on the Indians. The government knew that the matter was before the courts, and wanted to do nothing that would injure the case of either side. Before the Parkers' trip to Washington, the commissioner had tried to assure the Indians that no agent would be appointed, but when they heard it from the president himself, they were convinced and relieved to know that this administration was willing to let the matter be decided in the courts.[23]

The most important of the court cases, the case of *Joseph Fellows . . . vs. Susan Blacksmith and Ely S. Parker,* the administrators of John Blacksmith, was argued before the United States Supreme Court in January 1857. It was the case which had arisen in 1846, when agents of the Ogden Company had turned Chief Blacksmith out of a sawmill on the reservation and assaulted him, and John Martindale came to Washington to argue the case as he had at each stage of its travels through the courts. With him was Ely Parker, and those who followed the arguments before the Court were impressed with Parker's knowledge of the case and gave him credit for making valuable suggestions to Martindale during the arguments. Both the Indians and the Ogden Company hoped for a decisive ruling on the title to the reservation now that the case had come to the Supreme Court.[24]

After the arguments, Parker remained in Washington for some affairs of his own. When the construction of the Chesapeake and

Albemarle Canal had been successfully begun, Parker felt that he had done his duty to the company, and sometime during the winter he had resigned his position. He sought an engineering post with the federal government, through which he hoped to fulfill his old dream of going west. He applied to the Treasury Department for an appointment as superintendent for the construction of public buildings in Chicago. His references were impressive; they included such prominent New Yorkers as former Governor Horatio Seymour, former Canal Commissioner Frederick Follett, former State Treasurer Alvah Hunt, and former State Engineer and Surveyor William J. McAlpine, one of the leading engineers of the day.[25]

The Treasury Department did give him an appointment, but not at Chicago. He was appointed superintendent of light house construction on the upper lakes, and he was instructed by William F. Smith, an army engineer assigned to the Light House Board, to meet him on March 1, at Detroit where the Light House Office was located. Parker went to Detroit as instructed and soon learned the extent of the task before him. The Eleventh Light House District to which he was assigned covered lakes St. Clair, Huron, Michigan, and Superior and required extensive travel and equally extensive shipping arrangements to care for its share of the six hundred light houses and the five thousand buoys and beacons that the United States maintained in 1857. But Parker had barely begun his work at Detroit when Secretary of the Treasury James Guthrie gave him a new appointment as superintendent for the construction of a customhouse and a marine hospital at Galena, Illinois. Parker was instructed to remain at Detroit until the actual construction began, and then to proceed to Galena.[26]

Guthrie's appointment of Parker and the inauguration of President Buchanan, both of which occurred on March 4, 1857, were followed the next day by the announcement of the decision of the Supreme Court in the Blacksmith case. The Court refused, as had all the other courts, to deal with the question of fraud in making the treaties with the Senecas. Fraud or no fraud, the treaties had been ratified and had to be considered the law of the land. But the Court did rule that under the treaties only the United States government had the right to remove the Indians; if the Ogden Company attempted to remove them, it would be guilty of trespass. The decision was not all that the Indians had hoped for—it was a victory on narrow legal grounds rather than a vindication of their cause—but it was a victory. The Court's ruling meant that as long as the federal government was determined to take no action to remove them from Tonawanda, the Ogden Company was powerless to do so. (Important as the case was to the Tonawanda Senecas, it did not command the Court's entire attention. The newspapers noted that Chief Justice Roger Taney was not present to announce the decision in the Blacksmith case. He had remained at home to prepare the opinion in a case involving a slave named Dred Scott, which was to be announced the next day.)[27]

Parker was elated by the Court's decision and made a hurried trip back to Tonawanda to meet the Indians in council and tell them the news, stopping on the way in Rochester to give Martindale the opportunity of going with him and sharing in the celebration. Then he returned to Detroit to await orders from the Treasury Department to proceed to his new assignment in Galena, Illinois.[28]

Galena

~~~~~~

PARKER'S APPOINTMENT to the position in Galena was considered important enough to be noticed in the newspapers, but the notices revealed that few people knew who the new superintendent was. The *Chicago Times* assumed from previous appointments of this kind that he had been in the military service of the United States, while the *Galena Daily Courier* was under the impression that he was an editor of the Geneva, New York, *Gazette*. Senator Stephen Douglas of Illinois was chagrined that he did not know who Parker was, and he asked the Treasury Department for an explanation. The new secretary of the treasury, Howell Cobb of Georgia, assured Douglas that Parker was "a civil Engineer of known and tried capacity, who had been employed upon various public works in the State of New York & stood favourably before the late Secretary for his scientific attainments, integrity, and general fitness for the position." He also listed Parker's impressive references but did not mention that the new superintendent was an Indian.[1]

The New York newspapers soon arrived in Galena and answered the city's questions about Parker's identity. The Syracuse *Journal* remembered Parker as the "Indian Engineer who attended the military encampment in this city, and rode in the staff of Governor Seymour," and the *Buffalo Courier* described him as "the Chief of the Six Nations" and "an Indian of ability and cultivation." The *Courier* could not resist the opportunity of twitting the Know-Nothing party which distrusted foreigners and championed the rights of native Americans. "This is certainly a Native American appointment," it said, "but one from which no 'Know Nothing' need take encouragement."[2]

There was also some adverse comment. Nathaniel Strong, a Seneca who was closely connected with the mission station at Cattaraugus, New York, complained privately about the attention Parker was receiving from the whites. In spite of his missionary education, Parker was not meeting Strong's standard of Christian living, and Strong regretted to see Parker received by the whites "with open hands and hearts." He was also critical of Nic Parker, who was serving as United States interpreter and who was also on trial in Buffalo for breach of contract with a woman named Lucy Greenblanket. Lucy Greenblanket, like Nic, had been educated at the State Normal School, and she and Nic had lived together as husband and wife according to Indian custom for nearly two years. Strong said that Nic was accused of "getting *Babe* of her," after which he had left her and married Martha Hoyt, "and she has now got a Babe too!!" In Strong's opinion the Senecas were being represented by "knaves and scoundrels"; the Parkers were "perfect humbugs and always will be."[3]

After working in Detroit only five weeks, Ely Parker moved to Galena, arriving there on April 6, 1857, and settled into the town's best hotel, the DeSoto House. He had wanted to go west for years, but once there, he found that the West was not at all what he had expected. His first impression was that it was a "dark and benighted part of the globe" with no society or amusements "unless it be drinking whiskey, and plugging one's fist into somebody el[s]es mug." He was critical of the greed, the "abundant use, in every expression or remark made in any company, of hard epithets," and "the practice of cheating & bare faced lying and unconscientiously swindling a neighbor." On the other hand, he was favorably impressed by the richness of the country, the abundance of steamboats and railroads, and the lead mines for which Galena was named.[4]

Because of its lead mines, Galena had grown rapidly and had become one of the leading cities between St. Louis and Chicago. The town, built on the steep slopes of the Galena River overlooking the steamboat landings near its junction with the Mississippi, was a familiar sight to western travelers. Galena also had an aggressive congressman, Elihu B. Washburne, who had convinced the federal government that the busy town needed both a new customhouse to house the collector of customs and the post office, and a marine hospital to care for sick boatmen. It was the construction of these buildings that Parker was to supervise.

The buildings were a challenge to Parker's abilities. He found that the site chosen for the customhouse could not support such a building without piling, which had not been considered in the plans. Moreover, the customhouse was to be made of stone, and the marine hospital partly of stone, and yet there was no stone suitable for such a use

A daguerreotype by Alexander Hesler of the Galena, Illinois, levee, 1852–54, showing the steamboats *New St. Paul* and *Nominee*. In 1857 the secretary of the treasury appointed Parker superintendent for the construction of a customhouse and a marine hospital at Galena. While living there and in nearby Dubuque, Iowa, Parker became friends with several men who later gained prominence in the Civil War, among them John A. Rawlins and Ulysses S. Grant. *Chicago Historical Society.*

anywhere near Galena. And Parker found that government regulations required that he submit even his smallest decisions for review by Treasury Department officials in their remote offices in Washington. Within a few days of his arrival, he began a long series of communications about his work with Washington and then began to watch the mail for their replies, "waiting every day, Micawber like, for 'something to turn up.' "[5]

The authorities concurred with his judgment that the stone around Galena could not be used in the customhouse and authorized him to travel to other quarries to inspect other stone. After the ground had been broken for the customhouse, with suitable ceremonies and speeches by Parker and Congressman Washburne, Parker set out to visit quarries at Athens, Joliet, and LaSalle. But the stone he finally recommended he found at Nauvoo, on the Mississippi River some 240 miles below Galena. The ill-fated Mormon Temple at Nauvoo, burned by an anti-Mormon mob and later destroyed by a cyclone, had been built of the same white limestone Parker chose, yet even in the ruins of the temple the stone retained a good appearance. With the department's approval, Parker made arrangements to open a quarry at Nauvoo and to ship the stone up the river to Galena.

He had been in Galena less than three months when Indian affairs called him back to Washington. The Indians thought that the Supreme Court decision in the Blacksmith case had secured their homes at Tonawanda, but they were mistaken. It secured them only as long as the federal government took no action to remove the Indians, but the new Buchanan administration, with no prior notice, sent the commissioner of Indian affairs to Tonawanda in June 1857, to pay the improvement money himself and to give the Indians the choice of going to Cattaraugus or going west. The Tonawanda chiefs responded by sending Parker and three friendly white men, John Martindale, Frederick Follett, and William G. Bryan, to Washington to appeal to the president.[6]

In a series of meetings with the commissioner of Indian affairs, the secretary of the interior, and with President Buchanan in late June and early July, the delegates suggested a plan that would end the difficulties once and for all. The treaties of 1838 and 1842 had granted the Indians certain lands in Kansas where they were to be settled when they left New York. The delegates proposed that the Kansas lands be exchanged for a permanent title to the Tonawanda Reservation. On July 3, an agreement was signed under which the Indians would give up all claims to the lands in Kansas, and in return, money would be made available to the Indians to purchase part or all of the reservation from the Ogden Land Company. It would still be necessary to negotiate with the company, but everyone agreed that the company wanted money, not land, and that the arrangements could be made.[7]

Pleased with his role in the negotiations, Parker returned to Galena only to find that efforts had been made during his absence to have him removed from his superintendency. The Galena Democrats resented that the superintendent's position had been given to a stranger without their consultation, and while Parker was in Washington, Bushrod B. Howard, the Galena postmaster, appealed to Senator Douglas for Parker's removal and the appointment of a local politician in his place. In response, Douglas added his voice to those calling for Parker's removal.

Parker felt the mounting pressure and finally wrote to the secretary of the treasury about it. He said that he had been aware of the "strenuous and unremitting efforts" to remove him but preferred to ignore them and to spend his time performing his duties. He was writing now, he said, only because some influential Democrats, who did not want to see him removed, had urged him to, and he was writing only to ask that "should the Department contemplate a change in this Superintendency, they may give me due notice, to enable me to resign, instead of being subject to the ignominy of a discharge." Parker was proud of his reputation and wanted to save it, even if he could not save his job.[8]

But Parker had some influential friends who came to his defense. Frederick Follett, who had supervised Parker's work on the New York canals, was personally acquainted with Lewis Cass, the secretary of state, and appealed to him to intervene in the matter. Follett's endorsement of Parker was unqualified: "Mr. Parker, during the six years I was Canal Com^r, was an Engineer on my Division, and a good and faithful one, too, and left the service of the state with credit, and at his own request. He is an Indian, and the Grand Sachem of his tribe, a man of education, and a gentleman. He is one of that class that the Govt. should take a pride in helping along." Congressman Washburne also advised against the removal, and Richard Jackson, a Galena lawyer, wrote to Washington protesting against "the atrocious efforts of *pot house* politicians to remove Parker. . . . They have driven the red man almost from the American continent, and even after he is civilized and devoted to the institutions of the country they propose to wage a war of extermination!" In a second letter Jackson gave what he must have intended as a recommendation and a compliment: "He is a *gentleman,* tho' an Indian."[9]

Apparently a good many people in Galena agreed with Jackson, for a petition signed by the mayor and the aldermen of the city was circulated opposing Parker's removal. The Treasury Department, satisfied with Parker's work, ignored the appeals to remove him, and apart from a brief revival of the issue in the fall elections, nothing more was heard about replacing the new superintendent.[10]

On October 30, 1857, Parker received a telegram from New York asking him to return to the reservation to help negotiate a new treaty on the basis of the agreement made in Washington in July. He left

immediately for Tonawanda, where he and the other men who had
been in Washington met in council with Charles E. Mix, the chief
clerk of the Office of Indian Affairs. Agreement was quickly reached,
and a new treaty signed on November 5. Under its terms, the Tonawandas gave up all rights to the lands in Kansas and to the fund of
$400,000 which had been promised to assist in their removal. In return,
they were allowed up to $256,000 for purchases of land from the
Ogden Land Company. The price of the land was limited to twenty
dollars per acre unless specifically approved by the president, and the
Indians were guaranteed no less than 6,500 acres, or about half the
reservation. The improvement money, the $15,018.36 which had been
a source of contention for so long, was to be paid to the chiefs to
compensate any Indians who might lose their improvements in the
transfer of land.[11]

When the treaty was signed, Parker returned to Galena, but in
January 1858, he again passed through Tonawanda on his way to
Washington, where he met with members of Congress and went daily
to the Office of Indian Affairs to do what he could to ensure that the
treaty would be ratified. The treaty was finally ratified, and John
Martindale was selected by the Indians to make the land purchases
from the Ogden Company. A great deal was lost by the Tonawandas
under the treaty, for they were able to purchase only about three-fifths
of the land they held when the struggle for the reservation began. But
the smaller reservation was theirs by right of purchase, ownership the
Ogden Company understood and would respect.[12]

The long struggle was over. The Indians were grateful for the
assistance of friendly whites during the struggle, and especially for the
efforts of John Martindale, who as one observer said, had "for the last
fifteen years devoted his best powers, in the meridian of life," to defending the Indians' rights. (Years later, when Martindale died, one of
the Senecas wrote from Tonawanda, "I wish to know when our great
beloved friend is to be buried . . . for we are going to send some
Chiefs at the time, for he was a great Chief also.")

The Indians also appreciated Ely Parker's services and made him
a gift of fifty acres of their hard-won land to add to his farm. When
they asked Martindale's approval of the gift, he replied that "it was
something, still it was not *one-third* the compensation which the
Grand Sachem ought to receive at the hands of the Tonawandas for
his services." Parker himself took great pride in his part in the Tonawandas' struggle and boasted about it in a letter to his old principal
at Yates Academy: "Notwithstanding therefore the Presidents order

John Henry Martindale (1815–81). A West Point graduate who became a brigadier general in the Civil War, Martindale was better known among the Tonawanda Senecas for his persistent and successful defense of the Indians' rights to their reservation. *Courtesy of U.S. Signal Corps, photo No. 111-B-4083 (Brady Collection), National Archives and Records Service.*

to remove the Indians, I succeeded in staying his heavy hand, entered into negotiations with him, by which I raised $300,000 and out of that sum I bought back for the Indians the homes in which they had always lived. They are now comfortably settle[d,] fear nothing, owe nothing & have money in [the] bank. I am als[o] relieved of a great responsibility, which was shouldered upon me when yet a mere youth, the weight of which, I fear, has made me prematurely old."[13]

As a postscript to the whole affair, another court case reached the United States Supreme Court in February 1859. The case was a test of the New York law of 1821, prohibiting white intrusion on Indian lands, under which John Martindale had repeatedly tried to evict white settlers from the reservation, and again it was Martindale who argued the case before the Court. The Court's decision upheld the law and the actions taken under it, ruling that the law was a proper police regulation necessary to "protect these feeble and helpless bands from imposition and intrusion." The decision came too late to be of much practical help to the Indians, but it did add one final guarantee that the land owned by the Indians would remain theirs.[14]

With the Tonawandas secure in their homes, Parker devoted his full attention to his duties at Galena. There had been delays in the work on the federal buildings, most of them due to an exceptionally difficult contractor, but Parker dealt with them skillfully and won the respect of Galena's citizens as he did so. When the cornerstone of the customhouse was laid on April 15, 1858, both the Masonic Order and the Galena Brass Band came to assist in the celebrations.

Engineers were scarce in the West, and there were additional requests for Parker's services. The officials of Jo Daviess County called on him to make surveys and estimates for two wooden bridges in the county, and he provided Galena officials with a survey of the Galena River for a lock they hoped to build. Parker enjoyed his life in Galena, full as it was with "plenty of work, and troops of pretended friends." In fact, he was troubled that he enjoyed it so much. In August 1859, he had made a business trip to New York which included a visit with his old schoolmate Henry Flagler in Bellevue, Ohio, and a brief visit to his home at Tonawanda. But while he was in New York, he began to long for the West, feeling a kind of homesickness even when he was under his own father's roof, "surrounded by all whom I hold most dear on earth." The attraction of life among whites in the busy, driving West proved stronger than that of his own home among the Indians, and that realization set up a storm of emotions within him. He said that his visit home "almost [made] me weep to think that my fate had doomed me to walk in other channels. With such feelings raging within me, after a few days I turned my face westward, and made all possible haste to reach again the scene of my labors, that I might drive such thoughts far away from me. I wanted to look upon my friends, and yet dared not, le[s]t my countenance might betray the storm within." He had deliberately chosen to depart from the ways of his ancestors and was successfully traveling in the way of the whites. But the conflict between his two worlds was not yet resolved, and he was eager to forget it in his work.[15]

Masonry had become increasingly important to him as he sought acceptance in his new western home. Prejudice against the Indian was much more blatant in Galena than it had been in New York. Galena's citizens could still remember fortifying the town against Black Hawk and his warriors in 1832, and many were inclined to agree with Artemus Ward that "Injins is Pizin, wherever found." But whatever the attitudes of Galena's citizens, Parker found genuine acceptance in Masonry. He helped to organize a new lodge, Miners Lodge No. 273, and the members elected him their first worshipful master. As the men worked together to outfit new lodge rooms in Mitchell's Hall on Bench Street, Parker made some deep and lasting friendships with his fellow Masons.[16]

One of those friends was William R. Rowley, a former New Yorker who had taught school in Jo Daviess County, served as sheriff, and became clerk of the circuit court. Parker had two Masonic friends named John Smith. John Eugene Smith, the son of a Swiss soldier in Napoleon's armies and fluent himself in both French and German, was a jeweler with a shop on Main Street and an active interest in local politics. John Corson Smith was a carpenter and builder from Philadelphia who had built many of Galena's most substantial buildings. Parker introduced him to Masonry, and although Smith was only four years younger, he thought of Parker as his father in Masonry and showed his regard by naming a son for his Indian friend.[17]

Parker enjoyed the pageantry of Masonry and took a conspicuous part in the public dedication of the new lodge hall, but it was the brotherhood he found among Masons that he never tired praising. In September 1859, he attended a Masonic convention in Chicago and with deep emotion testified to the meaning Masonry had for him.

> He spoke of himself as almost a lone remnant of what was once a noble race; of his struggles in coming forward to manhood, and seeing his race disappearing as dew before the morning sun. As he found his

race thus wasting away, he asked himself:—"Where shall I go when the last of my race shall have gone forever? Where shall I find home and sympathy when our last council-fire is extinguished? I said, I will knock at the door of MASONRY, and see if the white race will recognize me, as they had my ancestors, when we were strong and the white men weak. I knocked at the door of the *Blue Lodge,* and found brotherhood around its altar. I knelt before the Great Light in the Chapter, and found companionship beneath the Royal Arch. I entered the Encampment, and found valiant Sir Knights willing to shield me there without regard to race or nation. I went farther. I knelt at the cross of my Savior, and found Christian brotherhood, the crowning charity of the masonic tie. I feel assured that when my glass is run out, and I shall follow the footsteps of my departed race, masonic sympathies will cluster round my coffin, and drop in my lonely grave the evergreen acacia, sweet emblem of a better meeting!"

When he had finished and had sat in silence a few moments, he rose and said:

I have omitted one thing which I ought to have said. I have in my possession a memento which I highly prize—I wear it near my heart. It came from my ancestors to me, as their successor in office. It was a present from WASHINGTON to my grandfather, RED JACKET, when your nation was in its infancy.

He took a wampum cord from his neck, drew out the Red Jacket medal, and passed it along the tables. The medal had become increasingly important to him as a symbolic tie to his Indian past, just as Masonry had become increasingly important to him as a symbol of his acceptance in his new white world.[18]

7

Captain Parker and Captain Grant

Parker was successful in completing his work on the Galena customhouse, and the building was formally inaugurated on August 8, 1859. It was a handsome two-story stone building, with the Galena post office on the first floor and the offices of the collector of customs and the inspector and surveyor of the port on the second floor. A Galena newspaper considered it "the most perfect structure north of St. Louis and west of Chicago" and gave due credit to Parker for his role in its construction. "Mr. Parker has discharged the duties of his important position to the satisfaction of everyone; and by strict attention, impartiality and perfect knowledge of every branch of work, contributed, in a very great measure, to the successful completion of the building."

The marine hospital, a large brick building surrounded by verandas and topped by an observatory with a splendid view of the river, was completed at about the same time, giving proof, the papers said, "that the Government has a public care for the lone and friendless Mariner in the time of his adversity from sickness." The only discordant note in the celebration was the Treasury Department's belated recognition that Congressman Washburne had acquired buildings for his district far larger than it needed. The small number of sailors who would be treated in the marine hospital, the Department learned, could be cared for much more cheaply under private contracts, and the massive customhouse and post office building was to be occupied by only three employees.[1]

At the same time that Parker was building the customhouse in Galena, the government was building a similar, but somewhat larger customhouse in Dubuque, Iowa, about seventeen miles away, and Parker also became involved in its construction. In December 1858, he had gone to Dubuque as consulting engineer, and during the following year he returned frequently as consulting superintendent, charged

71

U.S. Customhouse and Post Office, Galena, Illinois. Parker, who was an accomplished civil engineer, was selected to supervise the construction of this limestone building for the U.S. Treasury Department. Completed in 1859, it is still in use as the Galena Post Office. *Courtesy of the Galena Historical Society, Galena, Illinois.*

especially with settling differences between the superintendent at Dubuque, Joseph C. Jennings, and the local contractors, a task which he found "exceedingly unpleasant."

As the buildings in Galena neared completion, the Treasury Department decided to remove Jennings from his position and appoint Parker in his place. Jennings hurried to Washington to plead that he not be removed and even obtained an interview with President Buchanan, but to no avail. In October 1859, Parker took a leave of absence to visit Albany and then traveled to Washington, where he received the appointment as superintendent at Dubuque. Parker did not consider the Dubuque superintendency a desirable appointment. Jennings had not handled the work well, and the resulting difficulties with the contractors had become an issue in local politics. But Parker had made it clear that if the department assigned him to the position in Dubuque he would use his "best endeavors to advance the interests of the Government in that quarter."[2]

On his return to the West, Parker moved to Dubuque and took rooms in the elegant 125-room Julien House, which boasted water closets and bath rooms on each floor, rosewood chairs in the parlor, and its own omnibus and wagons to carry passengers and baggage free of charge. He soon became something of a public figure in Dubuque and made some new friends there, but he never formed the close ties with Dubuque that he had with Galena. There was hardly time for that, as he was spending a great deal of his time traveling. Early in 1860 he went to New York at Martindale's request to assist him in some affairs concerning the New York Indians. In July he traveled over two thousand miles to purchase iron work for the customhouse, visiting Chicago, Milwaukee, Cleveland, Cincinnati, Wheeling, Pittsburgh, and Rochester. He also made frequent trips to Nauvoo to visit the stone quarries and to other towns near Dubuque to procure materials for the customhouse. Early in 1861 he was back in Albany with John Martindale to introduce legislation on behalf of the Tonawanda Senecas.[3]

Parker also visited various Masonic activities. In June 1860, the Iowa Masons appointed Parker representative of the Grand Lodge of Iowa near the Grand Lodge of Illinois, and in October he was elected grand orator of the Grand Lodge of Illinois. Both Masonic activities and some remaining government business frequently took him back to Galena. It was on one of these visits that he met a former army officer who had recently moved to Galena from St. Louis, Ulysses S. Grant. Years later, Parker recounted the meeting:

My acquaintance with the general began in the summer of 1860, at Galena, Illinois, where he was employed in his father's store. I observed at our first meeting how very diffident and reticent he was. It was with difficulty that information on any subject could be obtained from him. Selling goods from behind a counter did not seem to be his forte, for if he was near the front door when a customer entered, he did not hesitate to make a pretty rapid retreat to the counting-room which was in the rear part of the building, leaving the visitor to be waited on by some other employee. I saw him quite frequently, becoming friendly by degrees as we became better acquainted, which friendship continued to the day of his death.[4]

Grant's diffidence and reticence proved no barrier to friendship with one who had been raised among the Iroquois. As Parker said on another occasion, "he reminded me a great deal of some of my Indian friends. It was necessary to break the ice before the good qualities of the general could be seen." But having broken the ice, Parker found him to be not only "companionable but possessed of a warm and sympathetic nature."[5]

The two men had a good deal in common. Both were known as military men. The people in Galena addressed the newcomer as Captain Grant, and because of Parker's military background the people in Dubuque called him Captain Parker. Grant, with his West Point education, may have been the only person in Galena whose training in engineering could be compared to Parker's. The two were also probably the only people there who had had a personal acquaintance with Franklin Pierce; Parker had met Pierce in his office at the White House, and Grant had played cards with him in Mexico City during the Mexican War. They shared, too, at least one experience which helped cement the friendship. Parker was once walking past a barroom when he heard loud noises from within it and recognized the voice of his new friend. There was a fight in progress with everyone opposing Grant. Parker went to his rescue, and the two military men took a defensive position back to back and successfully fought off the attackers.[6]

Grant also became acquainted with one of Parker's friends, John Aaron Rawlins, "a rising and promising young lawyer" then serving as the county attorney. Parker had known Rawlins since 1858, and said that in spite of political differences they had been "excellent friends" since their first meeting. Rawlins was a native of Galena, where as a boy he had helped to support his family by selling charcoal to the lead mines, and as an aspiring politician he was known as "the Coal Boy of Jo Daviess County." To Parker he was simply "Black John," his swarthy complexion, black hair, and flashing black eyes clearly setting him off from Parker's other friends named John. Rawlins was a champion of Stephen Douglas and a Democratic candidate for elector in the presidential election of 1860.[7]

The election of Abraham Lincoln and the scramble for office under the new administration posed an immediate threat to Parker's position. William Martin, a Dubuque brick mason who had worked under both Jennings and Parker on the new customhouse, solicited a "mammoth petition" asking that he be appointed to replace Parker. To add urgency to the matter, reports were sent to Washington charging Parker with drunkenness and interfering in politics in New York during the election.

The new secretary of the treasury, Salmon P. Chase, was prepared to remove Parker and appoint Martin in his place, but the removal was strongly resisted by those who knew Parker's work. William Buel Franklin, the engineer in charge of Treasury Department construction, told Chase that Parker's work had been entirely satisfactory, and Franklin "very respectfully but earnestly" recommended that the new secretary not make a change for political reasons. As to the charge of drunkenness, Franklin reported that "Mr. Clark, the chief Clerk in this office, inspected the Building at DuBuque last Season. He saw Mr. Parker there, travelled with him, and has seen him here on business. He avers that he never suspected Mr. Parker of being a drinking man. The letters and reports of Mr. Parker on file in the office, show that his business has been performed well and systematically and he has a clear head." Franklin supported his views with a recommendation from John C. Smith, which had been endorsed by Congressman Washburne.

Franklin admitted that Parker appeared to have made speeches for Douglas in New York during the presidential election and said that if another person just as competent for Parker's place could be found, it might be well to replace him, but he did not consider Martin such a man. Franklin insisted that politics had not been involved in Parker's appointment and asked that politics not be the cause of his removal. But Chase ignored his appeals, and on March 26, 1861, he directed Franklin to remove Parker and appoint Martin in his place.[8]

Parker was at Nauvoo when the order for his removal was issued, and he did not learn about it until his return to Dubuque on April 5. During the four days that were allowed him to settle his accounts, he wrote to S. M. Clark, Franklin's chief clerk, to thank him for his efforts to save the superintendency for him, saying unconvincingly that "your friendship in the matter, has taken away all the pain of decapitation." He received a "splendid certificate and a very complimentary letter" from the department, but his removal nevertheless appeared to him to be the end of his public career. "I do not expect," he wrote, "ever again to hold any public position."[9]

One of Parker's last public appearances in Dubuque was at an anniversary banquet of the Governor's Greys, a local military unit which had made him an honorary member. Captain Parker arrived partway through the festivities and was greeted with "vociferous cheers." He was escorted to a place of honor, after which the president of the group introduced him as the "Big Injun," and Parker responded to this joviality by calling the president "Tecumseh," and another official the "Little Injun."

The meeting grew more serious as the discussion turned toward news of the impending war. Finally Captain Parker was called on to speak, and as so often before, he shared his emotions with the help of his medal.

> After a short but eloquent speech, in which he alluded feelingly to the present distracted condition of our country and to the part his forefathers took in its earlier history, he presented for the inspection of the party, a testimonial received by his grandfather, the redoubtable Red Jacket, from General George Washington. It was a rare old relic of quaint design and valuable beyond all consideration, from its associations. . . . This memento of the days of the revolution was passed around the table by Sergeant Russell. It was regarded by every one with reverent curiosity, and it awakened every spark of patriotism that slept in the hearts of the gallant Greys.[10]

The spark of patriotism had also been awakened in Galena. The fall of Fort Sumter and Lincoln's call for volunteers resulted in public meetings and patriotic speeches, and Parker said that "the inspiriting notes of the drum and fife were heard on every street at all hours of the day and night." John Rawlins made it clear that his Democratic politics would not stand in the way of his response to the president's call: "We will stand by the flag of our country," he said, "and appeal to the God of battles!" John E. Smith was appointed aide-de-camp to Governor Yates with the rank of colonel and was soon preparing to leave for Springfield. In the midst of these affairs, Parker met Grant and asked him "whether he intended taking any part in the impending contest. He replied that he honored his country, and that having received his education at the expense of the Government, it was entitled to his services, and he should tender them to the proper authorities at Washington."[11]

Parker himself does not appear to have been as single-minded as his friends. As he prepared to return to New York State, he visited Davenport where the Governor's Greys had already been called into service. Going on to St. Louis, he stopped long enough to write to Captain Francis J. Herron, the commander of the Greys. Parker was interested in some "project" suggested by Herron and wrote that he was "entirely foot loose & ready, if the times will warrant, to engage in any undertaking promising profit." Nothing came of it, however, and summer found him at his home at Tonawanda, unemployed except for some farmwork and occasional surveying on the reservation.[12]

War excitement was as strong in New York as it was in the West, and even the tranquillity of the reservation was disturbed as the Indians began to speak of volunteering for the army. It was not long before Parker, too, decided to offer his services in the defense of the country, as his father had done before him in the War of 1812. He dutifully asked his father's permission and then proceeded to Albany to ask the governor for a commission. But in spite of his previous service as a captain of engineers in the militia and the obvious need for engineering skills, no commission was offered him.[13]

Never one to accept the thwarting of his own ambitions easily, Parker decided to seek a commission from the federal government. On September 2, 1861, John Martindale left for Washington to offer his West Point training to the government. Before the month ended, Parker was visiting Martindale, now a brigadier general stationed at Fort Corcoran near Washington. He also visited the Indian Office and tried to persuade the officials there to pay the Tonawandas some $13,000 in annuities that was owed them. It was probably at this same time that Parker offered his services to the War Department, only to be rebuffed again. He then appealed for assistance to Secretary of State William H. Seward, a fellow New Yorker who, only two years before, had spoken effectively in the Senate on behalf of the New York Indians. Seward bluntly refused to help. "Mr. Seward in a short time said to me that the struggle in which I wished to assist, was an affair between white men and one in which the Indian was not called on to act. The fight must be made and settled by the white men alone. He said, 'Go home, cultivate your farm, and we will settle our own troubles among ourselves without any Indian aid' ."[14]

"I did go home," Parker wrote, "and planted crops and myself on the farm, sometimes not leaving it for four and six weeks at a time." But he did not give up his efforts to enter the army. Recognizing that his lack of citizenship was a handicap to his ambitions, he submitted a petition to the United States Congress asking that they grant him citizenship. Speaking of himself as the petitioner, he wrote that "he is a freeholder, paying taxes in the states of New York, Iowa and Minnesota—that he has held various positions of trust and honor in the state and federal service, and that he has a high veneration for the laws and institutions of this, his native country, and he respectfully prays your Honorable Body to grant him the rights, privileges and franchises of an American citizen." The House Committee on the Judiciary, however, ruled that Congress had the power only to make uniform rules of naturalization, and that this did not include the power to confer citizenship on a single Indian, and therefore it refused his request.[15]

General John Martindale returned to Batavia in the fall of 1862 to recuperate from the effects of typhoid fever, which he had contracted in the army. He was Batavia's best-known soldier, and a public reception was held for him, where a crowd of thousands heard him speak. A forceful speaker, Martindale was a man of medium height, with brilliant hazel eyes and black, curly hair. He had a pleasant voice and spoke in "measured and well-balanced sentences," with "well-chosen words." His theme in Batavia was the need for more volunteers in the army. "He spoke of the war, and the imperative need of men to fill up our exhausted ranks, and earnestly and most eloquently appealed to our young men to rally to the support of the government in its present great emergency." But it had been a year since his friend Ely Parker had visited him at Washington and volunteered his services to the government, and those services still had not been accepted.[16]

Parker began to resign himself to a farmer's life on the reservation. Some Indian affairs had to be attended to—in June 1862, he was elected clerk of the Tonawanda Senecas, one of several new positions he had recommended to help adjust the old forms of government to changing times, and there were occasional trips to Albany and Batavia for the Tonawandas—but farming became his major occupation. Still it must have been clear to his Galena friend J. Russell Jones, when he received a letter dated October 30, from Parker, that his Indian friend had no desire to remain a farmer. "I have spent all my money and wasted a large proportion of my energies in farming, and it does seem that I have cast my seed upon stony ground, for I get no returns, nor is there much prospect of my getting any thing back very soon. I do believe it costs more to run a farm that [sic] it does a Mississippi steamboat. However I am stuck, and must remain so until I can get out."

The Parker house on the Tonawanda Reservation. The house, which was
fitted up for his parents by Ely Parker, is still standing on the reservation.
From Arthur C. Parker, *The Life of General Ely S. Parker.*

He spoke, too, about his need for a wife on the farm, but he
did not seem serious about it. "I suppose I ought to have one. In farming she might be useful, but should I at any time abandon farming,
what am I to do with the article. I suppose you would say set her up
as a parlor ornament. Well, I should think twice, before doing so
violent an act to my sense of proper usefulness. Do you know, among
your extensive list of female acquaintences, a good, strong, healthy
double breasted female, who would like to be a farmers wife. If so,
recommend me."

Farming did give him time for reflection, and his thoughts were
often on his western friends. As he wrote to Jones: "While my hands
labor, my mind loafs away to other scenes and holds silent converse
with absent friends. You cannot imagine how often during the past
summer while plodding after the plow, my mental hands have held 2
p^{rs} [two pairs] against your everlasting fulls [full house] or 'phoars'

[fours.] With Black John, I have had many good and glorious times; spiritually I mean. God bless & preserve the old Boy."[17]

Living at Tonawanda also gave him time for Masonic affairs. Parker helped organize a new lodge in Akron, near the reservation, and was elected its first master. Because he was living at Tonawanda, he was at home when his mother died. She had been ill only two or three days when she died early in the morning on February 23, 1862, at the age of 75. Parker and his brother Levi went to Akron to buy a coffin for her, and Newton Parker helped to lay her out in the Indian style, dressing her in a black broadcloth petticoat, a red figured dress, black beaded leggings, deerskin moccasins, and with an old style cape or collar around her neck. She was buried on a stormy day—two cutters and five sleighs made up her funeral procession—but in spite of the storm the Baptist Church was crowded for her funeral service. Nic was not able to be at home for her funeral, and Parker described the family's grief to him: "This sad and awful bereavement throws a great gloom upon our family."[18]

Mystifying as it must have been to Parker, other Indians were finding their way into the army. In October 1861, twenty-five Saint Regis Indians enlisted in the Ninety-eighth Regiment, New York Volunteer Infantry, and one of them was killed at the battle of Fair Oaks the following year. Several Indians were also observed by New Yorkers in some Wisconsin regiments that passed through Buffalo on their way to Washington. But the Indians in western New York had, like Parker, been refused entry into the army simply because they were Indians. Cayuga Chief Peter Wilson, who was eager to enlist as a surgeon, reminded the army officers that his father, grandfather, and great-grandfather had all served in the War of 1812, and that his uncle had been killed at the Battle of Chippewa fighting for the United States. He could not understand the present administration's refusal to accept Indian enlistments, and he offered to get a party of the Indians together for a game of ball so that the officers could see at first hand the Indians' "great agility and their powers of endurance."[19]

The issue became more confused when military officers in western New York suddenly began to recruit Indians for the army. Among those who were gathering the recruits was Parker's brother Newton. Newton, too, had been rebuffed on his first attempt to enlist in the army. "Glory to God!!!" he had written his wife, "I. N. Parker is not accepted in the volunteer service for the 'U. S. Army'. The officer . . . could not accept *me* because there is no regulation, that is no law for accepting the 'red man'." But less than a month later he appeared at the

Harrison Alexander (1841–1931), one of the New York Indians who served in the Union army during the Civil War. Born in Genesee County, Alexander enlisted in October 1861, in Company E, Eighth Regiment, New York Cavalry, and was discharged in June 1865. Like Ely Parker, many of the Indians were rebuffed in their first attempts to volunteer, but by the war's end, at least 162 and perhaps as many as 300 New York Indians served as soldiers and sailors for the Union.

meeting house at Tonawanda as a recruiter in a soldier's uniform. "Everybody bunged out their eyes, to see me dressed so," he wrote, ". . . something for the Injuns, I expect, to see an Indian dressed in soldier's uniform." But, after less than two months of recruiting and a promotion to sergeant, Newton and his recruits were all discharged from the army on the orders of Governor Edwin D. Morgan.[20]

In order to find out whether or not Indians would be accepted as soldiers, Parker wrote to the Indian Office in Washington. Commissioner William P. Dole replied that the War Department had assured him that although Indians would not be compelled to serve, neither would they be forbidden to serve, and the Indian Office, on its part, had no desire to interfere with enlistments. No sooner had this assurance been given, however, than Secretary of War Edwin Stanton arbitrarily ordered the military officers at Buffalo to limit the number of Indian recruits to three hundred.

Colonel John Fisk, who was raising a regiment in western New York, and who hoped to include two or three companies of Indians, asked Parker's help in raising the three hundred recruits. Fisk admitted that three hundred was a small number, but he believed it was a glorious number, the very number of Leonidas' Spartan troops, and he advised Parker to seize the opportunity and take a command over them. He acknowledged that the War Department's rebuff of Parker must have been discouraging, but he encouraged him to lay aside any feeling of indignation and go on to the renown and immortality he was sure would come to the head sachem if he were to lead the Indians into battle.[21]

For some reason, Parker never received a command over the Indian recruits. His brother Newton, however, did become one of their noncommissioned officers. Newton enlisted in June 1862, in the Fifty-third Regiment, New York Volunteer Infantry, and in September was transferred to the 132d Regiment. He became Third Sergeant in Company D, whose Second Lieutenant was a twenty-seven-year-old Tuscarora chief named Cornelius C. Cusick, and which included enough Indians to be known as the "Tuscarora Company." In the fall of 1862, the 132d Regiment was mustered into the service of the United States and left New York for Virginia, and finally was stationed at New Berne, North Carolina.[22]

After almost two years on the farm Parker had apparently exhausted all possible approaches to a commission in the army. His friends in the western armies, however, requested his services, and a commission finally came to him unsolicited. John E. Smith, the Galena jeweler, had become a brigadier general in command of a division in Grant's army. He had corrresponded with Parker and knew that his friend wanted to enter the army, and on April 2, 1863, he wrote to Washington to recommend that Parker be appointed as an assistant adjutant general and placed on his staff. He said that Parker was "well qualified for the position by Education and experience being also a good practical Civil Engineer, having been for several years in charge of the construction of Public works for the U. S. Government. His loyalty is unquestionable and [he] desires an opportunity to serve our country in this crisis." He did not mention that Parker was an Indian.

General Grant endorsed the request, and when there was no response to Smith's letter, Grant wrote to Washington himself to renew the request and to testify to his knowledge of Parker's qualifications. "I am personally acquainted with Mr. Parker and I think [him] eminently qualified for the position. He is a full blooded Indian but highly educated and very accomplished. He is a Civil Engineer of considerable eminence and served the Government some years in superintending the building of Marine Hospitals and Custom Houses on the upper Miss. river."[23]

Grant's letter was, however, unnecessary; the appointment had already been made. Parker's commission as assistant adjutant general of volunteers with the rank of captain, which bore "the great red seal of the War Department," was issued on May 25, 1863, and on June 4, Parker accepted it. For Do-ne-ho-ga-wa to accept a military commission was at variance with Iroquois custom. Traditionally, one who held the civil office of sachem could not retain his title if he went to war. But the Indians decided that since this was not a war against another tribe, Parker could remain a sachem and still accept his commission as a captain of volunteers.

A council of some six hundred Senecas gathered at Tonawanda later that month to bid him farewell. His niece remembered seeing Parker there on a fine black horse. She said that some were reluctant to have him go and asked "who would be their friend if he should be killed?" Parker replied that he was already determined to go and he thought he would come back all right. A feast was held in Parker's honor, and the council commended him to the care of the Great Spirit. With the blessing of the Senecas, Parker gathered the equipment he thought necessary, carefully including the Red Jacket medal among the possessions he would take to war, and prepared to join John E. Smith's division near Vicksburg, Mississippi.[24]

8

An Indian at Headquarters

THE MAN WHO PUT ON HIS NEW CAPTAIN'S UNIFORM and was preparing to leave for Vicksburg, made a striking appearance. He was thirty-five years old, stood five feet eight inches tall, and carried two hundred pounds on a sturdy frame. "A savage Jack Falstaff of 200 weight," Parker called himself; "200 pounds of encyclopedia," one of his friends called him, noting that for all his modesty and reserve, he was knowledgeable about almost any subject that arose.[1]

His shoulders and chest were immense. When he was still a young man, Parker had complained that he was getting so broad across the shoulders that he found it hard to buy clothes to fit; now that he was full grown, those shoulders gave him an exceptional strength which he used more than once in self defense. In a hotel lobby in the West a man had once started to fight with him. Parker grabbed the man around the upper arms and squeezed him until he cried out. A day or two later, the man met him again in the same hotel. Parker thought that he wanted to resume the fight and began to prepare himself, but the man had only returned to show him the damage he had done on the first occasion. His broadcloth coat still showed the marks from the pressure of Parker's grip, and the man's arms were still bruised. On another occasion a hotel keeper had tried to push him into the street. Parker shook him loose, and grabbing him by the shoulders, swung him around in a circle until his body stood straight out in the air. The two later became good friends, but Parker would sometimes playfully grab his new friend and give him a swing "just for old time's sake."[2]

His features were clearly those of a Seneca Indian, but so few people had had contacts with Indians that he was constantly being mistaken for a Negro, a Haitian, a Turk, or a South American. Those who observed him closely spoke about his dark brown complexion with its slight creamy tint, his straight black hair, his piercing black eyes with their hooded lids, and his broad, highly arched nose. His full lips and soft, round chin were partially hidden by the few straggly hairs which served as a mustache and beard. "Although his face in repose seemed stern and unrelenting," one of his contemporaries wrote, "his nature in fact was as gentle and kind as a woman's."

He had a very soft, musical voice, and spoke, as he did everything, correctly and precisely, clearly enunciating each syllable and never slurring his words. When he spoke English, there was no trace of an accent, and yet his native language had left its mark on his speech. Seneca has no labials; as Minnie Myrtle observed after her stay among the Indians, "The Senecas and Cayugas talk all day without shutting their lips," which explained why Parker seldom used his lower lip in talking, but rather seemed to talk from his throat.[3]

He walked with an erect, military bearing acquired during his service in the New York militia, holding himself "like an arrow." There was a confident manner about him, too, born of years of successfully proving himself to doubtful whites. But at the same time he seemed to have a compulsive need to be correct in the way he met people and carried out his responsibilities, as though he feared to make the mistake that would reveal that he did not really belong in this society, or the faux pas that people would use to banish him. He meticulously framed his words and actions in the best white manner, until in the end, his person had become like his pictures; he was clearly an Indian, but one carefully clothed in the ways of the whites.[4]

In business matters he could be aggressive. He was not reluctant to ask for a position or a promotion, nor was he hesitant to use the authority given him. He could assert himself, too, at a speaker's table or with a pen. But in his personal relations he was much more restrained. People described him as silent, reserved, taciturn. Casual acquaintances learned little about him. It was only with close friends, and usually then only when responding to their direct questions, that he revealed the depth of experience and emotion behind his impassive appearance. People always noted the imposing Indian's presence, but few knew the man.

This was the man who set out for Vicksburg. Traveling by way of Cincinnati and Cairo, Illinois, he arrived in Memphis on July 2. He was proceeding on down the Mississippi when a rumor reached his boat that Vicksburg had fallen to Grant's armies. The rumor was confirmed at Helena, Arkansas, and the boat's passengers began to hope that theirs would be the first boat to arrive at Vicksburg after the victory. The remaining stretch of the river, however, was infested with guerillas, and the boat was delayed while a convoy of gunboats was arranged. The boat finally reached Vicksburg on July 7, without incident except for the accidental drowning of two men, one from a gunboat and one from Parker's own boat.

No sooner had Parker arrived at Smith's headquarters than he renewed his acquaintance with his old Galena friend, Ulysses Grant. "Having reached Vicksburg, I immediately reported at these headquarters; and after refreshing myself, my Commanding General and myself called upon General Grant, by whom we were kindly and graciously entertained for over an hour. The General was in excellent humor, and well he might be, after having taken this place and broken one of the best appointed armies of the Confederate States."

Parker soon had his first view of the Confederates, for the city was full of the paroled remnants of Pemberton's army. He thought them "a hard-looking set of men, and their peculiar and dirty uniform only makes them look worse. They really look as if they were, or might make, splendid soldiers for the Evil One himself." When the Confederates left, they were two days marching out of town. Parker said that he watched them "until I got sick of the sight." Dead Confederates, too, were still visible. "I do not know how many have been killed in town during the seige, but the entire country within the rebel works is one vast cemetery; and what is worse, the dead are buried very carelessly, for we frequently see the head or some of the limbs protruding out of the ground. My horse one day stepped on a poor fellow's stomach, putting his foot clear through him. It did not, of course, hurt him, but it was very disagreeable to me."[5]

Although Parker had been commissioned as an assistant adjutant general, the division also lacked an engineer, and on July 10, General Smith assigned him to duty as division engineer of the Seventh Division, Seventeenth Army Corps. His duties were not arduous, and he found that he had considerable free time until September when the division was ordered to Little Rock to reinforce General Steele. As they set out for Little Rock, Parker made out a will, acting he said, only out of prudence, not fear, and directed that if he were killed his property should be divided equally among his father, Carrie, and Nic. The soldiers had gone only as far as Helena, however, when they received news that Little Rock had been taken, and they were ordered into camp on the river bank near Helena. For two weeks they stayed on the Mississippi flats without tents or rations, after which the division was ordered to Chattanooga to reinforce General Rosecrans. Parker, however, did not go with them. On September 18, he was ordered to return to Vicksburg, where he was assigned as assistant adjutant general on the personal military staff of General Grant.[6]

Charles A. Dana, the assistant secretary of war, had been with Grant during the seige of Vicksburg and had given the War Department a description of Grant's staff as it was before Parker's arrival. It was, he said, "a curious mixture of good, bad, & indifferent . . . a mosaic of accidental elements & family friends." There were some good officers on the staff: Grant's friend Rawlins, who had served with him since the beginning of the war, was one, and Joe Bowers, a former Illinois newspaperman who was now the judge advocate, was another. Dana also approved of James Harrison Wilson, the inspector general, and Cyrus Comstock, the chief engineer, both graduates of West Point. But there were some men on the staff who, in Dana's opinion, were of no use at all. He thought Colonel Clark Lagow "a worthless, whiskey drinking, useless fellow," and neither he nor Colonel Riggin "worth his salt, so far as service to the government goes." Captain Ross, a former stage driver who "violates English grammar at every phrase," Dana found of some use for he at least attended to the mail, but Captain Audenried's sole contribution seemed to be to ride after the general when he went out; "the rest of the time he does nothing at all."

Rawlins was then serving as assistant adjutant general on Grant's staff. Dana reported that Grant thought him a first rate adjutant, but Dana, who thought Rawlins generally industrious and conscientious, nevertheless did not think him qualified as an adjutant. "He is too slow and can't write the English language correctly without a great deal of careful consideration. Indeed, illiterateness is a general characteristic of Grant's staff, and in fact of Grant's generals and regimental officers of all ranks." Harry Wilson said later that it was through Rawlins' influence that Parker was transferred to Grant's staff. Perhaps Rawlins recognized that the addition of Parker to the staff would add the literacy that Dana had found lacking. Parker's assignment may have had the appearance of cronyism, but with his legal and engineering training, his previous service in the militia, and his ready pen, he brought with him to the staff some needed skills.[7]

His position as adjutant did not seem one that would bring him the renown and immortality that Colonel Fisk had depicted. Parker was, as Harry Wilson the dashing cavalry officer put it, an "indoor man," and not an "outdoor man" as he was. Grant himself was known to refer to staff officers like Parker as the "men with quills behind their ears." Yet the office of adjutant was a necessary one and had its own requirements. As Frederic T. Locke, another who held the office, described it: "[An adjutant] should be a man well posted in all arms of the service, know the right flank from the left, and from the front to the rear. He should be able to tell, without hesitation a jackass battery from one of one-hundred pounder Parrotts; should be able to ride a horse without falling off, and to handle his saber and revolver without wounding himself or killing his horse. He should know how to write both the name of the commanding general and his own; the larger the letters the better. He should be an adept in military correspondence, and be able with Chesterfieldian courtesy to apply the cold steel of official rebuke to subordinate commanders." There should have been little doubt that the new Indian adjutant could meet the requirements of his position.[8]

The presence of an Indian at army headquarters attracted considerable attention, but the assignment of the Seneca captain, who was apparently on such good terms with the commanding general, was accepted without question. Parker said that he was "very much flattered and pleased by the kind attentions of all Army men with whom I have been brought in contact officially," and he noted that the common soldier "does his duty & pays respect to my shoulder straps." He was abruptly reminded that he was an Indian, however, when he was addressed one day by the assistant secretary of war, Charles Dana, in the Seneca language.

Dana had been raised in western New York by an uncle who carried on a trade in dry goods among the Indians. He had learned to speak Seneca and had become familiar with the Indians' ways, and when he first met Parker at Vicksburg, he was sure that he was speaking to a Seneca. As Harry Wilson remembered the incident, he and Dana had just returned from a hard day's ride when they found the new officer at the campfire.

> Dana was duly introduced, but before taking off his side arms and making himself comfortable, he said to me, aside: "I think I know that man's people, and if he is a Seneca, as I think he is, I can speak his language. What do you think he would do if I were to address him in his own tongue?" As the gentleman was also a stranger to me, I could hardly venture an opinion, but as my curiosity was aroused, I said at once, "Try it on and let us see." Thereupon Dana, without a perceptible pause for reflection, addressed the captain in a well-sustained phrase filled with clicks and guttural sounds. Parker, although a man of grave and dignified bearing, looked puzzled and surprised at first, but as soon as Dana paused his interlocutor replied in words of the same kind.

A brief but animated conversation followed, and before it was ended a smile of gratification broke over Parker's face, and an acquaintance was begun which lasted till his death.

General Grant, who had himself learned some Chinook from the Indians on the west coast, was said to have been particularly impressed by Dana's unsuspected knowledge of Parker's language.[9]

Dana and Parker fell into the habit of conversing in Seneca, especially when they did not care to be understood by others, but their relationship was not as close as Wilson thought. Parker later maintained that the staff had considered Dana a spy for the War Department, and that they did not like him but merely tolerated his presence. Nor were they above making fun of the civilian in their camp. Grant's cousin, William Smith, told how he, Parker, Dana, and Captain Peter Hudson were quartered one night in a private home. "By the aid of many blankets, Hudson, Parker and myself make a very comfortable bed on the floor. I go to sleep while Dana and Parker are talking Indian. Parker grits his teeth and Hudson shakes with laughter, [as they] scare Dana by supposing we will have a night attack."[10]

Parker had been with Grant but a few days when he became ill with "the fever and ague." He was still ill, some days later, when Grant was ordered north to meet with Secretary Stanton. Grant and his staff left the same day, Parker walking the half mile to the boat in a high fever. That night he was delirious, and as his extremities became cold and his pulse appeared to die out, the doctor who was attending him did not expect him to live. He recovered and survived the trip, but he lost about thirty pounds during his illness and did not regain his strength for weeks. ("He almost ate strawberries," his people would have said, for among the Senecas strawberries were said to sprout along the road to heaven.)

Stanton ordered Grant to Chattanooga to take command of the new Military Division of the Mississippi. The rugged trip through the Cumberland Mountains left Parker sick again for two days, but then, although still weak, he resumed his duties at Grant's new headquarters at Chattanooga. William F. Smith, for whom Parker had worked briefly in Detroit, was now a brigadier general and the chief engineer at Chattanooga. Finding that Parker had little to do at the time, he requested the loan of his services, and Parker was soon working as adjutant in Smith's office as well as in Grant's.[11]

In spite of his duties, he found time to look over the countryside. He wrote to Carrie and Nic that the Southerners were poor by the Tonawandas' standards. "The country people of the entire South, so far as I have seen, do not live as well or as comfortable as the Tonawanda Indians. . . . The country houses are built of logs, generally round logs and chinked up, but very often entirely open, that is without chinks. Any Indian house is better, more comfortable and cleaner." "They use old fashioned fire places & sleep upon the floor. In short as a community they are not as civilized as our Indians." It also fascinated him to be in the old home of the Cherokees, and to be quartered near the birthplace of Chief John Ross, and he took the opportunity of speaking with people who had been associated with the Cherokees before they had been removed west.[12]

As preparations for battle increased, so did Parker's work. He apologized to Carrie for not writing sooner: "I have known for some days that a great battle was pending, but as I have to do all the writing, I was given no time to think of anything else but my work." The staff as well as the troops were under daily bombardment from the Confederate positions on Lookout Mountain, but Parker pretended indifference to the danger; "no more attention is paid to their firing, than to a boy playing with a pop gun," or to "the popping of a frozen tree in mid winter at the north."[13]

When the battle came, Parker thought it a "splendid affair." He was with Grant on Orchard Knob, where they could see the whole scene as the Union troops stormed Missionary Ridge, and he boasted that he had seen the whole of the five days' battle, "and was as much under fire as the Genl himself." It was his first view of Grant in battle, and his description of the General's nonchalance under fire was later printed and reprinted in the northern newspapers.

> It has been a matter of universal wonder in this army that General Grant himself was not killed, and that no more accidents occurred to his staff, for the General was always in the front, (his staff with him of course,) and perfectly heedless of the storm of hissing bullets and screaming shell flying around him. His apparent want of sensibility does not arise from heedlessness, heartlessness, or vain military affectation, but from a sense of the responsibility resting upon him when in battle. When at Ringgold, we rode for half a mile in the face of the enemy, under an incessant fire of cannon and musketry—nor did we ride fast, but upon an ordinary trot, and not once do I believe did it enter the general's mind that he was in danger. I was by his side and watched him closely. . . . Another feature in General Grant's personal movements are, that he requires no escort beyond his staff, so regardless of

danger is he. Roads are almost useless to him, for he takes short cuts through fields and woods, and will swim his horse through almost any stream that obstructs his way. Nor does it make any difference to him whether he has daylight for his movements, for he will ride from breakfast until one or two in the morning, and that too without eating. The next day he will repeat the dose, until he finishes his work. Now such things come hard upon the staff, but they have learned how to bear it.[14]

Demanding as it was to accompany Grant, Parker was glad that the fever which attacked him again after the battle had held off until it was over. "If I had been sick during the battle, I should have been very sorry, because beyond a doubt this is the grandest battle of this war."[15]

When the battle of Chattanooga was over Grant wanted to issue a congratulatory order to the army and asked Parker to write it because he was "good at that sort of thing." Grant made a few changes in Parker's draft and issued the order over his own name, but the order still conveyed the excitement that Parker felt at this, his first battle, and the order's key sentence pictured vividly the sweep of the battle as Parker had observed it. "You dislodged him from his great stronghold upon Lookout Mountain, drove him from Chattanooga Valley, wrested from his determined grasp the possession of Missionary Ridge, repelled with heavy loss to him his repeated assaults upon Knoxville, forcing him to raise the seige there, driving him at all points, utterly routed and discomfited, beyond the limits of the State." The battle had been a decisive blow against what he called "this unholy rebellion," and Parker was pleased with the role he had played in it.[16]

At the beginning of the new year, Grant moved his headquarters to Nashville. With three adjutants on the staff, Parker, Joe Bowers, and George Leet, and no battles expected, there was less work to do and time for some leave. Parker took advantage of the lull to acquaint himself with the city and its surroundings. With an engineer's eye he examined the State House, "a most elegant limestone, fire proof building," and the princely residence known as Belmont just outside the city, with its water tower, conservatories, amusement rooms, and chapel. He and another officer, wanting to visit Andrew Jackson's Hermitage but finding that it was beyond the picket lines, armed themselves "with 3 pistols each and our trusty sabres, took an escort of 10 men and rode out there." They had a pleasant visit with Andrew Jackson Donelson, the general's adopted son, and returned "without having seen a single guerilla."[17]

Parker was also becoming friendly with Samuel Beckwith, who was in charge of General Grant's cipher correspondence. Beckwith had originally been assigned to Grant's headquarters as a telegraph operator. Later he was set over the other operators and ultimately was entrusted with the army cipher and ordered to personally accompany the general day and night. Parker and the younger man had twice ridden side by side to the summit of Lookout Mountain, with the silent Parker hardly speaking a word. But as they spent more time together in Nashville, Beckwith began to draw a few words from his quiet friend.

> It was here, while indulging in companionship walks, away from the business streets, that Parker voluntarily, now and then, bubbled a bit concerning his early history. Then we had pleasant games of billiards, of which he was quite fond, but the clicking of the balls and the sliding markers were the only unprecluded methods of communication.
>
> After one of these enjoyable little three-game tournaments he invited me to his room on High Street, where he took from his trunk wonderful heirlooms, consisting of presidential gifts to his ancestors. The one most indelibly impressed on my memory was a large 5 x 8 oval polished silver medal presented by Gen. Washington in 1792. . . . I cannot recall the identity and dates of others which I was permitted to hold in my hands and read. I never knew of an equal concession.

As Beckwith came to know the Indian captain better, he learned to appreciate what he called his "unobtrusive ability." "Never disturbed, excited or hurried by passing events, his silent desk yielded its regular quota of handsomely-written sheets at the proper moment."[18]

From that silent desk Parker became aware of the efforts in Washington to create the rank of lieutenant general for Ulysses Grant. When President Polk had proposed the creation of the same rank during the Mexican War, young Ely Parker had termed it a "gross indignity to Congress and a downright base insult to Generals Scott & Taylor & in fact to the whole military talent," but now that the rank was being created for Grant, Parker rejoiced that "the truest and noblest among them all, has been so nobly rewarded." It was not clear at first whether Grant's staff would accompany him when he went east to assume his command, but on March 18, 1864, the new lieutenant general issued General Orders No. 1, naming the staff which was to accompany him to Washington, and including in it the name of Captain E. S. Parker, Assistant Adjutant General.[19]

9

Military Secretary

WHEN GRANT LEFT to assume his command in the East, Parker remained behind in Nashville for a few days and then went east himself, traveling by way of Tonawanda and Washington. His father had been ill for several months and was not expected to live, and Parker's brief visit to Tonawanda allowed him to spend two or three hours with his dying father. He also spent a weekend in Washington where he hoped to see Congressman Washburne, but could not, and then went on to Grant's new headquarters at Culpeper Court House, Virginia, arriving there on April 4, 1864. Later that month Carrie telegraphed that his father had died. With both his parents gone, Parker had lost his closest ties to the reservation and to his Indian heritage, and he confided to John E. Smith that he was "now afloat and without an anchor in this wide world." He was concerned about Carrie, left alone in his house, and asked Nic to look after her as well as he could, saying that he would not be able to return, "for I am bound to the Army until the War is over."[1]

Having failed to see Washburne personally, Parker wrote to him about the subject that was on his mind, a promotion for Black John. Rawlins had recently been promoted to brigadier general and assigned as Grant's chief of staff, but the Senate was reluctant to confirm the promotion because Rawlins was "only on staff duty," and some thought there was no need for Grant to have a chief of staff in the field when General Halleck was already serving as chief of staff in Washington. Parker wanted Washburne to use his influence to secure the confirmation as a "proper encouragement" for Rawlins. He knew both Rawlins and Grant well, and he agreed with those who were saying that the two were a team, and that without Rawlins' help, Grant's future success was uncertain. He told Washburne that, in his opinion, Rawlins was "absolutely indispensible to General Grant. . . .

93

Lieutenant General Ulysses S. Grant and his staff. *Left to right:* John A. Rawlins; Cyrus B. Comstock; Henry W. Janes; Grant; William M. Dunn, Jr.; Michael R. Morgan; Peter T. Hudson; Ely S. Parker; Orville E. Babcock. Rawlins and Parker formed a friendship at Galena, Illinois, in 1858. Both later became friends of Ulysses S. Grant. During the Civil War, Grant made Rawlins his chief of staff and Parker his military secretary. *Courtesy of U.S. Signal Corps, photo No. 111-B-26 (Brady Collection), National Archives and Records Service.*

I am also very confident that General Grant's continued success, will, to a great extent, depend upon his retaining General Rawlins as his privy counsellor or right hand man."[2]

Privately, Parker could be critical of Rawlins. He resented the way Rawlins spoke to Grant, continually calling him "Damned old Skeeziks" and generally treating him "like a dog." Parker said that the staff used to sit around the camp fire at night telling stories and singing songs, and Grant would sit quietly listening and smoking, with no

Lieutenant General Ulysses S. Grant and his staff. Grant is the seventh figure from the left (seated); Parker is the twelfth figure from the left (seated). *Courtesy of U.S. Signal Corps, photo No. 111-B-2205 (Brady Collection), National Archives and Records Service.*

one paying any attention to him. Sometimes Rawlins would begin to swear, and Grant would "good-naturedly remonstrate with his chief of staff for using too vigorous and sulphurous language, assuring him that his views would be quite as forceful and comprehensible if he did not try to clinch them with such hard words." Rawlins would agree to stop but would then turn around and say, "Damned old Skeeziks," which Grant would deal with by pretending not to hear him. But Parker nevertheless valued Rawlins' friendship and had a high regard for his

abilities, and he was pleased when the Senate finally confirmed
Rawlins' promotion.[3]

Walt Whitman visited Culpeper about this time and thought it
"one of the pleasantest towns in Virginia" with the sharp sound of the
soldiers' axes chopping, the "thin blue smoke rising from camp fires,"
and the Blue Mountains clearly visible in the distance. But Parker
arrived during a long siege of rain and thought it "an awful country—
a d——d mean country," and the people of Virginia a "miserable
spawn of humanity." The Army of the Potomac, however, pleased him,
made as it was of "splendid material . . . in fine condition and well
supplied with every thing." Its only shortcoming was the "inefficiency
and effeminacy" of its commanding officers, and General Grant rapidly
weeded them out. It was clear that the Confederates intended to resist strongly, but Parker had no doubt about the future of the campaign that was about to begin. "Richmond must & will be ours
before long."[4]

On May 4, Grant made his move toward Richmond by crossing
the Rapidan River, a move which precipitated the Battle of the
Wilderness. Parker's most vivid personal memory of the battle was of
saving Grant from almost certain capture by the Confederates. The
incident occurred after dark on May 7, when Grant and Meade were
moving their headquarters toward Todd's Tavern. Because the woods
were on fire and the road clogged, the party turned onto a side road
to the right. Parker, riding behind with Rawlins, became convinced
that the generals and their staffs were headed directly into the enemy
lines, and told Rawlins what he thought. Rawlins called out to Grant,
"Hey! General! Do you know where you are?" He said that he did not,
nor did Cyrus Comstock, who was leading the group, appear to know
where they were. When told what Parker had said, Grant asked if he
knew the way back to their own lines. Raised in the forest, Parker had
not lost his sense of direction, and he told Grant that he did know
the way back. Grant told him to lead the way, and Parker quickly
wheeled his big black horse in another direction and led the group to
safety. Long after the war, Parker was talking with Judge Roger
Pryor, who had served as a general in the Confederate Army. Pryor
had been in the Wilderness, and he told Parker that he had once seen
Grant and Meade with their staffs riding directly toward him. His men
wanted to fire on them, but he ordered them to be quiet so that the
group could be captured. He had never understood why the men
suddenly dashed off in another direction, until Parker told him what
had happened.[5]

Artist's sketch of General Ulysses S. Grant telegraphing the news of the crossing of the Rapidan, May 1864. The officer at the left with his hand on his sword appears to be Ely Parker, who was then an assistant adjutant general on Grant's staff. The drawing is attributed to Alfred R. Waud. *Courtesy of the Library of Congress.*

The new campaign was one in which even an "indoor man" like Parker was exposed to danger. He was riding with Rawlins once on a road where the teams had made two furrows with a ridge in between, and each of them was riding in one of the furrows. A rebel battery down the road fired at them, and Parker could see the cannon ball coming toward them. He said that had he sat up as a brave soldier should, the ball would have hit him, but he swung over to the side, and it merely brushed against his coat sleeve as it passed by. And he wrote to a friend: "This life, though dangerous, suits me charmingly.

At times I have been severely exposed to the death dealing missiles thrown at us by the enemy, thus far however, thanks to a Great over-ruling Spirit, I am unharmed. Without alarming my friends, I can truthfully say that I have had some narrow escapes, but having escaped it is needless to recount particulars."

His work as an adjutant kept him close to Grant. A combat artist sketched him standing by the general as Grant wrote out the telegram informing the War Department that he had crossed the Rapidan. Parker was on hand, too, when Grant wrote the letter which included the famous words: "[I] propose to fight it out on this line if it takes all summer." Parker said that Grant was sitting on a stump at the time, smoking a cigar, and that he puffed until his head was completely enveloped in smoke. Then he blew it away and wrote a bit. He smoked again and cleared the smoke and wrote again, and kept the process up until the letter was completed.[6]

Parker too was writing, continually writing, producing order after order in the clear, uniform handwriting which was much admired at headquarters, orders which he signed

By Command of
Lieut Gen Grant
E. S. Parker
Asst Adj't Genl

At the same time, his engineering skills were not forgotten. Many of the orders Parker prepared dealt with engineering matters, and he was sometimes ordered himself to engineering duties. A soldier in the Fourth New York Artillery remembered seeing him riding with an orderly behind him, showing soldiers where to lay down fence rails as an outline for new entrenchments. The soldier always supposed that "the Indian," as they called Parker, was one of Grant's chief engineers.

The soldier also noted Parker's shrewdness in dealing with some belligerent Southern women. As the troops were beginning to dig the entrenchments, one of the officers asked the women to vacate their house. They refused to go, and one of them said that her husband was in command of the opposing Confederate troops, and she was sure that her house would not be fired upon. Parker politely told her that she could stay, and then immediately called out to his men, "Throw up a redoubt directly back of this house and plant a battery there!" As the soldier said, "It was a clever bit of strategy for that battery did unmerciful work and it was a long time before the rebels sent a shell in our direction."[7]

As the Union army moved down to the James River, and the several corps commanders exasperated Grant by acting, as he said, "like horses in a balky team, no two ever pulling together," Harry Wilson proposed a different assignment for Parker. He said that Grant asked him "What is the matter with this army?" and Wilson replied: "'General there is a great deal the matter with it, but I can tell you much more easily how to cure it.' Whereupon he asked me: 'How?' 'Send for Parker, the Indian chief, and, after giving him a tomahawk, a scalping knife, and a gallon of the worst whiskey the Commisary Department can supply, send him out with orders to bring in the scalps of major generals.'"

The suggestion that a drunken Indian be used to bring the generals into line brought its intended smile, but there may have been more than humor in Wilson's words, for he also claimed that he had seen Parker drunk on the battlefield. At St. Mary's Church, he said, Parker met him "somewhat under the influence of liquor" and asked for a squadron of cavalry so that he could go out and capture General Lee and bring him back to Grant's headquarters. Wilson said that he was able to dissuade Parker from his mission only by telling the usually correct adjutant that his request was not properly authorized. And Wilson once characterized Parker by saying "when sober he was a man of sound judgment and excellent character but he was an Indian, and like all Indians, accustomed to getting drunk occasionally when he was sure to make a brute of himself."[8]

The prejudice in Wilson's statement is obvious, but there were also other witnesses to Parker's drinking. At Galena there had been accusations about his "dissipation," which his staunch defender Richard Jackson made no attempt to deny. "That he takes 'his toddy' when he pleases, and which, though an Indian, I presume he has a right to do, is not denied. How many of this vast audience don't do the same?" Mathew Brady, the photographer, told how after Parker had taken some "medicinal" whiskey at Nashville, "a series of loud war-whoops rang out," and the Indian was seen chasing Joe Bowers, who fled for his life. Amos Webster, an assistant quartermaster on

Grant's staff, said that "Parker was a fine man—an educated man—a writer and an orator. But when he got a little whiskey into him, he wanted rings in his ears." Sylvanus Cadwallader, the *New York Herald* correspondent who had "literally ridden with him from Vicksburg to Appomattox," said that Parker "was not a regular drinker, but once or twice a year when I knew him would have a 'carouse' for a few days, ending in extreme intoxication," which Cadwallader thought all came with being an Indian.

The drunken Indian was a stock character in the prejudice of nineteenth-century America, and there were many people who, like Wilson and Cadwallader, could not see an Indian without thinking of whiskey. But as the witnesses mount, it is hard to escape the conclusion that Parker did on occasion conform to the stereotype.[9]

After the Battle of Cold Harbor Grant moved his headquarters to City Point, Virginia. The new location, high on a bluff overlooking the junction of the Appomattox and the James rivers, was amply supplied by riverboats, so that Parker could boast of having ice cream and cakes at every meal. These headquarters, away from the battlefield, were a relief to the staff, and their memories of City Point were pleasant ones.

Parker liked to tell how on one occasion Grant had been compelled to obey his own orders. After lunch one day Grant asked Parker to accompany him on a walk to the newly completed quartermaster's wharves. They both lit up cigars and descended the long wooden stairs down the bluff to the river. They were walking leisurely to the wharf, enjoying their cigars, when a sentry halted them and told them it was against orders to smoke on the wharf. As Parker told it, "Nothing more was said, but our cigars went into the river. A few moments later the General remarked: 'I am sorry to lose my smoke, but the order is right.' I cannot say whether or not the guard knew the General, but he knew his duty, and doubtless would have arrested us had we disobeyed him."[10]

Horace Porter, a young aide-de-camp on the general's staff, told another story about Grant and Parker. Shortly after their arrival at City Point, Parker was busy at a writing table in Grant's tent, while Grant was outside talking with some of the staff.

A citizen who had come to City Point in the employ of the Sanitary Commission, and who had been at Cairo when the general took command there in 1861, approached the group and inquired: "Where is the old man's tent? I'd like to get a look at him; haven't seen him for three years." Rawlins, to avoid being interrupted, said, "That's his tent," at the same time pointing to it. The man stepped over to the tent, looked in, and saw the swarthy features of Parker as he sat in the general's chair. The visitor seemed a little puzzled, and as he walked away was heard to remark: "Yes, that's him; but he's got all-fired sunburnt since I last had a look at him."

Porter said that Grant was greatly amused by the incident and told it to Parker who enjoyed it as much as the others.[11]

When Congress had created the rank of lieutenant general for Grant, they had also authorized him to enlarge his staff. Soon after his arrival in Virginia, he made the additional appointments, mostly of regular army officers to complement the largely volunteer staff he brought with him from the West. Frederick Dent, Horace Porter, and Orville E. Babcock, all graduates of West Point, were among those added to the staff. Working with an Indian staff member may have been difficult for Dent and Babcock. Dent had fought against the Yakima Indians in the Northwest, and Babcock's brother had been killed by Indians near Fort Boise, Washington Territory ten years before.[12]

At the same time, Grant had been authorized to have two military secretaries to help him with his correspondence. These positions went to volunteers Grant had brought with him from the West. Adam Badeau, a newspaperman who had once worked as a clerk in Galena, was appointed as one of the secretaries. Parker's friend William R. Rowley, who like Parker had been attached to Grant's staff after first serving with John E. Smith, was the other. Rowley, however, soon resigned because of ill health and went back to Galena, where Parker kept him informed of the army's progress by sending him humorous letters, labeling one War Bulletin No. 5000 and another, two days later, War Bulletin No. 75,000. Interspersed with serious news of troop movements were reports like "The enemy have neither surprised us, or eat us up. They seem however to have been very much disappointed at our not giving them a grand Bear Dance on the 4th [of July]."[13]

On August 26, 1864, Grant wrote to Secretary Stanton requesting that Captain Parker be appointed military secretary with the rank of lieutenant colonel to take Rowley's place. Four days later the War Department announced the appointment, referring, however, to Parker's new position in less military terminology as "private secretary." Sylvanus Cadwallader, the *New York Herald* correspondent attached to Grant's headquarters, wrote about Rowley's resignation

Ely S. Parker as he appeared when he became General Ulysses S. Grant's military secretary. Parker was appointed assistant adjutant general on Grant's staff on September 18, 1863. On August 30, 1864, he became Grant's military secretary. In that capacity he stayed by Grant's side until the war's end, carrying the general's papers in a portfolio slung over his shoulder and his supply of ink in a wooden bottle which he tied to his buttonhole when he wrote. *Courtesy of the Illinois State Historical Library, Springfield, Illinois.*

and Parker's promotion. He saw the promotion as a "partial reward for invaluable services. . . . No greater compliment could well be paid him than to be named by General Grant as the successor of Lieutenant Colonel Rowley."[14]

Joe Bowers reported that "Parker feels fine over his promotion," a feeling which was shared by the members of the staff who had been with Grant in the West. There was some ill-feeling toward the new members of the staff and a satisfaction that the promotion had gone to a member of the old staff. Bowers expressed it in a way that the former charcoal burner Black John could understand: "I think we rather *charred* out the 'newcomers' this load of poles." George Leet added that "the old staff is exceedingly well pleased with his appointment—don't know how the new members feel about it." Parker himself had little doubt how the new staff felt. "We have the hardest kind of work to get along with the new people we are associated with. They look upon us with a jealous eye, and imagine, at least make one believe, that we are a set of know-nothings. We however carry a stiff upper lip and make them feel our power."[15]

The promotion placed Parker even closer to Grant during the rest of the war. He stayed at the general's side, carrying Grant's papers in a portfolio slung over his shoulder, and his supply of ink in a little wooden bottle with a screw on the top which he tied to his buttonhole when he wrote. It was the task of the military secretary to assist the general with his correspondence, and Grant readily confessed his need for the help. "The only place I ever found in my life to put a paper so as to find it again," he said, "was either a side coat-pocket or the hands of a clerk or secretary more careful than myself."[16]

Although Grant's new military secretary issued many an order "by command of Lieutenant General Grant," he claimed to have been in a position to give orders himself only once. In mid-September Grant left City Point with two staff members for a visit to General Sheridan in the Shenandoah Valley. So many others on the staff were absent because of sickness or away on orders that only Lieutenant Colonel Parker and Captain George Leet were left to "run Head Quarters." On the morning of September 16, an orderly came running into Parker's tent with the news that the Confederates had made a raid in the rear of the Union lines and captured some twenty-five hundred head of cattle. Parker, as the ranking officer at headquarters, gave the order to pursue the raiding force. The Union troops were beaten off, however, and Parker's comment when he repeated the story was, "You see I made a poor General."

On the same occasion City Point was threatened, and it became a matter of concern that there was no artillery there. General Benjamin Butler had some gunboats which could be brought up to take the place of artillery, but Butler's difficult temperament was well-known at headquarters, and when a message was sent to him about the gunboats, it was much less than an order: "It is suggested by Colonel Parker, of General Grant's staff, that the same be reported to you, and that a request be made to have such disposition made of the gun-boats as will remedy the want of artillery here."[17]

As the presidential election approached, the army granted leave to as many soldiers as possible so that they could go home and vote. Parker too, even though he had no vote, was given twenty days leave and used it to return to his home at Tonawanda. He was pleased to be reunited with his family and glad to learn of the affairs of the Indians generally, but he found himself completely out of sympathy with those who were leading the Indians. Parker's experiences had given him a larger view of Indian affairs, and the petty issues and dissensions on the reservation disturbed him. He discouraged Carrie from telling him of the Indians' "unending whims & imaginary troubles," and he advised Carrie and Nic to stay out of these affairs entirely: "You know that our family has always been grossly maligned by the Indians, and I for one want to give them as little cause as possible for doing so."[18]

His visit home also enabled him to learn about the activities of the twenty-eight other Tonawanda Senecas who were in the army, and especially about his brother Newton's experiences in North Carolina. Newton had enlisted for "3 years or sooner shot" and had been stationed near New Berne, North Carolina, since January 1, 1863. He was at first assigned as a copyist at the headquarters of the commanding general, then was assigned as an orderly sergeant, and finally became a color bearer, which he said meant that he did no guard or picket duty, but stayed in camp most of the time "lying in my tent wallowing over in my perspiration." When he wrote to Carrie, he made it appear that his greatest concern about army life was to get a pair of moccasins from her to replace his heavy government shoes. Army life, however, had exposed him to more danger than he would admit. Earlier that year he had been standing no more than four feet away from a storehouse full of mines when it exploded and killed thirty-five men in his regiment. The explosion threw Newton almost fifty feet away but left him unharmed. Lewis Henry Morgan had written to Major General Benjamin Butler in December 1863, recommending Newton for a captaincy, noting that his brother was a captain in General Grant's army, but Butler had taken no notice of the letter, and Newton was still serving as a third sergeant.[19]

Several other New York Indians were making a reputation for themselves in the Union army. There was an Indian in Newton's company known as "Big Ike" who was so accurate with his telescopic rifle that on one occasion he picked off the entire crew of a gun battery that had pinned down his regiment. And in the same company was Abram Powlis, an Onondaga scout, who somehow managed to go freely in and out of the Confederate lines where he was well-known as an Iroquois and a Union soldier. He was neither captured nor killed but always came back with valuable information for his regiment.

Better known still were the exploits of an unnamed Seneca in the Fourteenth New York Artillery who once made a bet that he could capture a Confederate sharpshooter perched in a tree between the lines near Petersburg. The method that he used convinced the correspondent of the *New York Herald* that "the wonders of Cooper's Indian heroes have not ceased." The Indian gathered a supply of pine boughs and wrapped himself in them from head to foot, attaching them to a branch fastened lengthwise to his body, so that when he was done he could hardly be distinguished from a tree. Concealing a musket in his boughs, he crept with almost imperceptible movements to the tree that held the sharpshooter. He waited patiently until the sharpshooter had fired and then aimed his musket at him, giving him no time to reload. The Confederate quickly surrendered, and the Indian triumphantly marched him back to camp and collected his bet.[20]

Caroline Parker's marriage may also have taken place while Parker was home on leave, for about this time she was married to John Mountpleasant, a widower who was the leading chief of the Tuscarora Indians and the owner of a large and prosperous farm on the Tuscarora Reservation. Fortunately Mountpleasant, like Carrie, was fluent in English, for as Carrie told people, "Mr. Mountpleasant cannot talk Seneca and I cannot talk Tuscarora, so we have to talk together in English." After the wedding Carrie moved to the Tuscarora Reservation, near Niagara Falls, and one more of Ely Parker's ties with home was broken. With Nic living at Cattaraugus and Newton in the army, only his brother Levi was left at the old home at Tonawanda.[21]

When his leave was over, Parker visited Washington, where he stayed five hours and had a "good long talk" with the commissioner of Indian affairs, and then he returned to City Point. The summer tents at City Point had been replaced by log huts as it appeared that the

Winter Headquarters, Army of the Potomac, November 1864. *Left to right:*
Lieutenant William M. Dunn, Jr.; Captain George B. Cadwalader; Lieutenant
Colonel Ely S. Parker; headquarters telegraph operator; headquarters army
clerk; Lieutenant Colonel Theodore S. Bowers; Captain George K. Leet;
Lieutenant Colonel William L. Duff. *Courtesy of the Illinois State Historical
Library, Springfield, Illinois.*

armies would not be moving during the winter, and Grant's headquarters had become a popular place for Washington officials to visit
when they wanted to see a little of the war. In fact, they came so
frequently that there were sometimes as many visitors as staff members at the headquarters mess table. One of the visitors was Secretary
of State William H. Seward. There is, unfortunately, no record of
Seward's reaction when he was introduced to Grant's staff and learned
that the Indian he had sent back to the farm had found his way to the
side of the most powerful general in America.

Abraham Lincoln was another visitor at City Point. He had made a brief visit in June 1864, and he returned in March 1865, and stayed at Grant's headquarters for more than two weeks. Robert Lincoln, who had been placed on Grant's staff as a captain and assistant adjutant general, was also present during his father's second visit, as were Mrs. Lincoln and Tad. When he was at headquarters, the president ate with the staff and sat in a camp chair at the fire with them, speaking candidly about the conduct of the war and entertaining them with stories. He would often go into the adjutant's tent or find a chair near Parker or Adam Badeau and eagerly read the military dispatches as they came in. "General Lincoln" and "the Indian," as the two were known at headquarters, discussed Indian affairs, and Parker found the president sympathetic to the Indians' plight and hopeful that the nation would someday make amends for the injustices done to them. Lincoln was still at City Point when Petersburg fell, and he went into the captured city and met there with Grant and his staff. Parker, however, was not present; he had ridden into Richmond which had been occupied that morning. The next day Lincoln, too, visited Richmond, but by this time Grant and the staff had begun the pursuit of General Lee's army in what was to be the last campaign of the war.[22]

One Real American

~~~~~~

Wɪᴛʜ Pᴇᴛᴇʀsʙᴜʀɢ ᴀɴᴅ Rɪᴄʜᴍᴏɴᴅ both in Union hands, General Lee attempted to escape with his army to the south. Grant was determined to block his way, and as the Union army moved west along the Appomattox River, Grant made his headquarters with them in the field. Most of the staff accompanied him, leaving only Joe Bowers and a few orderlies at City Point to oversee the supplying of the army. Parker was in the field with Grant, and in addition to his secretarial duties he was acting as adjutant in Bowers' absence.

It soon became clear that Lee's army could not escape, and on April 7, Grant wrote to Lee asking him to surrender the Army of Northern Virginia. Lee was not prepared to surrender, and further correspondence followed between the two commanders. Then on Sunday, April 9, Lee sent a note asking for an interview to discuss the terms of surrender. Grant received the note about noon on Sunday as he and the staff were riding around the lines to see General Sheridan. As Parker remembered it, Grant announced the contents of the note without showing any emotion, but "the Staff had a little jollification of their own on the lonely road in the woods by cheering, throwing up their hats, and performing such other antics as their tired limbs and dignity would permit." Grant then directed Parker to write his reply arranging for the interview, and the letter was given to Orville Babcock to deliver to Lee. Babcock found Lee resting under an apple tree, and he and Lee, along with Lee's military secretary, Colonel Charles Marshall, went into the village of Appomattox Court House to find a convenient place to meet with General Grant.[1]

As they came into the village, they were met by a man named Wilmer McLean, who offered the use of the parlor in his house as a meeting place, and the men waited there for the arrival of Grant and his staff. When they arrived, the staff sat down on the front porch

The residence of Wilmer McLean at Appomattox Court House, Virginia, where on April 9, 1865, General Robert E. Lee surrendered the Army of Northern Virginia to General Ulysses S. Grant. *Courtesy of U.S. Signal Corps, photo No. 111-B-6333 (Brady Collection), National Archives and Records Service.*

while Babcock escorted Grant into the parlor, but Babcock soon returned to the door and said that Grant wanted the staff to come in.

As they entered, Grant introduced them individually to Lee who was standing and who, Parker said, "shook hands with each in the most courteous, condescending and yet affable manner, making no remark further than passing the usual salutation." But when Parker was introduced, Lee appeared to be startled. Horace Porter said that "when Lee saw his swarthy features he looked at him with evident surprise, and his eyes rested on him for several seconds. What was passing in his mind no one knew, but the natural surmise was that he at first mistook Parker for a negro, and was struck with astonishment to find that the commander of the Union armies had one of that race on his personal staff." Another account of the incident says that "General Lee's face flushed with indignation, and that it seemed to him (Parker) that the negotiations were very likely to be broken off abruptly. General Lee evidently thought that a mulatto had been called on to do

"The Surrender of Lee," a drawing by New York artist James E. Kelly. Kelly consulted Parker, who was present at the surrender at Appomattox, as General Grant's military secretary, for the details of the drawing. Parker appears at the center of the window in the rear. The drawing was published in Bryant's *Popular History of the United States. Courtesy of the Cleveland Public Library: History Department.*

the writing as a gratuitous affront." But if those were his thoughts, Lee soon realized his mistake, and he extended his hand to Parker and said, "I am glad to see one real American here." Parker shook Lee's hand and replied, "We are all Americans."[2]

After Grant and Lee were seated and had chatted a while about old army days, Lee brought up the matter of the surrender and suggested that Grant put his terms in writing. Colonel Bowers had ridden out from Burkeville earlier that day and had already taken over a table, and Parker had helped him arrange his papers for business. Grant looked through the smoke of his pipe toward Bowers' table, and Parker handed him the manifold order book, a bound book of sheets of thin yellow paper with carbon inserts for copies, and a hard tipped stylus to write with. After Grant had written his terms in the book, and discussed them with Lee, they agreed on a few changes which Parker wrote in the book at Grant's direction. The manifold book was then returned to Bowers to make the official copy in ink. But Bowers was so nervous from his ride or from the gravity of the occasion that he could not complete the task. He began to write and then destroyed the paper, and after beginning and destroying three or four sheets of paper he said to Parker, "Parker, you will have to write this, I can't do it."

The imperturbable Indian took the manifold book and sat down to write, using ink from a small boxwood inkstand provided by the Confederate Colonel Marshall. After he had finished making the copy and Grant had signed it, Parker placed it in a large official envelope and returned it to Grant who handed it to Lee. Then on paper provided by Parker, Colonel Marshall wrote Lee's acceptance of the terms and gave it to Grant, who handed it on to Parker unopened. With that simple exchange of letters, the surrender was concluded. After the meeting, Parker remained at his table to write out several orders concerning the surrender. Before leaving he put one of the three yellow, manifold copies of Grant's terms of surrender in his pocket as a memento of the historic meeting.

The next morning Grant, his staff, and a number of other Union officers rode out to a high point overlooking the Confederate camps, and Lee rode out to meet them. Grant and Lee sat on their horses conversing for more than an hour while the other officers fell back out of hearing. Parker, however, remained by Grant's side, and as the two generals settled the details of the surrender, Parker wrote out the necessary orders, stooping over an old stump and using his portfolio as a desk. Parker thought that the meeting of the two generals on horseback with the other officers in "a most beautiful semi-circle" around them and the sun behind them was a "pretty sight," and he remarked that it was a pity there was no artist to record it.[3]

Grant was anxious to go to Washington to end the draft and to begin to reduce the huge military expenditures which Walt Whitman compared to "a heavy-pouring constant rain," and the general and his staff left for City Point that afternoon. There they boarded the steamer *Mary Martin* and arrived in Washington on the morning of April 13. Grant was soon invited to the White House to meet with President Lincoln, and sometime during the following day, Good Friday, Parker, too, met with the president. He used the occasion to show Lincoln the Red Jacket medal, which he had carried with him throughout the war, and he "spoke feelingly of the associations it represents."

The "Grand Photograph" taken by Mathew Brady at City Point, Virginia, April 12, 1865, just after Grant and his staff had returned from Appomattox Court House. General Grant is seated in the doorway; Ely S. Parker, his military secretary, is the fourth standing figure from the right. *Courtesy of U.S. Signal Corps, photo No. 111-B-13 (Brady Collection), National Archives and Records Service.*

Later that day Parker prepared to go to New York on leave, while the president left to attend a play at Ford's Theatre.[4]

Parker's leave took him to New York City and western New York, but he was back in Washington in time for the grand review of the Union armies in late May. For two full days city streets were filled with marching armies, a mixture of battle-hardened troops, preening generals, and homeless freedmen, who were greeted by the sound of bands, bells, drums, and cheers. A reviewing stand had been set up in front of the White House for President Johnson and his cabinet, where General Grant, arriving on foot with a few of his staff, joined them and received thunderous applause from the crowds. Beside him was "a huge colonel, dusky-faced," who was said to be "Grant's favored aid." The colonel was still bitter about Lincoln's assassination and remarked, "You white men are Christians, and may forgive the murder. I am of a race which never forgives the murder of a friend."[5]

"See, the conquering hero comes" was now the nation's cry, and Grant was the hero. Triumphantly he toured the nation, with a few of his staff along to shield him from the cheering crowds which constantly surrounded him. Among the staff who accompanied him were his two military secretaries, Parker and Badeau, now full colonels by brevet. (Brevets were honorary promotions which conferred the name of the higher rank without changing the actual rank or pay. They were given so often during the war that one quartermaster, whose mules had performed well in battle, requested that the mules "have conferred upon them the brevet rank of horses"!)[6]

In June Grant and the staff went to New York City, where they were received at the Cooper Union and dined at the Astor House, and then traveled on to West Point and a reception by General Winfield Scott. The "autograph army" there attacked the staff as well as the general, but Parker, as usual, "was untroubled and his signature came uniformly like copper-plate." At Troy, New York, however, the crowd was so unruly that it broke through even Parker's patience. Some overly enthusiastic firemen uncoupled the general's special car and declared that Grant, who was exhausted from handshaking and was sound asleep, must come out and shake hands with them. When one fireman, more rude than the others, broke in a window on Parker's side, Parker jumped up and said, "I have a great notion to fire on that villain!" His friend Beckwith was finally able to talk him out of it, and they went on uneventfully to Chicago and then back to Washington.[7]

In July the government began to make plans for a council with the Indians of the Southwest who had allied themselves with the Confederacy during the war. Some of these Indians had been slave-owners themselves, and being sympathetic to the Southern cause, had even provided troops for the South. Francis Herron, once the captain of the Governor's Greys in Dubuque, and now a major general in the army, had made a temporary treaty with the Indians, but now a commission was to be sent to them to clarify their relationship to the Union.

Lieutenant General Ulysses S. Grant and four members of his staff photo-graphed in Boston in the summer of 1865. *Left to right:* Ely S. Parker; Adam Badeau; Grant; Orville E. Babcock; Horace Porter. His sturdy frame and broad shoulders prompted Parker to call himself "a savage Jack Falstaff of 200 weight." *Lloyd Ostendorf Collection, Dayton, Ohio.*

General Grant, recognizing the value of including an Indian among the commissioners, recommended that Parker be appointed to the commission. Secretary Stanton approved the recommendation, noting that Parker was a "highly educated and accomplished Indian," and after a cabinet discussion on July 25, President Johnson appointed Parker one of the commissioners who were to meet the Indians at Fort Smith, Arkansas, in September.[8]

In the meantime, Parker was off on another tour with Grant. Colonels Parker, Porter, Babcock, and Badeau accompanied Grant and his family to West Point and Boston, and then on to Augusta, Maine, where "Colonel Parker, the Noble Indian," was one of those called on to speak to the crowd. The group had arrived in Quebec, when Rawlins telegraphed orders for Parker to report to the secretary of the interior for duty on the Indian commission. Parker accompanied Grant as far as Niagara Falls, where he took two of the Grant children, Jesse and Nellie, out to his sister Carrie's house on the Tuscarora Reservation. He then left the party to return to Washington to begin his duties as an Indian commissioner.[9]

The commission to which Parker was assigned was a diverse group. It was led by Dennis Cooley, a lawyer and Mason from Dubuque who had been associated with Parker as an honorary member of the Governor's Greys in Dubuque, and who had recently been appointed commissioner of Indian affairs. Serving with Cooley and Parker were Elijah Sells, the superintendent of the southern Indian superintendency, Thomas Wistar, a leading Quaker, and Brigadier General William S. Harney, who was well-known as an Indian fighter.

The commissioners assembled at Fort Smith on September 8, together with representatives of twelve Indian tribes: Creeks, Choctaws, Chickasaws, Cherokees, Seminoles, Osages, Senecas, Shawnees, Quapaws, Wyandotts, Wichitas, and Comanches. The commission was charged with telling the Indians that those who had made treaties with the Confederates had lost their rights under previous treaties with the United States and that they would have to abolish slavery and enter into new treaties with the federal government. Yet the commissioners were to treat the tribes leniently and to recognize the contributions of those who had fought for the Union. In spite of bitter feuding between loyal and rebel Indians, the council was successful in preparing an agreement with nine of the tribes in which the Indians pledged anew their allegiance to the United States.

Parker took an active role in the deliberations, at one time presiding over the council and at another addressing the Indians for the commission. But equally as effective as anything he said was the mere presence of an Indian on the commission. During the deliberations Parker was selected to leave Fort Smith and proceed farther west to participate in a council with the Indians of the Colorado Territory. But when the Choctaw and Chickasaw delegations at Fort Smith heard of the plan, they appealed to Commissioner Cooley to allow Parker to stay with them, saying that "the fact that the United States Government have seen fit to include a member of an Indian tribe with its commissioners, has inspired us with confidence as to its designs and

desires with reference to the Indian nations, and we are anxious to
have the benefit of his presence and counsel in any deliberations or
interviews with your honorable body." The commissioners quickly
agreed to keep Parker at Fort Smith, and General Harney volunteered
to go to the Colorado council in his place.[10]

On his return from Fort Smith in mid-October, Parker visited
John E. Smith in Memphis, his brother Nic in New York, and then
stopped in Philadelphia where Grant was visiting and traveled with
him to Washington. The next week Grant and his staff paid formal
calls on President Johnson and the members of his cabinet, and Parker
later reported to Nic that "the President & Cabinet were very much
pleased with the success of our mission west."[11]

Grant was still making tours, and Parker was sometimes included.
He was with Grant in New York City in November 1865, when some
two thousand people attended a reception for the general. But most
of Parker's time was spent at his desk in the little brick building at
17 and F streets in Washington which served as army headquarters.
The building was usually crowded with visitors. Some sought offices,
some had business with Grant, some came "to bore him with well-
meant but very officious advice," and others came simply to pay their
respects. An Englishman who came to meet Grant wrote about the
meeting in the *British Quarterly Review*. He described Grant's office
and the plain dress of the general, and then he described the officer he
had found with Grant. "A military officer was in attendance upon him
who was of old Indian descent, a person somewhat above the ordinary
height, whose complexion and features bespoke his origin, but whose
civilized experiences had given him a little more flesh than would seem
to have been common among his ancestors. This stately descendant
from the sons of the old wilderness, gave me a cordial grasp of the
hand on being introduced."[12]

Harper's New Monthly Magazine also took notice of General
Grant's Indian secretary. In the fall of 1865 Parker had put the Red
Jacket medal on exhibition in New York City, and an article about the
medal later appeared in *Harper's*. The article also described the
medal's owner and his career, giving particular attention to New York's
refusal to allow Parker to practice law, and suggesting that the matter
be reconsidered. "We wonder whether the man who was thought
worthy to be chosen Military Secretary by our Lieutenant-General
would now, should he desire admission, be excluded from the bar. If
there be any existing 'rule' of the Supreme Court of the State requiring
this, we very respectfully suggest to their Honors the Judges to

rescind it as soon as possible. We do not think that their judicial dignity would be seriously impaired should it happen that they were some day called upon to listen to a motion or plea from Mr. Parker, Successor to Red Jacket, Sachem of the Senecas, and Brevet-Colonel U. S. V."[13]

In January 1866, Parker was ordered away from his desk to make an inspection tour of the principal military posts and depots in Kentucky, Tennessee, and Mississippi, and to advise headquarters where it could make further reductions in the army's presence in the South. That month he visited Louisville, Nashville, Memphis, and Vicksburg, and reported on units which he thought could be mustered out of the service and buildings and supplies he thought could be sold. But when he had carried out his orders, he also volunteered his opinion on the continued need for a military presence in the South, an opinion which was thought significant enough to be passed on to the secretary of war, and by him to the president.

In Parker's opinion the presence of troops in the South was still "an absolute necessity" because of the plight of the Negroes. The slaves had indeed been freed, but Parker found the old black laws still being enforced against the freedmen by unreconstructed whites. With emancipation the Negroes had become wards of the government, as the Indians had been for decades, and just as Parker had pressed for government action on behalf of the Tonawandas when they were at the mercy of the whites, so he pressed for federal protection for the Negroes. It seemed to him

> an act of humanity to retain troops in the late slaveholding States in order to protect the negro in his life, person and the few rights he has acquired by becoming a freedman. . . . To guard against an unjust oppression of the negro, to prevent personal conflicts between the two races and to see that equal and just laws are enacted and executed seems to be the combined duty of the Freedmens Bureau and the military in the South, and until these things are accomplished it seems pretty clear that both of these institutions must be maintained in the South. The honor of the Government will demand that the work left unfinished at the close of the war be thoroughly completed ere military protection and the strong arm of the Government is withdrawn from the protection of the emancipated race.[14]

Parker had been back in Washington but a few weeks when Commissioner Cooley requested his services at the Office of Indian Affairs.

Cooley wanted Parker's assistance in negotiating with a number of delegations from the Indian country who had come to Washington to conclude the restoration of relations with the United States that had been begun at Fort Smith. Grant directed Parker to give Cooley whatever assistance he needed, with the result that Parker was partially employed all winter and the following summer making treaties with the Indians of the Southwest. Treaties were concluded with the Seminoles, the Creeks, the Cherokees, and the Choctaws and Chickasaws in which peaceful relations were restored, slavery abolished, and the former slaves given equal rights with the Indians, and Parker was one of the men who signed the treaties for the federal government.[15]

He was also acting for the Tonawanda Indians at the Indian Office. The commissioner routinely asked his advice on affairs relating to the Tonawandas, and Parker found himself passing judgment on such matters as the payment of Indian debts, a grant for a church bell, and plans for a new council house on the reservation. The situation pleased Parker, and remembering how he had sometimes been criticized by the Tonawandas, he bragged to Nic that "hardly any thing affecting the N. Y. Indians is acted upon without my being first consulted about it & whatever I say determines the matter. But this you need not repeat to any Indian, as they are too ignorant to comprehend how I can obtain such influence."[16]

General Grant also asked Parker's advice about some puzzling Indian affairs in Texas. The governor of Texas had demanded federal troops to protect Texans from Indian depredations on the frontier, but General Sheridan believed that the request was merely a ruse to remove federal troops from the center of the state. Acting on Sheridan's advice, Grant refused the request, but when President Johnson urged that the troops be sent Grant asked Parker for his advice. Parker said that the difficulties with the Indians were real, but he added that they were a direct result of the Texans' expulsion of the Indians from their reservations in the state before the war and their attempt to force the Indians to aid the Confederacy during the war. The Indians had refused to participate in "a white man's war" and had fled to Mexico. When they tried to return to their homes, they had been driven back by the Texans and many of them had been killed, with the result that the Indians began the warfare and plunder on the frontier that led to the call for federal troops. Parker's solution, which was endorsed by Grant and submitted to the secretaries of war and interior, was to reassure the Indians of the good will of the government by calling them to a peace conference and to give them safe military escort to the Indian lands west of Arkansas, where they could be both supported by the Interior Department and protected and watched by the army.[17]

It was clear that Indian affairs in the West would continue to be a major concern of the army, and Grant therefore asked Parker to prepare a general plan for dealing with the western tribes. In January 1867, Parker submitted a four-point plan "for the establishment of a permanent and perpetual peace, and for settling all matters of differences between the United States and the various Indian tribes"—a lofty goal, but one which Parker, after twenty years of experience in Indian affairs, was certain could be reached.

First, he proposed that the control of Indian affairs be returned to the War Department. When the Department of the Interior had been created in 1849, the Indian Office was transferred to its jurisdiction, but as the tide of western settlers rose, and the Indians' treaty rights were disregarded and their reservations disturbed, Parker concluded that the Interior Department's civil agents were incapable of protecting the Indians. "If any tribe remonstrated against the violation of their natural and treaty rights, members of the tribe were inhumanly shot down and the whole treated as mere dogs." Nor did Parker have any confidence in the integrity of the civil agents, "the ruling passion with them being generally to avoid all trouble and responsibility, and to make as much money as possible out of their offices." Military officers, Parker thought, would not only be capable of protecting Indians' rights but would also discharge their duties as Indian agents honestly and faithfully because their military honor would be at stake.

With Indian affairs under the control of the military, the notoriously corrupt system of Indian traders could be abolished. "It is a fact not to be denied," Parker wrote, "that at this day Indian trading licenses are very much sought after, and when once obtained, although it may be for a limited period, the lucky possessor is considered as having already made his fortune." Parker quoted both Washington and Jefferson on the need to furnish the Indians with goods which could lead them "to agriculture, to manufactures, and civilization," and he also urged a return to their policies of having the government provide the goods directly, in this case through the military, without enriching the traders.

Second, Parker recommended that the Indians be guaranteed territories of their own in which white settlement would be prohibited and that a permanent plan for governing the Indian territories be adopted. When the Indians had been removed to the West, they had been promised lands of their own, but with the rapid settlement of the West not only their lands but also their lives were threatened. "The Indian races are more seriously threatened with a speedy extermination than ever before in the history of the country. And, however much such a deplorable result might be wished for by some, it seems to me that the honor of a Christian nation and every sentiment of humanity dictate that no pains be spared to avert such an appalling calamity befalling a portion of the human race."

Third, he proposed that until the Indian Office was transferred back to the War Department an inspection board be created to oversee the Indian agencies and "see that every cent due the Indians is paid to them promptly as may be promised in treaties, and that proper and suitable goods and implements of agriculture are delivered to them, when such articles are due." Such a board would not only curb dishonest agents, but Parker thought that the very fact of its creation would convince the Indians of the government's intention to deal with them honestly and fairly.

Parker's fourth proposal was for the creation of a permanent Indian commission composed of both whites and educated Indians who would visit all the Indian tribes and "hold talks with them, setting forth the great benefits that would result to them from a permanent peace with the whites, from their abandonment of their nomadic mode of life, and adopting agricultural and pastoral pursuits, and the habits and modes of civilized communities." The commission would attempt to convince the Indians that "the waves of population and civilization are upon every side of them; that it is too strong for them to resist; and that, unless they fall in with the current of destiny as it rolls and surges around them, they must succumb and be annihilated by its overwhelming force." Parker was aware that many people were pressing for that very annihilation, but he argued that such a policy was inhuman and unchristian and would expose the country "to the abhorrence and censure of the entire civilized world." He admitted that the work of the commission he proposed would be difficult and slow but argued that it would be much cheaper than any military solution to the Indian question and, more important, it would be just and right.[18]

Parker's Indian plan was well received. Secretary Stanton submitted it to the congressional committees on military affairs, and in the Senate Henry Wilson asked Parker to draft a bill containing his proposals for Wilson to submit to Congress. And the *Cleveland Leader* took favorable notice of the plan, referring to its author as "the most accomplished representative of the aborigines of our country."[19]

Even though Parker's proposals were not adopted, a new voice had been heard in Indian affairs. Government officials were becoming aware that the Indian colonel at the headquarters of the army was unusually qualified to advise them in their dealings with the Indians, and they were carefully listening to what he said.

Minnie

~~~~~~

IN SPITE OF PARKER'S INVOLVEMENT in Indian affairs and some talk at headquarters about his going among the western Indians in a civil capacity for a year or two, he remained a member of General Grant's military staff and continued to receive military promotions. In March 1866, Grant's adjutant, Colonel Bowers, was killed by falling under a railroad car on a visit to West Point. Parker accompanied Grant and the staff to the funeral at the Military Academy and then found himself "compelled to run the desk he [Bowers] vacated." In July, when Grant became general-in-chief of the army, Parker was assigned as colonel and aide-de-camp to the general.

Grant also made sure that he would not lose Parker's services when the volunteers were mustered out of the army by obtaining a commission for him as a second lieutenant in the regular army. That was soon followed by successive brevets as first lieutenant, captain, major, lieutenant colonel, colonel, and brigadier general in the United States Army, in addition to a brevet as brigadier general, United States Volunteers. People usually referred to him now as General Parker, although he always remained Colonel Parker to some.[1]

He still returned to New York when he could. In the fall of 1866 he spoke at an agricultural fair at Albion and attended the Senecas' Green Corn Festival at Tonawanda, where he spoke to the Indians in Seneca, advising them to advance themselves in the arts of civilization, emulating the virtues and shunning the vices of the whites. But he had committed himself to the army, and he offered the use of his farm at Tonawanda to Nic, asking only that any of his colts that might make good trotters or runners or saddlehorses be sent to him at Washington.[2]

Some showy horses would be a useful asset in the capital, for just as Parker had found a place for himself in the army, so he was also finding a place for himself in Washington society. Among the social events surrounding New Year's Day, 1867, the newspapers reported that General Grant's staff officers had entertained at Parker's residence and that Parker was among those who attended a reception and later a levee held at the White House. In spite of the impeachment proceedings then threatening Andrew Johnson, the reception at the White House was a splendid one, marred only by the embarrassment of the theft of $100 from the secretary of the treasury by a pickpocket on the White House portico.[3]

But Indian affairs once again claimed Parker's services when the massacre of Captain William Judd Fetterman and eighty men, who were protecting a wood transport train outside Fort Phil Kearny in December 1866, thrust the Indian question back into the center of attention. The Senate demanded an explanation of the massacre, and President Johnson appointed a special commission to visit the Indian country to learn what had happened and to do what they could to prevent future troubles with the hostile Indians. General Grant had to be convinced of the wisdom of sending a commission to the Indians, but he finally agreed to appointing army officers as members of the commission and included Ely Parker among them.[4]

The commission, composed of four military officers (Alfred Sully, John B. Sanborn, Napoleon Bonaparte Buford, and Parker) and two civilians (G. P. Beauvais and Jefferson F. Kinney) met in Omaha in mid-March. In spite of a snowstorm which kept them in Omaha, the men began to take testimony about the Fetterman massacre, and Parker soon reached his own conclusions in the matter. In an unofficial letter to Rawlins he said that he was "perfectly satisfied, that Carrington [the commander of the fort] had no sort of discipline in his garrison, and although the Indians had been hostile ever since his arrival there, he took no unusual precautions against them." Fetterman himself was at fault for disobeying orders, Parker thought, but Carrington shared the blame by not trying to find out why his orders were disobeyed and by not sending reinforcements until it was too late.

At the same time Parker was reaching some conclusions about the general conduct of Indian affairs in the West. "The whole conduct of Indian Affairs shows a great lack of judgment and efficiency on some one's part." The military movements he observed seemed only to be arousing the hostility of previously peaceful Indians with no effect on those who were already hostile, and Parker used his close relations with Rawlins to suggest military movements which he thought could end hostilities without alienating still more Indians.[5]

From Omaha, the commission traveled to Fort McPherson, Nebraska, where they took testimony from Colonel Henry Carrington, the commander at Fort Phil Kearny at the time of the massacre. Parker's previous opinions about Carrington were readily confirmed: "In my opinion he is not fit to be in this Indian country. He is no fighter and does not understand the Indian character or their mode of warfare." Parker learned, however, that a court of inquiry had been ordered to examine Carrington's case, and he consequently lost interest in pursuing it, "since it can result in no good, and our work would be 'love's labor lost.' "

The commission turned its attention to the Indians. It reported to Washington that a state of war existed with the Tongue River and the Powder River Sioux, and Parker agreed that these Indians had to be dealt with by force: "These hostile Sioux will not come to terms and they should be promptly & severely punished." But many of the Indians were friendly, and the commissioners planned to visit as many of the friendly Indians as possible to try to dissuade them from joining in the war.[6]

Parker and Beauvais, who owned ranches in western Nebraska, were sent ahead to arrange a meeting with the leaders of the Brule and Oglala Sioux, and in late April a meeting was held on one of Beauvais's ranches at the old California Crossing, near Fort Sedgwick. Chiefs Spotted Tail and Swift Bear came to the council with about ninety armed warriors and another ninety women and children, representing in all some twenty-five hundred Indians.

General Sully, who was the president of the commission, opened the council and explained that the commissioners had selected Parker to speak for them. Assisted by an interpreter who translated his speech sentence by sentence, Parker spoke in what the *New York Herald's* correspondent called a "very appropriate and impressive manner." He explained that the commission had been sent by the Indians' "great grandfather, the President of the United States," who had been made "sick in his mind" by the warfare of the Indians and the murder of white settlers.

> Your great grandfather will not pass this by in silence. His ears have been open to the cries of his white children. He has determined to punish these bad Indians; but he does not want to strike anybody who does right, and he has sent us to find who among you are friendly and peaceably disposed. . . . He wants all Indians to live at peace with each other, as good brothers; and, by and by, when all the bad Indians are punished, he would like to have all the Indians live together

as good neighbors, but to do this they must have a permanent home. They must have a place where the white man will not disturb or molest them.

He urged the Indians to let the commission know what part of the country they would like for a permanent home and promised to send their answer "to your great grandfather who is a wise man and will do for you what is right." He also promised to tell the president about any grievances they might have.

The Indians listened with great attention, and then Spotted Tail and Swift Bear replied that they had previously approved the government's request to build a road through their lands but had never received the presents they had been promised for doing so. Moreover, they were poor and made poorer by the Indian agents who stole from them. The Indians showed no intention of going to war, and the meeting ended in a friendly spirit. Parker was selected with two others to give presents to the Indians, and Sully reported to Washington that over 700 warriors had been prevented from joining the war party. With this success, Sully was also convinced of the importance of the commission's visiting as many Indians as possible, to gather the friendly Indians onto reservations, and to prevent the war from spreading.[7]

The commission went on to Fort Laramie and held further meetings with the Indian tribes, and then in May, in order to reach even more Indians, the commission split into three groups, Parker and General Sully leaving for Omaha to travel up the Missouri River to meet with the Indians there. They traveled by land from Omaha to Fort Randall and then on to Fort Sully, reporting that they found the Indians in that vicinity peacefully planting their crops but bitter because the agricultural implements promised them by the government had never arrived.

At Fort Sully they were joined by Father Pierre-Jean DeSmet, a Belgian-born Jesuit priest known to the Indians as Black Robe. Because he had the confidence of the Indians, DeSmet had been appointed an "envoy extraordinary" to meet with them for the same purposes as the commission. The three men joined forces, the Seneca Indian, the Belgian Jesuit priest, and the white soldier with a reputation for Indian fighting, and they began a steamboat trip up the Missouri that would take them as far as Fort Buford, at the border of the Montana Territory. They stopped at the principal military posts along the way, called the Indians to councils, and tried to convince them to remain at peace. They found the Indians generally peaceable but angered both at the military presence in their lands and the bad faith of the whites, who had been free to make promises to them, but whose "many fine words and pompous promises always come to nothing, nothing, nothing." Father DeSmet took an active part in the councils but also busily conducted masses for the Indians and baptized nearly 900 children and forty-six adults along the way.[8]

If the presence of a black-robed priest in the western forts seemed unusual, so did the presence of an Indian wearing the uniform of a United States Army officer. Yet Parker was not the only Indian officer in the West. Cornelius C. Cusick, the Tuscarora chief who had served in Newton Parker's company during the Civil War, was a second lieutenant in the regular army and was serving in the Dakota Territory during Parker's visit. A year later he was wounded in a fight with the Indians, suffering a blow on the right shoulder by an Indian war club.

Inevitably, there were those who viewed Indians like Cusick and Parker with suspicion. After spending two months on the Missouri, Parker and his companions returned as far as Yankton, where a nervous official, called to deal with the two white men and their obviously Indian associate, thought it wise to consult Washington with a curt telegram asking, "Who is Eli S. Parker?" On the other hand, when Sully and Parker reached Omaha, Henry M. Stanley, who was visiting there, reported their presence, but seemed much more interested in an Englishman who had recently been scalped and was carrying a bucket of water containing the scalp, "somewhat resembling a drowned rat, as it floated, curled up, on the water."[9]

His mission completed, Parker traveled back to Washington by way of New York State and visited with Carrie and John Mountpleasant at the Tuscarora Reservation. The *Buffalo Express* used the occasion to comment on the career of the area's famous resident: "Colonel Parker is a good example of the success which almost any man of determination and fair ability may attain in republican America.—It must be refreshing to him to remember that a few years ago he was denied admission to practice at the New York State Courts, . . . but this rebuff was the means, several years later, of giving Gen. Grant a valuable officer. He is spoken of as a man of varied acquirements, and of much ability."[10]

When he returned to Washington about September 1, 1867, after an absence of nearly six months, Parker reported that "it took me sometime to post myself as to what had occurred in the civilized portion of our country, during my sojourn in the wilds of it." Yet a month later he was traveling again, this time as an engineer. The

Minnie Orton Sackett (1849–1932), the pretty eighteen-year-old Washington socialite who married Ely S. Parker. Minnie was described as "friendly and vivacious" and one of the most beautiful belles in Washington, D.C. *Courtesy of the Buffalo and Erie County Historical Society, Buffalo, New York.*

secretary of the treasury was considering selling the government's interest in the Dismal Swamp Canal in Virginia and North Carolina, and had requested the loan of an officer from the Corps of Engineers to report on the condition of the canal and the wisdom of selling the government's shares in it. General Grant, however, directed his own aide-de-camp to do the work, and Parker was soon on his way to Norfolk to examine the canal. The area was familiar to him—the Dismal Swamp Canal was near the site of Parker's earlier work on the Chesapeake and Albemarle Canal—and Parker quickly completed the survey and was back in Washington in less than three weeks.[11]

With a flurry of excitement, Washington society learned in December that General Grant's thirty-nine-year-old Indian aide was to be married to Miss Minnie Sackett, a pert and pretty socialite who was eighteen years old, and white. And thereby hangs a tale.

Minnie lived in Washington with her mother Anna, the widow of Brevet Brigadier General William Sackett of the Ninth New York Cavalry. Both mother and daughter were prominent in Washington society. President Johnson, for example, when he returned in September 1866 from a visit to Chicago to dedicate a monument to Stephen A. Douglas, had received a personal note from the two: "Mrs. and Miss Sackett present their compliments to his Excellency Andrew Johnson and hope that he will give an afternoon Reception, that his lady friends may congratulate their President upon his safe return home. God has received the offering of a widow's prayers and protected our beloved President." Parker probably met Minnie at one of the many social events they both participated in, but Parker's acquaintance with her mother may have gone back to the summer of 1864.[12]

In July 1864, Anna Sackett appeared at General Grant's headquarters at City Point accompanied by an ambulance load of canned fruits and meats and other supplies for distribution to the members of the Ninth New York Cavalry. Her real errand was to obtain news of her husband, Colonel William Sackett, the commanding officer of the Ninth Cavalry, who had been wounded on June 11, near Trevilian Station, Virginia. She hoped to enter the Confederate lines to look for her husband, and General Grant directed that a letter be written to General Lee, asking permission for her to visit her husband if he was still alive. Ely Parker was present at headquarters at the time of her visit and may have written the letter himself. Lee replied that it would not be possible for Mrs. Sackett to enter their lines but that he would inquire about her husband's condition. She finally learned that he had died of his wounds on June 14.[13]

Lieutenant Colonel William H. Sackett of the Ninth New York Cavalry, stepfather of Minnie Orton Sackett who married Ely Parker. Sackett was killed at Trevilian Station, Virginia, on June 14, 1864. *Courtesy of the Library of Congress.*

Ely S. Parker about the time of his marriage to Minnie Sackett in 1867 in Washington, D.C. Parker was then a brevet brigadier general and aide-de-camp to General Grant. *Smithsonian Institution National Anthropological Archives, Bureau of American Ethnology Collection.*

Minnie Orton Sackett at the time of her marriage to Ely S. Parker, December 23, 1867. Although Parker failed to appear on their scheduled wedding day, he and Minnie were married a week later, and Ulysses S. Grant gave the bride away. Of her marriage Minnie explained: "Some people thought I married the General because he was an Indian. Now I don't care for Indians—I married the General because I loved him." From Arthur C. Parker, *The Life of General Ely S. Parker.*

Although Minnie was known in Washington as "the daughter of the gallant Colonel Sackett," she was not really his child. Anna and William Sackett had only been married in 1862, and Minnie was then thirteen years old. Her real father was Thomas Orton, and she called herself Minnie Orton Sackett until her marriage.[14] Minnie was described as "gay and lively, . . . friendly and vivacious." She was "blonde" in complexion, with brilliant eyes and dark brown hair and was said to be one of the most beautiful belles in the capital. Harry Wilson considered her "a very beautiful, modest and accomplished woman," and James E. Kelly, a New York artist who knew her later in life, described her as "tall slim and merry—and handsome." Kelly spoke with her about her marriage and she told him, "Some people thought I married the General because he was an Indian. Now I don't care for Indians—I married the General because I loved him."[15]

The wedding was scheduled for Tuesday, December 17, at the Episcopal Church of the Epiphany in Washington. The invitations were issued, the bridal gown was made up at Madame Demorest's Branch on Pennsylvania Avenue, and on the Saturday before the event, Parker went to General Grant's house to borrow a military sash to wear at the wedding. General Grant had agreed to give the bride away, and on the appointed day Grant and his staff were among the "*creme de la creme* of Washington society" who assembled at the church for the wedding. But the groom failed to appear. When a search for him proved unsuccessful, the crowd "quietly dispersed with many heartfelt prayers for the lady so cruelly deserted." The search continued to be fruitless, and rumors about the missing groom spread through the city, and by means of the newspapers, through the country. It was said that he was ill with a violent cold, that he had been seen in Baltimore, that his body had been found under the ice in the Potomac, and that he had been married to another woman in Buffalo. Through it all the bride was reported to be "in tears, and the mother in a passion."[16]

Two days later the newspapers reported that Parker had been found and gave his explanation for his absence. He said that on Saturday, after he had gone to General Grant's house to borrow the sash, he had taken a walk and met one of the New York Indians. The Indian had taken him to his room and given him a glass of wine. As they talked, Parker began to feel drowsy and lay down for a rest. When he awoke, the Indian told him that he had been ill and gave him some medicine to take. By the time Parker woke again, the day of the wedding was past. Some of Parker's friends thought that the Senecas were opposed to his marrying a white woman and had sent the Indian to

Washington to drug Parker in order to prevent the marriage. The Indians who followed Handsome Lake's religion were indeed opposed to intermarriage. Parker's grandfather, Jimmy Johnson, often repeated the prophet's warning: "It is a great sin to intermarry, and intermingle the blood of the two races."[17]

Two of Parker's fellow officers had a simpler explanation for his disappearance. Horace Porter wrote the next day that "Parker has disgraced us more than usual. He was to have been married to Miss Minnie Sackett yesterday morning, but instead of appearing he went on his habitual four days drunk, and has not yet turned up." Even Parker's good friend William Rowley, when news of the affair reached him in Galena, wryly expressed his disbelief of Parker's explanation by asking Adam Badeau, "Have you caught and *bottled up* the Indians that captured Parker[?]"[18]

Whatever explanation Parker offered Minnie must have satisfied her, for the wedding was rescheduled for December 24. The publicity given to Parker's disappearance brought a great crowd of the curious to the church; an estimated three thousand people gathered around the building, "all intent on seeing the white woman married to the red man." But as the people began to fill the church, elegantly decorated with greens, they were told that the decorations were for the Christmas service; the wedding had been performed at the rectory the night before, at which only a small group, including Grant and some of his staff, were present. Grant had given the bride away as originally planned, and Parker and Minnie had left the same evening for New York City and Rochester. The disappointed crowd complained loudly that the affair had been a "sell," but no apologies were made, and no further explanations of the wedding fiasco or its happier sequel were ever given.[19]

Parker's marriage did little to change his style of life, except perhaps to keep him closer to home. Apart from an official visit to Forts Porter and Niagara in New York State in November, he remained in Washington during all of 1868. He appeared at receptions at the White House and at General Grant's, followed Tonawanda affairs at the Indian Office, and kept his friends informed about the "impeachment excitement" in the capital. But events that were to change his life greatly began their course as his friend Ulysses Grant became the Republican nominee for president of the United States.[20]

Parker had remained close to Grant both officially and personally. He was by Grant's side on the celebrated occasion when General Winfield Scott Hancock refused to salute Grant. Parker and Grant were walking down Pennsylvania Avenue when they met Hancock, whom Grant had recalled from a command in New Orleans, and who had angrily blamed Grant for what he considered a reflection on his honor. Grant saluted him, but Hancock, who was Grant's subordinate, refused to return the salute. Grant characteristically said nothing, but Parker observed that he did get "red in the face."

Parker showed his loyalty to his friend by giving him his political support in the election of 1868, support which he described in a letter to his brother Nic's young children. "General Grant you know is the republican candidate for President of the United States, in opposition to Seymour of your State, and this fact has made my work a great deal heavier, as we are compelled to see and talk with politicians from every part of the country. I want to see Grant elected, because I think he is the best patriot, and that he only can bring peace to the country. He is a very nice man indeed. He is a great general and has a good heart."[21]

After his election Grant gave the staff a prominent place in his inauguration. The president-elect and his military family left army headquarters for the Capitol, and afterward the staff accompanied him to the White House grounds. The next day the staff was called back to the White House, where Grant announced the new positions that were to be given them. Horace Porter was appointed Grant's private secretary, with Orville Babcock to assist him. Grant's brother-in-law, Fred Dent, was assigned as military secretary. Adam Badeau was given a room in the White House to complete his military history of the war, and Parker was to become commissioner of Indian affairs.[22]

Parker was assigned to temporary duty in the office of the secretary of war while the way was prepared for his appointment as commissioner. Grant had no need of formal recommendations of Parker—he knew him as well as any who might recommend him—but recommendations were still made. Senator John Thayer of Nebraska, a onetime Indian fighter who was considered an expert in Indian affairs, was quick to urge Parker's appointment: "I can think of no one whose appointment to that position would give greater satisfaction to the country. What appointment so appropriate? Who could exercise so favorable an influence upon the Indians?"[23]

Others were not so positive. Samuel B. Treat, the secretary of the American Board of Commissioners for Foreign Missions which had missionary work among the Senecas, was alarmed about the possibility of Parker's appointment. He had heard in Washington that Parker's "habits, in the matter of drinking, were not unexceptional" and had written to Asher Wright, a missionary who had spent his entire adult life among the Senecas, to obtain his opinion about Parker. Wright's reply was much more favorable than he had expected, and Treat passed it on to Washington. Wright thought Parker "competent for the place" and

> very well versed in Indian matters generally;—that his policy, fore-shadowed in his published replies to the Senate's Investigating committee is in accordance with that of President Grant. (In fact I believe that he has done more than any other man towards shaping Grant's policy towards the Indians:) and that his appointment will break up the system of plunder which has been a disgrace to the country and so ruinous to the Indians. I have seen him but a few times since he entered the army, and know not what habits he may have acquired there. The President probably knows better than any one else whether there is danger in that respect. . . .
>
> In some respects Grant could not do better than to appoint him. In many respects he would be in danger of doing worse; and yet, if he should appoint him, I shall be continually anxious in regard to the result of the experiment: not from personal considerations; but because he is an Indian: and will, on that account, be tempted on the one hand, and criticized on the other: while his success or failure will have vast influence for good or evil upon the race which, for the first time in the history of the country, he represents in high official position under the Government.[24]

There was still one question to be answered: was Parker eligible to hold the office? Grant had been embarrassed in one of his early appointments to learn that the man he had selected was not eligible to serve, and this time he first asked the attorney-general for an opinion on Parker's eligibility. No Indian had ever held the office, and since Indians were not citizens, it was reasonable to ask whether an Indian could hold the office. Yet Parker had held other federal positions, both military and civil, without citizenship, and times were changing. Congress passed a civil rights act in 1866, which granted citizenship to all persons born in the United States regardless of race, color, or previous condition of servitude. The act did exclude "Indians not taxed," but that presumably meant Indians living on reservations and not those who lived as Parker did. A good case could be made that Parker was a citizen and qualified to serve, and Attorney-General Ebenezer Hoar, without giving his reasons, ruled that Parker was eligible to become commissioner.[25]

Grant nominated Parker for the position on April 13, 1869. Two days later the Committee on Indian Affairs reported favorably on the nomination, and the following day the Senate confirmed it by a vote of 36 to 12. The official appointment was then made, and on April 26, Parker resigned his commission in the army and began his duties as the first Indian ever to hold the office of commissioner of Indian affairs.[26]

Commissioner of Indian Affairs

THE OFFICE OF INDIAN AFFAIRS, over which Parker presided, was responsible for the government's relations with the almost 300,000 Indians who lived in the United States and its territories in 1869. Those relations were governed by some 370 treaties which had been made with the various tribes over the years, but they were also governed by the idea that the Indians were "wards of the nation." As Parker explained the situation to his superior, Jacob Cox, the Secretary of the Interior: "The Indian is the ward of the Government. The management and direction of *all* his affairs and relations in a civil capacity has been conferred by the Act of 1832 exclusively upon this Office. . . . It regulates his estate both real and personal. It supervises his domestic relations. And it exercises all the power over him of guardian and ward." As commissioner of Indian affairs, Ely Parker was the one through whom the Great Father in Washington dealt with his Indian wards. But the new administration was not content with the Indian as ward; the Great Father himself had made it clear in his inaugural address that he would "favor any course toward [the Indians] which tends to their civilization and ultimate citizenship."[1]

Grant and Parker believed that civilization and citizenship for the Indians was a practical necessity lest they "be overwhelmed in the advancing wave of white civilization." The rapid settlement of the West, hastened by the new transcontinental railroads and the discovery of gold, was bound to bring Indians and whites into close contact and possible conflict. The policy of the new administration was to avoid conflict by bringing the roving bands of Indians onto reservations where they could be protected from the whites and at the same time prevented from engaging in violent acts themselves. On the reservations provision could be made, in Parker's terms, for their "humanization, civilization, and Christianization."

Photograph of Ely S. Parker by Mathew Brady. President Grant's appointment of Parker as commissioner of Indian affairs was the first appointment
ever of an Indian to that office. Parker served as commissioner from April 26,
1869, to August 1, 1871. His resignation from the office followed a congressional investigation of charges that he defrauded the government in the
purchase of Indian supplies. Though cleared of any wrongdoing, Parker's
actions were severely criticized by the investigating committee, and he sub-
sequently severed all connections with the government. *Courtesy of U.S.
Signal Corps, photo No. 111-B-5272 (Brady Collection), National Archives
and Records Service.*

To carry out the policy, Grant obtained an appropriation of $2 million over and above the $5 to $6 million annually appropriated for the Indian service. The additional money would provide the means to remove the Indians from the path of the western settlers and to educate them in the agricultural and mechanical skills necessary to save them from extinction and which would eventually allow them to assume the role of American citizens. President Grant's new commissioner of Indian affairs was himself a silent testimonial that the Indian, when educated, was fully capable of assuming his place in American society.[2]

Parker's background suited him admirably for his work as commissioner. His legal training equipped him to deal with the maze of laws and treaties which governed Indian affairs, and his work for the Treasury and War departments had made him a skillful administrator. He had represented his own people before the commissioner of Indian affairs for more than twenty years and had served on two important Indian commissions in the West, as well as helping the Indian Office negotiate treaties in Washington. Not only was he close to the president and sure that his policies would receive support from the White House, but for the first time in the nation's history an Indian directed the government's Indian policy. To be sure, there were great differences between the sophisticated Indian in "citizen clothes" seated behind his desk in the magnificent Patent Office Building and the "blanket Indians" who came to call on him, but his callers nevertheless had confidence in him because he was an Indian, and an Indian obviously endowed with power.

Indian delegations continually called at his office. They came from all parts of the country, those from the wilder parts generally avoided the chairs, sat on the floor, leaned on the furniture, or stood by the walls, and came dressed in their traditional clothes, with tomahawks or pistols in their belts. Interpreters came with them who translated the speeches of the officials and the visitors sentence by sentence. The peace pipe, too, was often smoked in the commissioner's office just as it was in western councils. Among Parker's visitors was his brother Newton, who came to Washington with a petition asking for the abolition of the Tonawandas' government by chiefs, a proposal, however, which received little sympathy from his brother, who was a chief and a sachem himself. But in most matters Parker could no longer speak simply as an Iroquois sachem, or even as an Indian. As commissioner he spoke for the public interest as well as the interests of the Indians. He said that if the Indians' "semi-civilized customs and forms of society" conflicted with the public interest, they would have to yield to it. Parker even found himself in the novel position of defending the Supreme Court's decision in the case of Fellows versus Blacksmith, explaining what had been so often explained to him, that treaties once ratified must be obeyed, whether the Indians had assented to them or not.[3]

To carry out his duties as commissioner, Parker had the assistance of an office force of thirty-eight clerks, many of them specialists in Indian laws and treaties. One of them had charge of some $4 million in trust funds, which had accumulated from the sale of Indian lands and which the Indian Office administered for the various tribes. Others looked after such matters as the numerous land surveys involved in creating new reservations, the purchase of annuity goods promised in treaties, and the settlement of Indian claims. Although it increased the work of his clerks, Parker insisted that all claims concerning Indians be settled through his office to make sure that the whites who represented the Indians had no opportunity to cheat them.

The Office of Indian Affairs also employed nearly seventy agents in the field and fifteen superintendents to whom the agents reported. The agents dealt first hand with the Indians, taking censuses, distributing annuities, providing emergency food and clothing, and overseeing the work of the other employees of the Indian agencies, the interpreters, teachers, doctors, farmers, millers, carpenters, and other artisans who were to care for the Indians and to lead them to civilization. In all, Parker's office employed more than 600 people in Washington and at the various agencies.[4]

Parker and Grant wanted to insure that the employees of the Indian Office dealt with the Indians justly, and their first step in that direction was the removal of the agents and superintendents from the arena of politics. It was widely believed that the Indian agents were corrupt, and that they, the politicians, and the contractors who supplied provisions for the Indians had formed an "Indian Ring" with the purpose of defrauding the Indians. The vigorous competition for appointments to the modestly paid position of Indian agent made the belief entirely credible. One story popular at the time told of the chief who described his agent to General Sherman. "When he come he bring everything in little bag, when he go it take two steamboats to carry away his things."[5]

Shortly before Grant's inauguration, delegations of both orthodox and Hicksite Quakers called on the president-elect to discuss their views on Indian affairs. Their call suggested an alternative to the politically appointed agent, and on February 15, 1869, Grant directed Parker to write to the Quakers asking if they would nominate members of their own societies who could serve as Indian agents. The Quakers accepted the proposal, and as a result two entire superintendencies which included fourteen agencies were assigned to them, the Central Superintendency to the orthodox Quakers and the Northern Superintendency to the Hicksites. Under the new "Quaker Policy" the two groups of Quakers would not only nominate superintendents and agents, but would also oversee their work after they had been appointed. Parker assured the Quakers that any attempt they might make for the "improvement, education, and Christianization of the Indians under such agencies" would receive the president's full encouragement.[6]

For the balance of the agents, Grant and Parker turned to the army. Both men favored returning the entire Indian Office to the War Department, but since that was politically impossible, they took advantage of an old law which permitted the assignment of army officers to duty with the Indians, and with a few exceptions army officers soon replaced the remaining politically appointed agents and superintendents. A few of the officers were men Parker knew. General Sully became superintendent in Montana, and Parker assured his brother Nic of the good character of the officer who was to be assigned to the New York Indians. For the other positions Parker asked the War Department, where possible, to assign officers who had some knowledge of the Indians, and in any case to assign men "of rank experience and sobriety as they are more useful on this duty."[7]

Some members of Congress, angry at the loss of patronage under the new policy, opposed the appointments of both Quakers and army officers, but Grant would not give up the experiment. Grant and Parker both had confidence in the honor of military officers, as they did not in the civilians who had been serving as agents, and the Quakers' reputation for peacefulness and honesty gave hope for a new era of integrity and peace in the nation's relations with the Indians.[8]

Parker carefully instructed his agents in their duties. They were to carry out the administration's policy of locating Indians on permanent reservations, and they were to prepare the Indians "to submit to the inevitable change of their mode of life to pursuits more congenial to a civilized state. You will endeavor to keep constantly before their minds the pacific intentions of the government, and obtain their confidence by acts of kindness and honesty and justly dealing with them, thereby securing that peace which it is the wish of all good citizens to establish and maintain."

When the Indians came onto the reservations, the agents were to protect them "in all their legal rights" and to give them every assistance in learning "agricultural pursuits and the arts of civilized life." The agents were also to distribute clothing, provisions, and agricultural implements to the Indians who settled on the reservations, both as a reward for settling there and "with a view of removing from them every temptation to murder and plunder."

"Roving Indians" who refused to settle on the reservations or Indians who were hostile to the government were in no case to be given presents, nor were the agents to have any authority over them. They would be "subject wholly to the control and supervision of the military authorities, who, as circumstances may justify, will at their discretion treat them as friendly or hostile."[9]

Parker's policy of coaxing the Indians onto reservations with kindness and presents and threatening roving and hostile Indians with the power of the army depended on a good understanding between the Indian Office and the War Department. With Parker's friend John Rawlins serving as secretary of war, and with their mutual friend Ulysses Grant in the White House, that understanding was readily achieved. Parker's use of the army set him apart from the many humanitarians who had taken an interest in the reform of the Indian Office. In many respects Parker's policies were exactly what the reformers had called for, but the reformers generally thought that the army had no place in the conduct of Indian affairs.

As a military man himself, Parker saw the use of the army as a necessity in dealing with the Indians. He frequently called on the military to quiet hostile Indians and to protect his agents from Indian hostilities, just as he called on them to protect the Indians on the reservations from the intrusions and hostilities of white men. In common with the humanitarians, Parker insisted that the Indians be dealt with justly and kindly, but he was also aware of what he called "the difficult task of humanizing and taming the wild Indian," and he was willing to use force where necessary against Indians as well as whites.[10]

The country's humanitarians were also enlisted in the new Indian policy. Two years earlier, in 1867, Parker had suggested that a board of inspection be created to oversee the agencies, to curb dishonest agents, and to convince the Indians of the government's intention to treat them honestly and fairly. Others had made the same suggestion, and one of Grant's first acts as president was to establish a Board of Indian Commissioners composed of ten men "eminent for their intelligence and philanthropy" to serve as the inspectors Parker had proposed. The board was empowered to inspect the records of the Indian Office and its agencies, to be present when annuities were paid to the Indians or goods bought for them, and generally to advise the government on its Indian policies.

The new commissioners took their task seriously. The board was determined to remove all dishonesty from the Indian service, and as a group of committed Protestants, the board members were equally determined to civilize and Christianize the Indians, pronouncing in their first annual report that "the religion of our blessed Saviour is believed to be the most effective agent for the civilization of any people." William Welsh, a Philadelphia merchant and Episcopal churchman with a long history of humanitarian interests and a somewhat pompous manner, was elected chairman of the board. At their first meeting the commissioners divided into three committees who were to visit Indian reservations and inspect agencies, and with Parker's encouragement the commissioners visited half the tribes in the country in their first six months in office.[11]

Parker's chief concern as commissioner was the purchase of supplies for the Indians, and he spent weeks at a time in New York City and Philadelphia attending to the purchases. It was useless to encourage the Indians to give up the hunt and settle on reservations if they were not well supplied with food and clothing and the agricultural implements necessary to begin a settled life, and Parker wanted to be sure that when appropriations were available the goods were purchased and shipped as quickly as possible. The purchase and transportation of Indian goods had also been a main area of fraud and theft, and rather than delegate those tasks to anyone else, Parker chose to oversee them himself.

A few days after he took office, Parker left for New York City to attend to the spring purchases which were expected in the West before the time of the summer hunts. He personally employed inspectors who went into the stores, checked the quality of the goods, and watched as they were packed for shipment, to make sure that the merchants did not substitute inferior goods. But if Parker anticipated trouble from the merchants, he was mistaken; his troubles appeared in the form of the Board of Indian Commissioners. One of the commissioners, George Hay Stuart, a Scotch-Irish banker from Philadelphia who had been chairman of the United States Christian Commission during the

Civil War, was also in New York, and not content with having the
merchants inspected, he was determined to inspect Parker's work,
too. After Parker's inspectors finished their work, Stuart wanted to
cart the goods to another building, unpack them, and reinspect them
before they were shipped. What is more, he insisted on being the one
who would certify the bills for payment for the goods.

Whatever his personal feelings about Stuart's obvious distrust of
him, Parker believed that such procedures would only delay the
shipment of goods which were urgently needed in the West, and he
hurriedly returned to Washington to discuss the matter with the
secretary of the interior. Cox agreed with Parker, and Parker informed
Stuart that the board's inspectors were welcome to work with his inspectors, but that the delay of repacking and reinspecting the goods
could not be tolerated. He also told Stuart that the merchants would
be paid only on the certificates of Parker's men. To make sure of his
position, Parker reported the incident the next day to Grant, and
when he was sure that Grant approved of his actions, he let Stuart
know that he had the backing of the president. Stuart reported to Cox
that he was entirely satisfied with Parker's conduct in the matter. But
Chairman Welsh said bluntly that Stuart and William E. Dodge,
another member of the commission, "more than suspected frauds,"
with the clear implication that Parker was a party to them.[12]

After Welsh learned of the incident and discovered that he could
do nothing to change the president's mind, he promptly resigned from
the Board of Indian Commissioners. Welsh had assumed that the
board would have the final authority in the expenditure of all Indian
appropriations, and he believed that unless it was given that authority,
fraud and theft would still prevail. When it became apparent that
Parker and not the board had the power to make purchases, he resigned and began to "work for the Indians in his own way and upon
his own account." Working with the Episcopal mission board, he
continued to visit the Indians and kept a strict watch on the operations
of the Indian Office, "with a view," as Parker supposed, "to detecting
irregularities and exposing them, and thereby taking from it the
management of the Indian funds."

Although he no longer had any official position, Welsh continued
to make suggestions to the Indian Office and the president in a manner
Parker found offensive. Parker said that "the communications from
Mr. Welsh relative to Indian affairs have not always been couched in
those terms which might be expected from one not authorized to
dictate or control, but as there was a probability that his motive was a

desire to promote the welfare of the Indians, his wishes have, as far as the same were practicable and not incompatible with existing laws, been complied with." But the harshest of Welsh's letters was still to come.[13]

In addition to his trips to New York and Philadelphia, Parker traveled in November 1869, to Louisville, Kentucky, to attend a reunion of the Society of the Army of the Tennessee. Parker had attended a similar meeting of the society with John Rawlins at Cincinnati in 1866, where Rawlins had been elected president of the society, but Parker was going to Louisville to present a eulogy in Rawlins' memory.

Although Rawlins had been ill for some years with what probably was tuberculosis, Grant had appointed him secretary of war in his cabinet. Six months later, and only in his thirty-ninth year, Rawlins lay dying in Washington. Parker was at his deathbed, and in his last hours Rawlins dictated his will to his Indian friend. Parker was impressed with Rawlins' loyalty to Grant. He had named "my friend Genl Ulysses S. Grant," along with his wife, as guardian for his children and executor of his will. His last desire was to see Grant once more, and his last question was, "Hasn't the old man come yet?" In his speech at Louisville, Parker praised Rawlins lavishly, calling him "a most valuable executive officer" and "an almost indispensable aid to his chief." He also praised Rawlins' directness of speech and his integrity of purpose. Both were qualities that would be sorely missed in the president's cabinet.[14]

Parker and his wife were also enjoying the social life of the capital. One Washington observer reported seeing "General Parker and his little, decidedly pronounced blonde wife" at an afternoon "five o'clock" given at the home of a wealthy citizen. His description of Parker, though not too accurate, reveals the impression he was making on Washington society. "He was a full-blooded and strongly individualized Mohawk Indian; a classical scholar, graduate of an Eastern university; a large, affable, courtly, gallant gentleman, in evening dress-suit." A newspaper reporter also noticed the couple at a reception given by the Speaker of the House of Representatives, James G. Blaine. "Back of General Sheridan, who will persist in dying his mustache, stands Colonel Parker, of Indian renown, and his wife, who is said to entertain as well as any lady in Washington."

But not everyone in Washington society welcomed the Parkers. Another reporter who observed the couple at the Speaker's reception voiced her strong disapproval of the white woman married to the

Minnie Sackett Parker. Although some objected to the white woman married to the Indian man, Minnie Parker played a prominent role in Washington society while her husband was commissioner of Indian affairs. She was said to "entertain as well as any lady in Washington." *Courtesy of Madeline Bullard Perry.*

An engraving by R. O. O'Brien made from a photograph of Ely S. Parker taken by New York photographer Napoleon Sarony. *The New-York Historical Society, New York, New York.*

Indian man. After mentioning Parker's presence, she said: "His wife is fair, standing beside him, and attracts attention because she has broken a law; but why should she be received in society for the same reason that puts the poor Irish washerwoman, who links her fate with another race, beyond the pale of association, only the newspapers can answer. And yet no half breeds have made their appearance, which proves there is a destiny which has something to do with shaping our ends."[15]

The Parkers' social life included invitations from the White House, where they were sometimes guests of the Grants. On one occasion they dined informally with Grant and his family just after

Grant had been to Philadelphia, where he had been persuaded to attend an opera at the Academy. Grant was notoriously tone-deaf; he once said that he knew only two tunes: "one is 'Yankee Doodle,' and the other isn't." When Minnie asked him how he had enjoyed the opera, Parker said that Grant "replied that he did not know. He had heard a great deal of noise, and had seen a large number of musicians, most of them violinists, sawing away upon their instruments. Here he exemplified by imitating with the carving knife and fork the actions of a violinist, and added that the noise they made was deafening, unintelligible, and confusing to him."[16]

As Parker prepared his annual report at the end of 1869, he admitted that in spite of the government's policies toward the Indians, "hostilities to some extent, though not to that of war by tribes, have unfortunately existed more or less during the past year." His words had hardly been printed when an even more serious threat to the peace was posed by the Piegan band of the Blackfoot tribe in Montana. When Parker learned from General Sully of thefts and murders committed by the Piegans, he referred the information to the War Department "with the request that prompt measures may be taken by the Military to check the lawless acts committed by these Indians." The response of the military was more severe than Parker had anticipated. Major Eugene M. Baker was ordered to attack a Piegan camp on the Marias River, and General Sheridan added his personal instructions: "Tell Baker to strike them hard!" On January 23, 1870, Baker led an early morning raid against the unsuspecting camp in which 173 Piegans were killed, many of them women and children. Many people, especially in the East, were outraged at what they called the "Baker Massacre," but Parker's opinion was that the Piegans had brought the trouble on themselves, and he pointed out that, whatever its faults, the army's show of force had brought peace to the area. "Although the consequences were deplorable, yet they were effectual in completely subduing the Indians, and the entire nation has since not only been quiet, but even solicitous to enter into arrangements for permanent peace and good behavior in the future."[17]

As summer approached, the brittle peace was threatened again, this time by the Sioux. Parker received reports of hostilities on the Missouri River and immediately went with Secretary Cox to the White House to meet with the president, the secretary of war, and the general of the army, where it was agreed to send reinforcements to the western forts. Parker's agent at Crow Creek in the Dakota Territory had also reported unfriendly Brule Sioux in the area, and Parker specifically asked that troops be sent to protect the agent and his employees "against any violence with which they may be threatened, and if possible to maintain quiet among these Indians."

In order to defuse what appeared to be a serious threat to the peace, Grant and Parker agreed to invite some of the Sioux chiefs to Washington, to hear their complaints, and to try to convince them of the futility of war. Parker sent instructions to his friend General John E. Smith to escort the Indians to Washington, and he also invited G. P. Beauvais, who had served with him on the Fetterman Commission and who had the Indians' confidence, to come to the capital to assist in the negotiations.[18]

Four Brule Sioux led by Spotted Tail and Swift Bear, whom Parker had met in Nebraska in 1867, arrived in Washington in late May. The Indian Office regarded them as generally friendly to the United States, and when they met in the council room of the office, Parker told them he was glad they had kept their promises of peace. He said that the president had heard of their troubles and had invited them to Washington to hear their complaints. Parker let them know that Red Cloud and his party, who were considered unfriendly, would be arriving in a few days and that the government hoped to win their friendship, too. After Parker promised to take them to see the president, "a pipe which the red men had brought with them was then lighted and passed around the small number of persons present, nearly all of whom indulged in a few whiffs, and after a few moments the delegation shook hands with the Commissioner and passed on their way to dinner." Spotted Tail and his delegation stayed in Washington for two weeks, professing their friendship and asking that their people be allowed to go on the hunt lest they starve. When they left, they presented Secretary Cox with "an elegant pipe" and Parker with "an elaborately-worked Buffalo robe."[19]

On June 1, Red Cloud and sixteen other leaders of the Oglala Sioux arrived in Washington. Unlike Spotted Tail, Red Cloud had remained defiant to the government and freely expressed his dissatisfaction with the reservation assigned to him and to the roads and forts placed in his lands. In a ritual as old as the republic, Parker took Red Cloud and his party on a tour of the Navy Yard and the arsenal, to demonstrate the superior power of the nation they had chosen to defy. The Sioux were, however, not as naive as Parker thought; when cannons were fired to impress the Indians, someone noticed that the women they had brought with them put their hands over their ears before the guns were fired, "proving that they knew all about that long ago." Parker later took them to meet the president, where Red Cloud appealed for food and clothing for his people who were "poor and naked," and on the evening of June 9, they were formally entertained at the White House.[20]

The Indians held a series of councils with Parker and Secretary Cox, who explained again the treaty the Sioux had agreed to in 1868, which Red Cloud claimed not to understand. They also encouraged the Indians to settle on the reservation and to adopt the ways of the whites. During the discussions Cox held up Parker as an example of the kind of Indian the government respected. "Here is the Commissioner of Indian Affairs," he said, "who is a chief among us. He belonged to a race who lived there long before the white man came to this country. He now has power and white people obey him, and he directs what shall be done in very important business. We will be brethren to you in the same way if you follow his good example and learn our civilization."

When the negotiations had been completed, Parker had John E. Smith take the group home by way of New York City, where the Indians were permitted to buy presents at the government's expense, and where Red Cloud presented his case before a distinguished audience at the Cooper Institute. From New York they returned west, carrying with them the government's promise that "if you shall stay quietly in the home assigned to you we shall keep adding to your presents."[21]

The negotiations with Red Cloud and with the delegations of Cheyenne Sioux, Pawnees, and Osages who followed him were successful. Red Cloud reluctantly became an advocate of peace, and Parker later reported that since his visit to Washington, Red Cloud had kept his band "quiet and peaceable."

Parker's main concern was to provide the Indians with the supplies that had been promised them to keep them peaceable. The Indian agents reported severe shortages of food along the Missouri River, and Parker was convinced that unless food was purchased and shipped quickly, the Indians would lose faith in the government and leave the reservations. He said later that "it was known and admitted by all who had dealings with them that it was only the food and clothing that kept them about the agencies; and it was the unceasing apprehension of all that the moment their supplies ceased they would abandon their agencies and at once resume their nomadic habits, taking from citizens whatever property they might fancy, and inaugurating a war, if deemed to their advantage." The governor of the Dakota Territory was in complete agreement; he urgently requested Parker to send food, saying that "we must feed or fight the Indians in this superintendency."

But the army's commissary department, which had previously been purchasing supplies for the Indians, gave notice that it could not continue to supply them after July 1. More important, the appropriation which provided for feeding the Indians extended only until July 1, and as that date approached the Congress appeared to be making no progress in passing another appropriation. Parker had assured the Indians that if they stayed on their reservations and remained at peace they would be fed, and rather than risk war while waiting for Congress to act, he made an arrangement with a large contractor, James W. Bosler, who agreed to furnish the necessary beef and flour immediately, taking the risk that he would be reimbursed when the appropriation passed. The arrangement worked well. Parker later reported that "an abundance of good provisions was soon supplied, the Indians did not abandon the agencies, and an apprehended expensive Indian war was averted." The negotiations in Washington and Parker's boldness in furnishing supplies for the Indians were the turning point in the western situation. While local incidents of violence continued to occur, the major threats to the peace appeared to have ended.[22]

A different kind of threat to Grant's Indian policy came from the Congress. When Congress passed the army appropriation bill on July 15, 1870, a provision was added that prohibited the assignment of army officers to duty with the Indian service. The prohibition was in part a reaction to the army's massacre of the Piegan Indians. It was also Congress' way of regaining political influence in the appointment of agents. But President Grant was not prepared to return to a system of political appointments with all its risks of corruption. Instead he decided to expand the Quaker experiment, and he invited a variety of religious bodies to nominate candidates for the agencies vacated by the army officers. The first appointments were men nominated by Protestant groups, but Parker also encouraged the appointment of Catholic agents, and even a Jewish superintendent was finally appointed. With almost the entire field service of the Indian Office in the hands of religious groups, Grant's celebrated Peace Policy toward the Indians was full-blown. Complete justice toward the Indians might never be achieved, but the Grant administration had made every effort to put the Indians' fate into the hands of the men most likely to understand what honesty and justice meant.[23]

Parker was away from his office for long periods during the latter part of 1870. He spent almost two months in New York during the summer, purchasing goods for the Indians, and then visited Chicago and St. Louis in September and October. In December he traveled to Okmulgee in the Indian Territory, where the various tribes had been called together to organize a new territorial government. Parker's arrival at the council on December 12, "produced a lively sensation among the delegates," and they listened with approval as he told them that the object of the council was to create a government exclusively of Indians, "by which the Indians could hold power as long as they pleased." The president, he said, had no desire to open the territory to white settlers, but rather wanted the Indians to create a government for the territory so that it could eventually come into the union as an Indian state. The tribes worked together in harmony and drew up a constitution and a bill of rights for the new government of Oklahoma. The three members of the Board of Indian Commissioners who had also attended the council were impressed with its "great importance" as an example of "the humane policy of the administration." On their return to Washington they reported that during their visits to the Indians they had "witnessed much to encourage us in the belief that the present policy of the President and Congress in behalf of the Indians of the United States is showing evidence of success."[24]

When Parker returned to Washington early in January 1871, he learned that another, very different report had also been made on Indian affairs. During his absence William Welsh had written a letter to Columbus Delano, the new secretary of the interior, indirectly accusing Parker of defrauding the government in the purchase of Indian supplies. Welsh had also published his letter in the newspapers, with the result that the Committee on Appropriations of the House of Representatives was preparing to call Parker before it to investigate the charges. And the committee had invited Welsh himself to attend the investigation and personally press his charges. In effect, Parker was to be placed on trial for his conduct as commissioner.

On Trial

WILLIAM WELSH had just returned from the West where he had gone to introduce five new Indian agents of the Episcopal Church. While he was there, he visited twelve different tribes on the Missouri River and came back full of enthusiasm for the church's work among the Indians. He said that Indians that were once "blood-thirsty and thriftless" and "fond of whisky and paint and feathers" were adopting the civilization and the religion of the whites. "Our holy religion," he wrote, "will soon displace the superstitious rites that are fast losing their influence over the heathen people." He had met some excellent army officers working among the Indians, too, and had defended them against those who called them "Indian exterminators." But Welsh also came back to Washington convinced that both the Indians and the government were being defrauded in the purchase of Indian supplies.

Welsh had learned of the beef and flour that James Bosler had delivered to the Indians on the Missouri River under the contract Parker made in June, and Welsh claimed that "a few adroit manipulators of contracts and purchases have made at least $250,000" on those supplies alone. The Indian Office, he said, bought the supplies on the open market, without advertising for bids, and as a consequence paid outrageously high prices for them. In at least one case, the beef was not even needed; Commissioner Parker had to compel his agent to receive it. In another case bribes had been given to certify a false weight for the cattle. And Welsh said that in none of the purchases had Parker consulted the Board of Indian Commissioners as the law required.[1]

A week after Welsh's letter was published, Edward P. Smith, a Congregational minister who had just been appointed to one of the Indian agencies, had occasion to call on Welsh in Washington. Welsh

William Welsh (c. 1810–78), Philadelphia merchant, philanthropist, and chairman of the Board of Indian Commissioners. Welsh brought charges against Ely Parker in 1870 for his conduct as commissioner of Indian affairs, which resulted in a trial in the House of Representatives. From Charles Morris, ed., *The Makers of Philadelphia*.

informed Smith that he was very busy, yet Smith found him not too busy to give him "a full report of his past life to date" and a detailed account of his connection with Girard College and several Reformatory Institutes in Philadelphia, "and whatever else is important in the world." Welsh was also anxious to talk about the frauds he had discovered in the West. He said that the speculators were covering their tracks, but he was convinced that "Col. Parker is very closely in with the ring." He also emphasized that Parker had violated an express law of Congress in making purchases without consulting the Board of Indian Commissioners. Smith came away from the meeting with the impression that Parker's real crime was in not consulting Welsh, and he concluded that "it seems to me quite possible that Col. P will have to leave."[2]

When Parker returned to Washington and learned of Welsh's letter, he went to see the president and then prepared a formal reply to the charges. In his reply Parker reviewed the events of the past summer, telling how his agents had reported that, unless the Indians were fed, they would "commence depredating, and perhaps inaugurate a general Indian war." The delay in passing the Indian appropriation had created an emergency; there was no money to buy the supplies, and no time to ask for bids. The contract with Bosler had been made because Bosler was willing to risk a large expenditure while waiting for Congress to act, and under the circumstances, Parker did not think the prices he paid had been extravagant. Parker dismissed the charge that he had been at fault in not consulting the board about the purchases by pointing out that the law which required him to consult them was part of the appropriation bill which was passed almost a month *after* he had made the contract with Bosler. He concluded his statement by saying that Welsh's charges seemed to him an attempt to take the management of Indian funds away from the Indian Office. "I will not assert," he said, "that he and his associates, or any other religious organization, are not as competent to manage and disburse Indian funds as the Indian Bureau, but there being at present no law authorizing such a course, the Bureau is bound to repel all such attempts."[3]

The tone of Parker's reply was calm and confident, but it masked his real feelings. The charges hurt him deeply. When he became a sachem, Parker had been told that the thickness of his skin would be seven spans, as a proof against criticism, but it was not. So disturbed was he at Welsh's charges and his impending trial that he took to his bed. A Washington matron reported that "Gen'l Parker is confined to

Norton P. Chipman (1838–1924). As a judge advocate in the army, Chipman earned a reputation in the prosecution of Henry Wirz, the commander of the Confederate prison camp at Andersonville. He later defended his friend Ely Parker when Parker was tried in the House of Representatives because of accusations about his conduct as commissioner of Indian affairs. *Courtesy of U.S. Signal Corps, photo No. 111-B-4902 (Brady Collection), National Archives and Records Service.*

his bed by illness [,] and the severe ordeal he is at present passing [through] . . . makes his power feeble." He was still ill at home when the investigation began.[4]

Three members of the House Committee on Appropriations, Aaron A. Sargent of California, William Lawrence of Ohio, and James B. Beck of Kentucky, were appointed to investigate the charges, and they invited William Welsh to attend the investigation and examine the witnesses. Attending with him, and apparently cooperating with him, was Vincent Colyer, the secretary of the Board of Indian Commissioners. Parker elected to be represented by counsel and for his counsel chose a personal friend, Norton P. Chipman, a lawyer from Iowa, and a Mason. Chipman had served as a judge advocate in the army, and had made his reputation as the prosecutor in the trial of Henry Wirz, the commander of the Confederate prison camp at Andersonville.

Thirty-four people were called to testify in the investigation, many of them businessmen who generally supported Parker's contention that the prices he paid Bosler were not extravagant under the circumstances, and who testified to Bosler's good reputation in the West. Parker, too, was called from his sickbed to testify and later recalled for further testimony. He defended his actions as he had in his previous reply to Welsh's charges, but under continued questioning about his failure to consult the board or to ask for bids when the Indian supplies were purchased, his confidence began to melt away. At one point he told the chairman: "If the committee will allow me I wish to say that at no time have I pretended to be an expert in regard to the management of Indian affairs. I entered the office of the Indian Bureau with the duties perfectly new to me, and it may be very probable that mistakes have been made. In looking back I can see many things which I would change." But he also strongly asserted that he had never defrauded anyone. "I do say, and I speak it in as solemn a manner as I am capable . . . that I have never profited pecuniarily, or indeed otherwise, by any transaction in my official capacity while I have been serving as Commissioner of Indian Affairs. . . . I have never sought to defraud the Government out of one penny, or have knowingly lent my aid to others with that view."[5]

An important part of Parker's testimony was his insistence that Secretary Cox had been fully informed about the contract with Bosler. Parker said that as commissioner he had daily conferences with the secretary during which he had spoken frequently about the contract with Bosler and that Cox "was aware of the whole of it." So confident was Parker that Cox had known and approved of the contract that he had Cox called out of retirement to testify for him. But Cox disclaimed all knowledge of the matter, saying that he had never heard or seen Bosler's name before the investigation and had never been consulted in regard to any contract with him.[6]

Cox's testimony called Parker's integrity into question, but the testimony James Bosler gave also questioned the integrity of William Welsh. Bosler said that before the investigation Welsh had invited him to Philadelphia to talk with him, but that he had become suspicious when Welsh began "acting as a detective." Welsh told Bosler that he had investigated him and found everything in order, "but in the course of the conversation he spoke of General Parker, and said that his connection with those parties in New York was not very creditable, and further that the general was the representative of a race only one generation from barbarism, and he did not think that he should be expected to be able to withstand the inducements of parties who were his superiors in matters of business."

Welsh also told Bosler about his earlier disagreement with Parker and his resignation from the board, and told him that if the rest of the board "had followed his example, they would have had General Parker out of office at that time." He apparently still resented President Grant's support of Parker, for according to Bosler, "He said something about the President's desire to serve General Parker, and what he thought of it; I do not remember the exact words; but he attributed it to the President's goodness of heart. He asked me, in the same connection, if I had ever seen General Parker drunk; and he said that in New York he had been 'feasted and wined'; that 'tables had been kept up there'; and that he was satisfied that General Parker did not have the moral courage to withstand temptation."[7]

After the testimony had been taken Welsh summed up his case against Parker, and then Norton Chipman made his concluding remarks. The committee ruled the discussion of Welsh's motives in making his charges out of order, but Chipman managed to emphasize Bosler's testimony about Welsh's animosity toward Parker. He brought in documents showing how Welsh had probed into Bosler's private bank account, and probably into Parker's, but without finding any irregularities. And he called attention to the role of Vincent Colyer in the investigation. As the secretary of the Board of Indian Commissioners, Colyer worked closely with Parker and might have been expected to support him, yet he had been at Welsh's side throughout the investigation, "aiding the prosecutor in the accomplishment of a

purpose to remove the Commissioner of Indian Affairs." Colyer testified that Parker personally bought blankets for the Osage Indians that
were of such poor quality that it was reported that "a baby can slip
through them without breaking a warp or filling." But Chipman noted
that expert testimony had shown that only one bale of blankets was
defective and then only in its color, and that Colyer had not brought
the matter to Parker's attention or taken advantage of the merchant's
offer to replace the blankets, but had preferred to use them as one
more charge at Parker's trial.

Chipman also reviewed the arrangements that Parker had made
with James Bosler. He said that Parker believed there was an emergency when he acted, and he showed that the law allowed for
purchases on the open market, without bids, in an emergency. General
Sherman and General Harney had done the same thing for the
Indians, spending even more money without the authority of law
and paying even higher prices in other emergencies, and had not been
censured for it. (Had Chipman been aware of it, he could also have
pointed out that Welsh himself and the Episcopal committee on
Indians that he chaired had, in fact, commended General Harney for
doing exactly what Parker had done.) The charges against Parker,
Chipman said, were motivated simply by the desire to remove him
from his office. Chipman also introduced documents showing that in
spite of his testimony, Secretary Cox had been aware of the contract
with Bosler and had raised no objection to it at the time. Parker, with
Cox's concurrence, had acted to meet an emergency, and Chipman was
convinced that if he had not done what he did and an Indian war had
begun, Welsh "would then have held the commissioner responsible for
not doing the very thing of which he now complains."[8]

Once his own testimony had been given, Parker seems to have
regained his composure. While the investigation was still going on,
the Parkers appeared at a reception given by Postmaster General and
Mrs. Creswell, where Minnie stood out among the assembly of the
capital's fashionable women. "One of the most Frenchy looking toilets
that appeared was worn by Mrs. General Parker. The profusion of
pink roses with which it was sprinkled contrasted beautifully with the
blue tarlatan of which it was composed, and diamonds sparkled among
the Valenciennes lace which covered the low corsage."

Two weeks later a carnival was held on Pennsylvania Avenue to
celebrate the replacement of its old cobblestones by a new wooden
pavement. Horse races were held, and then the avenue was opened to
private vehicles so that the owners could show off their horses. General

Sherman was there, as were the Peruvian minister, cabinet members, and senators. Among them "General Parker, of the Indian Bureau, drove leisurely along with a pair of fine blacks." But even there he could not escape the Board of Indian Commissioners. On the second day of the carnival, in a masquerade spoof of a government of all women, "Indian Commissioners were represented by two stalwart Indian chiefs hobnobbing with a couple of prim Quakeresses."[9]

Several days later the committee published its report. The members of the committee agreed that there had been an emergency the previous summer and that something had to be done to supply the Indians. They criticized Parker, however, for not having referred the matter to the president for his action. It was a dangerous practice, they said, "to allow a subordinate officer to make large purchases at his own discretion in the absence of appropriations." Norton Chipman had shown that Cox was aware of the contract with Bosler and had apparently seen no necessity of referring it to the president, but Cox was no longer in the government, and the blame for not obtaining Grant's approval fell squarely on Parker.

After reviewing the testimony, the committee expressed its belief that the Indian Office had serious faults, but that fraud was not among them.

> To the mind of the committee, the testimony shows irregularities, neglect, and incompetency, and, in some instances, a departure from the express provisions of law for the regulation of Indian expenditures, and in the management of affairs in the Indian Department. But your committee have not found evidence of fraud or corruption on the part of the Indian Commissioner. With much to criticise and condemn, arising partly from a vicious system inherited from the past, and partly from errors of judgment in the construction of statutes passed to insure economy and faithfulness in administration, we have no evidence of any pecuniary or personal advantage sought or derived by the Commissioner, or any one connected with his Bureau.

The committee was especially critical of Parker's refusal to consult the Board of Indian Commissioners about the purchases of Indian supplies. Even after the appropriation act required him to consult the board, Parker insisted that the act referred only to the purchase of dry goods, a matter in which the board had been consulted. "Goods" and "supplies," he said, had always been treated separately in the Indian Office, and he did not believe the act compelled him to consult the

board in the purchase of "supplies." Parker thought it would be impossible to conduct business if the act was interpreted to include
supplies as well as goods; the board would have to come to his office
and supervise every disbursement that he made. The committee dis-
agreed and suggested that Congress pass a new bill which would
make it clear that the board was to supervise every expenditure of the
Indian Office.[10]

Congress quickly passed the bill the committee had recommended. In spite of the broad powers now given to it, the board at
first asked only to see vouchers for payments Parker made under
contracts, but in June 1871, they asked that all vouchers from the
Indian Office be submitted for their approval. When their request
came to his attention, Parker asked the advice of the secretary of the
interior, who said that the law required Parker to do just what the
board was asking. Faced with the prospect of submitting every expenditure of his office to the Board of Indian Commissioners for their
review, Parker submitted his resignation to President Grant, effective
August 1, 1871.

In his letter of resignation he complained that the actions of Congress had almost completely stripped the Indian Bureau "of all its original importance, duties and proper responsibilities." The commissioner
of Indian affairs had become "nearly a supernumerary officer of the government, his principal duties being simply that of a clerk to a Board
of Indian Commissioners." Parker said that he was willing to aid in
promoting the president's "wise and benificent Indian policy," but he
said that he could not "in justice to myself longer continue to hold the
ambiguous position I now occupy as Commissioner of Indian Affairs."
His mind was made up; the resignation was submitted "most respectfully but firmly." But his decision to resign had been a difficult one.
The same day he submitted his letter of resignation, he left Washington for Schooley's Mountain in New Jersey, "for the benefit of his
health."[11]

Parker's resignation, Grant said, "severs official relations which
have existed between us for eight consecutive years without cause of
complaint as to your entire fitness for either of the important places
which you have had during that time." He said that Parker's management of Indian affairs had been "able and discreet" and "in entire
harmony" with his policy. But Parker's continued opposition to the
Board of Indian Commissioners may also have been a political embarrassment to Grant, and the resignation was accepted. A few days later
Grant assured Commissioner George Hay Stuart that his next appoint-

ment to the office of commissioner of Indian affairs would be someone who had the full confidence of the board.[12]

With Parker out of office, William Welsh assumed a charitable attitude toward him. He told Lewis Henry Morgan that "Parker meant well but conviviality and a fashionable wife made him the prey of astute and polished augurs. I always liked him." He was less charitable toward Grant. He helped spread a rumor that Grant had rewarded Norton Chipman for his defense of Parker. "I heard that he got Delano to employ Chipman and it is certain that he rewarded the Defender by making him Secretary of the District [of Columbia]." And he could understand Grant's support of Parker only by saying that Parker was an "infatuation" with him, "heightened by a sentiment in favor of an Indian civilizing his brethren." In 1875 Welsh published an open letter to Grant in which he said, "Every suggestion I ever made to you was promptly responded to, save only the investigation of frauds allowed by your appointees. . . . Your protection of Gen. Parker when he was convicted of misfeasance or malfeasance as Commissioner of Indian Affairs, and of those who had control of that office, seems wholly unaccountable except on the hypothesis that love in you is blind."[13]

He had served as commissioner only a little more than two years, but Parker was proud of what he had accomplished. He had succeeded in organizing the Peace Policy for which Grant was to become famous. He had fought to end the practice of making treaties with the Indians, maintaining that the Indian tribes were not sovereign nations and lacked the power to compel their people to obey treaties. He said that the treaties were "like the handle to a jug. The advantages and the power of execution are all on one side." The result was that the same act which compelled him to bow to the Board of Indian Commissioners also put an end to the treaty system. But above all, he boasted that the country had been spared expensive Indian wars while he was in office. There had been isolated instances of violence on both sides, and the Piegan massacre had been followed by a similar massacre of Apaches at Camp Grant in April 1871, but a general peace with the Indians had been established in the West.[14]

Newspapers in different parts of the country were agreed that peace had indeed been achieved. The *Erie Daily Republican* said that "the last twelve months has been more entirely free from Indian hostilities and outrages than any similar period that we can now recall during the last ten years," and the *Troy Daily Times* extended the period to one hundred years. The *Portland Daily Press* quoted

Grant's inaugural statement, "Let us have peace," and went on to say "and we have had peace. The expensive and bloody Indian war that was raging upon his accession to power has ceased, and . . . there is every probability that a lasting peace has been established." And the *Philadelphia Post* said that the president's Indian policies had wrought "marvels" in his first two years. "There are no more armed warriors, stung to deeds of murder and outrage by the robberies of unprincipled politicians acting as agents. The nomadic tribes are settling on reservations, exchanging the wigwam for the house, the scalping knife for the plow, and, from the descendants of Penn, forgetting barbarity and wrongs in the lessons of civilization."[15]

Parker's two years as commissioner of Indian affairs resulted in a national success but a personal defeat. His experiences with the Board of Indian Commissioners left him bitter about the government and Indian affairs, and when he resigned his position as commissioner at the age of forty-three, Parker severed all connections with the government, put Indian affairs behind him, and turned to the world of business. Perhaps, too, his fashionable young wife influenced his choice of a new career. Whether she did or not, one of Minnie's friendships played a part in the Parkers' choice of a new home.

Josephine Jones, a friend of Minnie, and "one of the reigning belles of Washington," had married Arthur Brown, a native of Fairfield, Connecticut, Brown was the son of William H. Brown, the prominent shipbuilder who had built the *America,* the yacht whose speed is still celebrated in the America's Cup races. Through their friendship with the Browns, the Parkers purchased a home on the main street of Fairfield, Connecticut in September 1871, and there Parker began a new life as a businessman and Wall Street investor.

Parker's friendship with Brown was somewhat unusual. Brown, a man of "pleasing personality" who "resembled the late Napoleon III in appearance," was a staunch Democrat who had been a Southern sympathizer during the war. The federal government had once arrested and confined him at Fort Lafayette for writing a subversive letter (which was, however, later proved a forgery). But business associations overcame political differences, and Parker soon acquired an interest in the Read Carpet Company in nearby Bridgeport as had his new friend Brown.[16]

Parker's business activities while he lived in Fairfield are somewhat obscure, but he appears to have become an investor in other businesses besides the carpet company. Among them may have been investments in the new Standard Oil Company. His home in Fair-

"Robin's Nest," Ely and Minnie Parker's house in Fairfield, Connecticut, as it appeared in 1872–73. The Parkers owned the house from 1871 until 1887 and were frequent visitors in Fairfield until Parker's death in 1895. *Courtesy of Madeline Bullard Perry.*

field stood next to that of Oliver Burr Jennings, a brother-in-law of William Rockefeller and one of Standard Oil's original stockholders and directors, and it seems likely that the very wealthy Jennings guided Parker in his investments. Parker also had ties to Standard Oil through his former schoolmate at Yates Academy, Henry M. Flagler, who had gone into business in Ohio with John D. Rockefeller, and who was also one of the directors and original stockholders in the new company.

Fairfield was on the New York and New Haven Railroad, and Parker, like many other residents of the town, pursued his investments in Wall Street during the day and then returned to the "peaceful quiet" of Fairfield, where the commuters were "met at the station by the female contingent in stylish vehicles and becoming apparel and whirled thence in a twinkling to the pretty homes on either side of the long, wide shady main street."[17]

The town was popular as a summer resort, and many wealthy New Yorkers had summer homes in Fairfield. Parker, too, referred to his handsome house on three acres of land as his "summer home" and gave it the seasonal name "Robin's Nest," but he found Fairfield "so agreeable, the charm of its old families so pleasing to him" that he decided to make it his permanent home. Whatever his investments were, they were apparently good enough to allow him to live in the elegance that his new surroundings demanded. A neighbor and friend of the Parkers, George Mills, said that "his wine cellar was unparalleled in these parts. His span of blooded horses paced through the little Fairfield streets like a circus rider in the Coliseum. His footman and coachman were distinctively, but tastefully caparisoned, and when he sometimes attended band concerts in Seaside Park in the fashion of the era, all eyes were turned toward the distinguished Indian. . . . He brought his Negro bodyguard and a retinue of servants from the south." Minnie involved herself in Fairfield society, gave "brilliant entertainments," and joined St. Paul's Episcopal Church, where she sang in the quartet.

Fairfield remembered Parker as a "well-informed and highly cultivated man." George Mills recalled "once being at his home for dinner, when one of the guests was telling about her trip up the Nile river, and the general, though he had never left his native shores told the traveler as much and more about Egypt and the Nile than she, who had returned from her trip, knew. He was a widely read man." But the display of knowledge was unusual; Mills also described Parker as "modest and retiring and despite his glamorous life, had little to say about himself, unless drawn out."[18]

Well-to-do and without children, the Parkers invited Nic's teenage daughter Minnie to come to Fairfield and live with them, but the change from the Cattaraugus Reservation to Fairfield, Connecticut, was too great for her—"she was unhappy in this white man's heaven"—and the Parkers finally had to send her back to the reservation. Parker occasionally returned to the New York reservations, and once at Nic's urging wrote to the Indian Office about his brother's job as United States Interpreter, but the affairs of the Indians were no longer of great concern to him. He had cast his lot with the Connecticut Yankees in Fairfield, and he was as much at home there among them as his niece had been ill at ease among them.[19]

But Parker's new prosperity did not last. With many others he lost money in the failure of Jay Cooke and Company in 1873, and still more money in the collapse of the Freedman's Bank the following year. There were said to be losses, too, in the failure of an insurance company and a publishing venture. The most revealing loss was suffered when a bank cashier, who apparently worked in New York City and for whom Parker was a bondsman, embezzled funds, with the result that Parker was called on to make the bond good. His lawyers reminded him that he could not be compelled to pay, for in order to protect the Indians from unscrupulous businessmen, a law had been passed in New York State which guaranteed that no contract could be enforced against an Indian for the payment of money. His grandnephew related the conclusion of the story as it had come down in the family. "But General Parker gave a single answer. 'I fully intend to make that bond good,' he said, 'I executed it in good faith. I am a *man* and if the law does not compel me to pay, my honor does.' And he paid, though his fortune was wrecked. Years after the defaulter became wealthy and respected, but he never repaid a penny."[20]

His losses may have been exaggerated in the telling of the tale. Parker had enough money left to keep his "summer home" in Fairfield for more than a decade after these events, and during part of that time he maintained another home in New York City as well. But his losses were serious enough to make him consider resuming his career as an engineer. He soon learned, however, that during the fifteen years since he had left Dubuque, the profession had passed him by. Bitterly he wrote that "while I was soldiering the profession ran away from me, other and younger men had stepped in and filled the places. Young men were wanted for their activity and the old men were discarded." But as had happened so often in his life, help came from an influential friend. William F. Smith, for whom Parker had worked at Detroit and at Chattanooga, was now president of the Board of Commissioners of the New York City Police Department, and on September 30, 1876, the board appointed Parker to the position of clerk in the New York Police Department at the modest salary of $2,400 a year.[21]

Mulberry Street

~~~~~~

THE HEADQUARTERS of the New York City Police Department were at 300 Mulberry Street, and here Parker labored for the rest of his life. He complained constantly that he was "overwhelmed with work," "driven with work," and "very, very busy," but busy as he was his position was one of little authority and, one suspects, little satisfaction. His career, someone commented, had been "side-tracked in Mulberry Street."[1]

Parker worked for the Committee on Repairs and Supplies of the Police Board of Commissioners. All requisitions for repairs or supplies in the department were made to that committee which then referred them to Parker, who was to look into the necessity for the requisitions, determine the cost of them, and report his findings in writing to the chairman of the committee. When the requisitions were approved, Parker might prepare contracts for the work, and when the work had been done, he also reviewed the bills. But Parker had no authority for approving requisitions himself or for paying bills; that lay entirely with the commissioners. Parker's work frequently took him out of his office, and he was a familiar sight on the city's streets, usually dressed in a suit of slate-colored cloth, a Prince Albert coat, and a sugar-loaf hat with a stiff, flat brim.

Politics infested the police department, and commissioners and clerks came and went, but Parker remained at his desk, attending to the repair of the department's station houses, steamboats, and telegraph, and overseeing the purchases of pencils and erasers and brooms and shovels, for nineteen years. After Parker's death, John C. Sheehan, a member of Tammany Hall and a former chairman of the Committee on Repairs and Supplies, was accused of padding the bills in his committee. His defense was to show that all his expenditures had been reviewed by General Parker, but he was strongly denounced

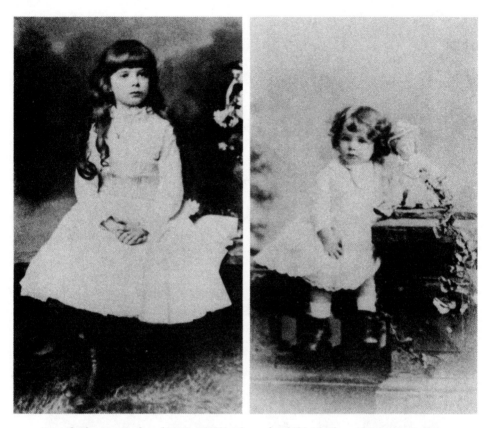

Maud Theresa Parker (1878–1956), the only child of Ely and Minnie Parker. When Maud was born in Fairfield, Connecticut, Parker was fifty years old and Minnie twenty-eight. The picture at the left was taken when Maud was six years old. Maud married Arthur Bullard of Wayland, Massachusetts, and later had three children, including Madeline Bullard Perry. *Courtesy of Madeline Bullard Perry.*

for attempting to implicate the dead man. The *New York Tribune* reminded its readers of Parker's good reputation and noted that his work for the police department was done entirely under the orders of the commissioners. It was true, the paper said, that "General Parker was of Indian blood and birth, but he was not a Tammany Indian."[2]

After he went to work for the police department, Parker and his wife moved to New York City, living for a time in the Sturtevant House on Broadway, later on West Thirty-second Street, and finally

Ely S. Parker, Do-ne-ho-ga-wa, in his later years. Although he resigned from the army in 1869, Parker was active in the Grand Army of the Republic, the Loyal Legion of the United States, and the Society of Colonial Wars. *Courtesy of the Fairfield Historical Society, Fairfield, Connecticut.*

settling on West Forty-second Street. For many years they kept their home in Fairfield, making it truly a summer home like those of their neighbors. It was in Fairfield, on August 14, 1878, when Parker was fifty years old and Minnie twenty-eight, that a daughter was born to them. They named her Maud Theresa, and Minnie had her baptized in the Episcopal Church in Fairfield. Parker also called her Ah-weh-ee-yo, "Beautiful Flower," but the Indian name was mostly romance. There was little to draw the child to Indian ways in New York City, and the Indians she did meet considered her to be white, since clan and status among the Iroquois always descended through the mother rather than the father.[3]

Like many other veterans, Parker became a member of the Grand Army of the Republic and busily engaged himself in the affairs of Reno Post Number 44, which met on East Fifty-fourth Street in New York City. As a former officer he was also eligible for membership in the Military Order of the Loyal Legion of the United States, and in 1887, he was elected a member of the Legion's New York Commandery. Shortly before his death the Society of Colonial Wars also accepted him as a member because of the service his ancestors had given to the British colonies in their wars against the French. These military associations provided him with the ceremony and the companionship that Masonry had when he was younger. His friend John C. Smith invited him to Chicago in 1889, to speak to the Masons on the fiftieth anniversary of the Grand Lodge of Illinois, and he went and displayed the Red Jacket medal as he had at many previous Masonic gatherings, but he had found his place among the veterans of the Civil War, and he no longer needed Masonry as he had before.[4]

His military associates often asked Parker to write about his experiences in the Civil War, but he seldom did. He did speak on "The Character of Grant" before the Loyal Legion in 1889, and later allowed the speech to be published. A few of his anecdotes about Grant were also published in *McClure's Magazine* in 1894, but in general he considered it unnecessary to fight the rebellion over again. When General Lew Wallace revived an old controversy about the war, Parker asked a friend, "Let me ask you please, for whose special benefit is this business reopened now, so long after the principal and positive actors, who alone could tell the whole truth of the thing, have passed away. Has Wallace any old axes to be refurbished, or is it only a stray literary bee buzzing in his bonnet?" On another occasion he decried "the perfect diarrhae of war papers and the innumerable controversies" that were being revived. Characteristically, he wanted

Draft of the terms of surrender offered by General Ulysses S. Grant to General Robert E. Lee at Appomattox Court House, Virginia, April 9, 1865. Ely Parker, General Grant's military secretary, used this draft to make the

until properly exchanged

government of the United States, and
each company or regimental commander
sign a like
parole for the men of their
commands.

The arms artillery and public
property to be parked and stacked
and turned over to the officer
appointed by me to receive them.
This will not embrace the side
arms of the officers, nor their
private or baggage. This done
each officer and man will be
allowed to return to their homes
not to be disturbed by United
States authority so long as they
observe their parole and the
laws in force where they may
reside.
Very respectfully
U.S. Grant

official copy of the terms for General Lee and then kept the draft as a memento of the occasion. After Parker's death, it was purchased from his widow and is now in the collection of the New-York Historical Society. *The New-York Historical Society, New York, New York.*

to be fair in anything he wrote, and he hesitated to put his own opinions about the complexities of the past in writing. But it is possible, too, that sitting in his little office at police headquarters, the memory of those exciting days was painful to him, and it was easier not to write about them.[5]

When he did write or speak, it was often about his associations with Grant and in what he said always showed him the greatest loyalty. He resented the "dastardly attempts" to blacken Grant's name by reviving stories of his drinking during the war, and although he refused to comment on the stories publicly, privately he called them the work of "small minded persons who would magnify his petty faults into grave and damning defects of character."

He continued to see Grant when he could, but since he had left the Indian Office he was no longer close to him. In December 1879, he went to Philadelphia with other members of the old staff to welcome Grant back from his world tour. But the staff, which had once been so close to him, had to wait until after midnight to see him and then received only a "short, but a most happy" interview. The following year he visited Grant in New York City, taking with him his copy of the draft of the terms of surrender at Appomattox, which he had enclosed in a hinged wooden case, along with the pen he had used to make the final copy. He asked Grant to certify the copy as authentic, and Grant wrote on it, "The document below is one of the original impressions from the manifold on which I wrote the terms of surrender of Gen. Lee's Army, at Appomattox Court House, Apl. 9th 1865. It is one of the three impressions taken by the manifold. New York City, Oct. 21st 1880. U. S. Grant."

During Grant's last illness Parker went "twice a week to see him, but without success," although he was kept informed about Grant's condition by his son Fred. At Parker's request, he and those who remained of the old staff were included in the funeral procession when Grant died.[6]

When Grant was gone, Parker continued to show his loyalty to him. Adam Badeau, after he had assisted Grant in preparing his *Memoirs,* claimed that he had been their joint author with Grant and eventually sued the Grant family for his share of the profits. In the midst of the Grants' difficulties with Badeau, Parker wrote a personal note to Fred Grant, offering his support and denouncing Badeau's "grasping and rascally operations." "I loved your father dearly, deeply and sincerely," Parker wrote, "and nothing Badeau, or any one else, can say can swerve my loyalty to him & his honored memory."

Yet, intertwined with his loyalty was a seldom-expressed resentment that Grant on his part had not been more loyal to his old staff when he became president. It was partly a personal resentment, fed by an exaggerated sense of his own importance to Grant, and partly a resentment that Grant seemed not to have appreciated Rawlins' services, and Parker's loyalty to Rawlins was even stronger than his loyalty to Grant. The feelings he could never express publicly, he shared privately with John E. Smith, who had known all three of the men.

I suppose that myself with Rawlins, had more to do with shaping Grant's military and civic schemes than any body else, up to the time that he threw us off, which was when his royal highness became firmly settled in the Presidential chair. Rawlins, Bowers and myself did all the work of the staff, and for a long time Grant seemed to appreciate it. But the West Point influence about Grant undermined us all. However Rawlins and myself sincerely loved Grant and never abandoned his colors. Rawlins died looking for Grant who never came until death had sealed his eyes forever. Grant was held back from doing a last kind act by West Point influence. There are a great many things I could say of Grant and his friends, but which are better kept locked within my own bosom. I may only say that one great fault of his life was the abandonment of his early best and truest friends, and the taking unto himself of false and strange gods who at last ruined him utterly. Next to Rawlins, I flatter myself, I knew as much of Grant's real character in its every shade than any other living person, but my love for him and respect for myself, I think never will permit me to discuss him otherwise than favorably. Politics was not his forte and the love of filthy lucre floored him. Requiescat in pace.[7]

Parker shared his resentment toward Grant with one other friend. On Memorial Day, 1886, he met General Thomas Kilby Smith in New York City, and Smith said that he "had a long conversation with General Parker the Indian about Grant & Rawlings & old times. He feels just as I do. We all suffered alike from the ingratitude & neglect of Grant. It broke Rawlings heart. Parker attributes a good deal to Mrs. Grant & her worship of wealth & wealthy men."[8]

Even though he no longer took an active part in Indian affairs, Indian concerns continued to claim Parker's attention. In 1878 he visited the Indian Office in Washington, representing the Seneca Nation, which was seeking permission to lease some oil wells on the Allegany Reservation. (Parker was careful to see the chairman of the

Board of Indian Commissioners first, and to secure his approval of the leases before he saw the commissioner; he had learned where power resided in the Indian Office.)

He was also consulted on occasion by the Indians, some of whom came to see him in New York City, but just as frequently he was consulted by whites who were seeking information about the New York Indians and who looked to Parker as one of the few people who could provide it. Even his own brother Nic was finding it difficult to answer questions about traditional ways. Lewis Henry Morgan was still interested in the Indians and asked Nic for some information, but Nic told him that he was not familiar with the matter and that everyone he asked gave him a different account. "The difficulty," he said, "seems to be that there is now no one who actually understands the laws of the 'Confederacy' as it was."

Ely Parker knew as much as anyone, and readily shared what he knew with those who sought information, but he had lived so long away from the Indians that he was no longer certain about their present practices. On one occasion he described an Iroquois festival as he had known it, but then added candidly: "But things may have been changed." His visits to the reservation were infrequent. He made a point of speaking Seneca when he did go, saying that he "went back home, to loosen up my tongue," but the stamp of the white world on him was unmistakable. On one of his trips he spoke to a little girl on the reservation, saying to her in English: "Get me a drink of water." Remembering it years later, she said, "I thought he was a white man."[9]

Parker's dormant interest in Indian matters was reawakened about 1881, when he met a white woman with a passionate interest in the New York Indians, Harriet Maxwell Converse. Parker's friendship with Mrs. Converse also brought out a previously hidden aspect of his personality; their correspondence reveals a meditative, poetic, and even fanciful side of Parker which had not been apparent in the military secretary or the commissioner of Indian affairs. And theirs was a friendship which caused Parker, even if only briefly, to question whether he had done the right thing in abandoning his Indian ways.

Harriet Maxwell Converse was born in Elmira, New York, in 1836. Her father, Thomas Maxwell, and her grandfather, Guy Maxwell, had both been interested in the Indians and had both been adopted by the Senecas, the Indians having shown their respect for her grandfather by naming him Ta-se-wa-ya-ee, "Honest Trader." After the death of her first husband, the well-to-do Harriet married Franklin Converse, "an erect dapper little gentleman" best known as "the father of the banjo"

Harriet Maxwell Converse (1836–1903), author and poet. Her interest in the New York Indians resulted in a close friendship with Ely Parker, who called her "the best posted woman on Indian lore in America." *Courtesy of the University of Rochester Library.*

for his work in developing that instrument. Mrs. Converse was an author, having published both prose and poetry before she met Parker. Her friendship with Parker nourished the interest in the Indians she had inherited from her family, and her subsequent writings about them and her work for them led to her adoption as a Seneca and then to the unusual event of her election as an Iroquois sachem. Parker himself once called her "the best posted woman on Indian lore in America."[10]

Harriet and Franklin Converse lived on West Forty-sixth Street in New York City, near the Parkers, and the two families became good friends. The strongest ties, however, were between the Indian sachem and the poet, who expressed their friendship through frequent visits and letters. Their letters, even when they concerned serious matters, were often playful. Parker addressed her by her Indian name, Gayaneshaoh, or because she had been adopted into the Snipe Clan as "The Snipe," or sometimes simply as "Cousin," for the members of the Snipe Clan were cousins to the Wolves. When she was traveling, he called her "The Wandering Snipe." In his letters he was Donehogawa or "The Wolf," and in one of his more fanciful letters he told her:

> I know well that the snipe is a restless, uneasy, harmless little bird, hence I was not surprised to find that my Uncle's gray uniformed, light-footed messenger had today left another note on my table from you. Yes, notwithstanding the known character for rapacity and cruelty of the wolf, real and mythological, in all countries and among all peoples, it is yet a noble animal. It was the father and mother of the founders of ancient Rome, and it deceived poor Little Red Riding Hood. I am not certain whether the fidgety snipe figures in ancient or modern history. I hope it does. Since you desire it, I promise that the restless, flighty, prodigal, but good little snipe, shall receive nothing but kindness and protection from the wild, ferocious, untameable Wolf of North America, for it is very probable that the two are cousins.[11]

On another occasion, the Snipe wrote that she was ill and depressed, and the Wolf attempted to lift her spirits by directing her to the peace and rest of the world about her.

> You say yourself that you [are] in a most lovely country with beautiful views all around you, the silent, but peaceful, murmurings of the babbling brooklet near by inducing quiet repose, the heavenly music of the feathered songsters in your ears constantly, the almost intelligible prattle and scolding of the pretty, tiny red squirrel to amuse you, the

endless grinding of the cricket on the hearth encouraging reflection and the unceasing hum of thousands of insects, seen and unseen, in the grass and shrubbery about you, all this, I say, would seem unmistakeable aids to drive dull care away, and to bring rest, peace and happiness to the weary body and soul. . . . They say that when you are in Rome you must do as the Romans do, therefore if every thing about you, animate and inanimate, is peaceful, restful and speaks of happiness, then you, who are so susceptible, impressable and imaginative, should drift into the same mood and spirit of your environment, and thus disperse the gloom, desolation and inky darkness in which you are attempting to enshroud yourself.[12]

The Snipe was charmed by the Wolf; she called him great and good, and when he protested, she assured him that she "knew him." Parker's reply was that he was not sure that he knew himself. "There are so many sides to my nature," he wrote to her, "that I sometimes scarcely know myself on my introspection inspections. I sometimes fancy myself like a chameleon, ever changing color in thought with every varying circumstance. If you do know me, you have a far deeper insight into dark, mysterious human nature than I possess over my own earthly kingdom." Again, he spoke to her of "that variegated and kaleidoscopic character of mind and fortune, which thus far in my life has been my lot." But her interest in his Indian nature brought that pattern of the kaleidoscope back into focus, and he allowed himself to question whether he had been right in abandoning his Indian ways:

Sometimes the idea obtrudes itself into my obtuse and lethargic brain, whether it has been well that I have sought civilization with its bothersome concomitants, and, whether it would not be better even now, being convinced of my weakness and failure to continue in the gladiatorial contests of modern life, to return to the darkest and most secret wilds, (if any such can be found,) of our country and there to vegetate and expire silently, happily and forgotten as do the birds of the air and the beasts of the field. The thought is a happy one, but perhaps impracticable. I mention it only as a stray ignis-fatuus of a bewildered and erratic brain.[13]

Under the prodding of the Snipe, the Wolf also came to question his previous assumptions about the civilization of the Indians in general. As commissioner of Indian affairs, he spoke about the necessity of the "humanization, civilization, and Christianization" of the

Indians. But the activities of the Christian reformers left him with doubts about both their religion and their civilization, and Mrs. Converse's denunciation of the attitudes of whites had reawakened those doubts. Parker told her that he had no faith in the "American christian civilization methods of treating the Indians of this country. It has not been honest, pure or sincere." He was especially opposed to the reformers' favorite plan of breaking up the reservations, allotting the lands to individual Indians, and granting them immediate citizenship, a plan he had urged himself when he was commissioner of Indian affairs. He came to believe that it was only the Indians' tribal organizations and religious traditions which could save them from extinction. "When they abandon their birth right for a mess of christian pottage they will then cease to be a distinctive people."

His own solution to the Indian problem was education: "secular and industrial schools in abundance," but education that would allow the Indian to remain on the land, for "his good life is bound up and interwoven with his land, his women and his children." The members of the popular Indian Aid Associations and the Indian Rights Association, who were promoting citizenship and the allotment of lands, he thought were entirely misguided. In fact, he blamed them for most of the Indians' troubles and said in one bitter moment: "What with Congress, the 'Indian Defense' and 'Indian Rights' Associations and the various christian organizations, our United States Indians, are being ground into impalpable dust between the upper and nether millstones of their dogmas and contentions." Some of his animosity may have been due to the fact that the allotment of lands had been one of William Welsh's favorite schemes and that Welsh's nephew, Herbert Welsh, was the secretary of the Indian Rights Association.[14]

In 1884 Parker was invited to Buffalo to participate in the reinterment of Red Jacket's remains in Forest Lawn Cemetery. Some time after his death his remains had been exhumed by George Copway, the Ojibwa lecturer, and some white men who wanted to give them a better burial, but the Indians had claimed them and for some years they had been hidden in the home of Red Jacket's stepdaughter. The Buffalo Historical Society finally acquired the remains and proposed to give them a permanent resting place in Buffalo. Parker had earlier objected to the plan, but when the Seneca Nation approved it, he agreed to attend the ceremonies. Harriet Converse went to Buffalo with the Parkers, where they joined a group who assembled at the Historical Society on October 8, to pay their last respects to the Seneca orator. Parker spoke to the group in English as his brother Nic translated for the Indians who were present. The next day, when ceremonies were held at the cemetery, Parker appeared in full military uniform, seated by his sister Caroline and her husband, while their brother Nic came in full Indian dress, including a sash and a tomahawk.

That evening Parker addressed a crowd of three thousand at the Buffalo Music Hall. He spoke about the history of the Iroquois and emphasized their long allegiance to the United States. After their power had been broken by General John Sullivan's army during the Revolution, Washington had established peaceful relations with them, and the New York Indians had been careful never to break the peace. He told how they had fought for the United States in the War of 1812 and again in the Civil War. After he spoke, Parker exhibited the medal Washington had given to Red Jacket. To him it was a perpetual symbol of the peaceful ties between the Iroquois Indians and the United States.[15]

The Buffalo Historical Society also had plans to erect a monument to Red Jacket at his new burial place. Mrs. Converse began to raise money for the monument, and Parker prepared a design for it. He wanted it to be a monument to the entire Iroquois people and not simply to Red Jacket, and he found his theme in words spoken by Red Jacket just before his death. "I am an aged tree," he had said, "and can stand no longer, My leaves are fallen, my branches are withered and I am shaken by every breeze. Soon my aged trunk will be prostrate." The aged tree, Parker thought, was a fitting symbol for the dying Confederacy as well as the dying orator.

He asked James E. Kelly, a New York artist, to prepare plans for a monument with the bronze trunk of a tree set "solitary and alone" on an unhewn granite boulder. Bronze reliefs of Red Jacket and various symbols of the vanishing Iroquois Confederacy would be the monument's only adornments. Parker's design and Kelly's sketch of it were widely publicized, but the monument was never made. The Red Jacket Monument Committee in Buffalo had found a donor willing to contribute $10,000 toward the monument, but who rejected "the design of a granite tree and Red Jacket on a stump as horrid and grotesque," and the monument finally erected was a large heroic statue of Red Jacket, the creation of a prominent sculptor from Cleveland.[16]

James E. Kelly, who worked with Parker on the design of the monument, was too young to have participated in the Civil War, but he was fascinated by the war's heroes and dedicated to capturing their likenesses and recording their conversations. His mother was fascinated

Parker's conception of a statue to commemorate Red Jacket and the Iroquois Confederacy as drawn by James E. Kelly and published in the *Magazine of American History* in 1890. The broken tree set on a granite boulder was suggested by Red Jacket's statement just before his death: "I am an aged tree, and can stand no longer. My leaves are fallen, my branches are withered and I am shaken by every breeze. Soon my aged trunk will be prostrate." Parker thought his words also described the dying Iroquois Confederacy. The design was considered too unorthodox, and a more conventional statue of Red Jacket was erected in Forest Lawn Cemetery in Buffalo. Ely Parker is buried near that statue. *Courtesy of the Cleveland Public Library: History Department.*

by Indians, and out of his own interest and her urging, Kelly aggressively pursued a friendship with the Indian General Parker.

He had first met Parker in his office at Police Headquarters where he had been sent by the editor of Bryant's *Popular History of the United States* to get his advice on a sketch he was preparing of the surrender at Appomattox. The "dark looking man with a straggling goatee and mustache" gave him the advice he needed, and when the print was finished, Kelly was pleased to note that Parker put a copy in the frame which contained the terms of Lee's surrender. Kelly later made a bust of Parker, showing him in the uniform of a brevet brigadier general with the Red Jacket medal hung from his neck. Because of Kelly's friendship with Parker, he was adopted by the Senecas and became a Wolf and the adopted brother of the Parkers. He was named Ga-nos-qua after some ancient monsters who were mailed in stone. Ga-nos-qua had been Spencer Cone's name, and Parker thought it appropriate for his new sculptor brother.[17]

About 1890, when Kelly was working on the Red Jacket monument and the Parker bust, he became "quite intimate" with the Parker family, and with an artist's eye for detail, left a vivid description of the Parkers at home. Parker was at this time greatly troubled with a sore on his foot (he was found to be diabetic) and was confined to the house. While Kelly worked on the bust, Parker sat in a large armchair with his foot propped out in front of him and smoked a large walnut-colored meerschaum pipe. In spite of Parker's ailment, Kelly thought him "the picture of comfort and kindly humor." Maud Parker was then ten or twelve, and she would perch on the end of the sofa behind Kelly with her knees up to her chin and her hands clasped around her ankles, watching him work, sometimes making suggestions "with [the] wisdom of a child." At times Parker would interrupt to tease her by pointing to her cowlick and saying, "Now get her scalp lock." Kelly described Maud as a "bright pretty and winsome little spright," who like her mother had a fair complexion and dark hair, and who he thought showed no trace of her Indian ancestry. The Parkers later enrolled Maud in St. Mary's boarding school on Forty-sixth Street, and Kelly gave her instruction in painting. Maud's grandmother Sackett was also living with the Parkers, a woman whom Kelly described as "ever so fine looking friendly and attractive." She was somewhat larger and more robust than Minnie, whom Kelly also thought a handsome woman.[18]

Other visitors to Parker's home were sometimes shown his Indian mementos, especially the Red Jacket medal and the purple and white

Plaster copy of a bust of Parker made by James E. Kelly in 1890. Kelly pictured Parker in the uniform of a brevet brigadier general and wearing the famous medal he had inherited from Red Jacket. Because of Kelly's friendship with Parker, he was adopted by the Senecas and became a member of the Wolf clan. He was named Ga-nos-qua, which had also been the name of Parker's oldest brother, Spencer Cone. *From the collections of the Rochester Museum and Science Center, Rochester, New York.*

wampum belt which had been given to Do-ne-ho-ga-wa to signal the tribes of the Confederacy in case of war. He might also show them the mementos of his army days: a cane made from the oak tree under which Pemberton surrendered at Vicksburg; a watch fob made from the apple tree where Lee rested while waiting to meet Grant at Appomattox; and the draft of Grant's terms of surrender. Sometimes "in his quieter reminiscential moments," he would rehearse the scene at Appomattox for his fascinated listeners.[19]

Another person who sought out Parker's friendship was Jacob Riis, the Danish-born reformer and author. Riis worked as a police reporter on the *New York Tribune* and the *Evening Sun* and came to know Parker in his office at Police Headquarters. Riis's tribute to their friendship in his *Making of an American* captured the pathos of the declining years of the sachem and general spent among the police supplies on Mulberry Street.

I suppose it was the fact that he was an Indian that first attracted me to him. As the years passed we became great friends, and I loved nothing better in an idle hour than to smoke a pipe with the General in his poky little office at Police Headquarters. That was about all there was to it, too, for he rarely opened his mouth except to grunt approval of something I was saying. When, once in a while, it would happen that some of his people came down from the Reservation or from Canada, the powwow that ensued was my dear delight. Three pipes and about eleven grunts made up the whole of it, but it was none the less entirely friendly and satisfactory. We all have our own ways of doing things, and that was theirs. He was a noble old fellow. His title was no trumpery show, either. It was fairly earned on more than one bloody field with Grant's army. Parker was Grant's military secretary, and wrote the original draft of the surrender at Appomattox, which he kept to his death with great pride. It was not General Parker, however, but Donehogawa, Chief of the Senecas and of the remnant of the once powerful Six Nations, and guardian of the western door of the council lodge, that appealed to me, who in my boyhood had lived with Leather-stocking and with Uncas and Chingachgook. They had something to do with my coming here, and at last I had for a friend one of their kin. I think he felt the bond of sympathy between us and prized it, for he showed me in many silent ways that he was fond of me. There was about him an infinite pathos, penned up there in his old age among the tenements of Mulberry Street on the pay of a second-rate clerk, that never ceased to appeal to me.[20]

15

The Broken Rainbow

In September 1891, the members of Tammany Hall and the survivors of the Tammany Regiment (Forty-second New York Volunteers) invited Parker to be one of the speakers at the dedication of a monument to the Tammany Regiment at Gettysburg. Standing before the thirty-one foot statue of the Delaware chief Tammany and his wigwam, Parker spoke of the chief and the good qualities he was reported to have had. "I believe that if ever there was a good Indian," he said, "he was one; and that too before he was a dead one." He also spoke about the battle of Gettysburg, comparing it to the battle at Thermopylae but noting also the importance of Grant's victory at Vicksburg, which had been won at the same time. He closed by reciting a poem to "Immortal Tammany, of Indian race." The trip to Gettysburg was to be his last public appearance away from home.[1]

Parker's health was failing, and travel became difficult. He had suffered from rheumatism for some years and said as early as 1883 that his arm was "quite useless." In the spring of 1890 he developed a sore on his foot, and Harriet Converse led him to Dr. James H. Salisbury, who diagnosed his trouble as diabetes and prescribed hot water and the diet meats (Salisbury steaks) for which he was famous. Salisbury may also have been the doctor who prescribed whiskey for him, a medicine which Parker refused. William F. Smith, who knew Parker both in the army and in the police department, was one of those who charged Parker with drunkenness during the war. But, he said, Parker had since gotten over his "bad habits," and when his doctor ordered whiskey for him, he refused it, saying that "he could die but he need not take whiskey." Dr. Salisbury offered to see Parker as a "social patient," without charge, and Parker saw him frequently, but the sore on his foot refused to heal.[2]

He was also suffering the pain of illness and death within his

Caroline Parker Mountpleasant, photograph taken in 1888. Ely Parker's only sister Carrie was married to John Mountpleasant, a widower who was the leading chief of the Tuscarora Indians and the owner of a large and prosperous farm on the Tuscarora Reservation near Niagara Falls, New York. Thousands of visitors, who came to see her collection of Indian relics, knew her as "the most remarkable woman of the Iroquois Indians." From Arthur C. Parker, *The Life of General Ely S. Parker*.

family. His brother Newton died about 1870 in Montana, where he was superintendent of schools among the Crow Indians. In September 1891, Carrie suffered a stroke while visiting at Tonawanda, where she died on March 19, 1892, and two months later, on May 13, 1892, Nic died of a stroke at Cattaraugus.

Carrie's home on the Tuscarora Reservation had been a showplace for the Indians. Her husband, John Mountpleasant, had until his death a few years earlier, operated such a successful farm, owning over 200 acres of land, two reapers, two threshing machines, and one mowing machine, and raising over fifteen hundred bushels of wheat a year, that his white neighbors thought him "not far from the kingdom." Carrie played hostess there to thousands of American and foreign visitors who came to see her collection of Indian relics and who called her "the most remarkable woman of the Iroquois Indians" and "the Queen of the Tuscaroras," a title which she amiably ignored. She was well-known as the sister of General Ely Parker, and it was said of her that she was "proud of her race, and more so of her brother."[3]

Nic had served for more than twenty years as United States Interpreter for the New York Indians and had been highly praised by the agents for whom he worked. About 1877 he lost his position and soon after left his wife and children at Cattaraugus and went to live with an Indian woman at Tonawanda. Laura Wright, the widow of Asher Wright the longtime missionary to the Senecas, had been living with Nic and his family, and she said at the time that "he seems like a poor broken down man and avoids all his former associates, both whites and Indians." But Nic seems to have mended his ways and at the time of his death was referred to as a "well-to-do farmer" at Cattaraugus, "a man of education and much intelligence, with great influence among his fellow men," and the father of five children by his white wife, the niece of Laura Wright. He had also served for many years as clerk of the Seneca Nation, and the Nation, in spite of its republican philosophy, had recognized him as a chief by bestowing on him the name Gy-ant-wa-ka, which had once been borne by the great chief Cornplanter.[4]

In spite of his ailments, Parker and his family managed to spend at least part of their summers outside New York City. Doctors convinced him that children should be taken out of the city each summer because of the impurities of city air, and Parker wanted to lay a good foundation for Maud's health. The Parkers kept their home in Fairfield until 1887, and either spent their summers there or rented the house to others. When the house was finally sold, its contents were also sold at

Nicholson Henry Parker in 1892, the year of his death. Ely Parker's brother
Nic lived most of his life on the Cattaraugus Reservation in New York. He
served the federal government for many years as U.S. Interpreter for the
New York Indians. His home was on a farm adjacent to the mission station,
and he was married to Martha Hoyt, the white niece of the Reverend and
Mrs. Asher Wright, missionaries at Cattaraugus. From Arthur C. Parker, *The
Life of General Ely S. Parker.*

A photograph of Ely S. Parker taken in 1894, the year before his death, and after he had suffered several disabling strokes. The death of Levi Parker, his brother, in April 1895, left Parker the last surviving member of his family, but he continued to work for the New York City Police Department until three days before his death on August 30, 1895. *Courtesy of the Buffalo and Erie County Historical Society, Buffalo, New York.*

auction. Parker had a fine library which was especially rich in the field of Indian history. It also included a first edition of Henry Ward Beecher's sermons, and the local minister appeared, hoping to receive some of the books. He found Parker up on a ladder, taking down his books, and dressed in full Indian costume. Parker seldom wore the clothes, but "some impish motive impelled" him to retrieve them from an old trunk and put them on. It was said that the bewildered clergyman, when he saw the Indian poised on the ladder, "scurried away, a bit perturbed, and the general had a good laugh over it."[5]

During two of his last summers the Parkers stayed at the old Pawling House in Pawling, New York. A boy whose family shared a table there with the Parkers remembered him as a very restrained man with impeccable manners, who was very quiet, but who when he had something to say always said something worthwhile. Maud was with the Parkers, a very excited, intense girl in pigtails who loved to run, running like a deer around the park and beating everyone in the footraces, including the boys. The other children would tease her, saying that she could run so well because she was an Indian, but Maud would stamp her feet and say, "I'm a real American, and the only one here."[6]

Parker still made some public appearances in New York City. After Grant's death, Horace Porter and General Sherman, among others, began an annual celebration of Grant's birthday, and Parker was invited and given a place of honor from at least 1892 until his death. At the celebration in 1893, he was asked to prepare a narrative of the surrender at Appomattox, and after he had written it, handsome copies were distributed to the guests, who gathered at the Waldorf Hotel for the occasion. But Parker's health continued to decline and his public appearances were few. In 1892 he applied for a veteran's pension as a permanent invalid, and the next year, having discovered that he had Bright's disease, he applied again. While the application was still pending, he suffered a stroke.

For several days he had complained of pain and numbness on his left side, yet he continued to go to his office at police headquarters. Shortly after noon on July 11, 1893, he lay down on a lounge there and asked to have a doctor called. The doctor found his left arm and leg paralyzed, but Parker was still conscious and able to speak. Because his family was spending the summer in Denver, Parker was sent to the New York Hospital and put in a private room. There he had three more slight strokes. A month later his doctor reported that "power has returned to a considerable extent, but impairment of sensation is still marked; mind and speech are not affected." Minnie's comment was

Ely S. Parker with his daughter Maud. The picture was taken during Parker's last illness, shortly before he died. *Courtesy of Madeline Bullard Perry.*

that "the General is improving slowly. His arm and leg are useless. I doubt if he is ever able to do for himself again." But helpless as he was, Minnie found him still hopeful. She said that he "rebels at his condition, *proud* to the last, and well he may be, for grander nobler man *never* lived."[7]

In September a pension of twelve dollars a month was finally approved. The small payments were of some help, but Parker was continually concerned about money in his last years. He told Harriet Converse on one occasion that he was so desperate for money that he was even thinking of pawning the Red Jacket medal. A few months after his stroke, he did put many of his possessions up for auction, including rugs, porcelains, watches, Indian curios, silver medals, and engravings, but not the Red Jacket medal. At first his concern about money seemed unreasonable. It was true that his salary had been cut to $2,000 as an economy measure in 1881, but even after that he employed at least one servant and spent his summers in expensive resorts. But as his illnesses progressed, his money drained away, and when he died Minnie was left with no property except a few pieces of furniture ("sufficient to furnish one or two rooms"), her own clothing, and no income of any kind.[8]

Concerns about money and health took their toll. In July 1894, Parker told Harriet Converse: "I am very tired and care not how soon the end comes." In October he suffered another stroke while in Fairfield and was not able to return to his office until the following March. In March he also learned that his brother Levi had suffered a stroke and was dying at his home at Tonawanda. When Nic died, Parker told James Kelly that "I have yet one brother left, should he also go before me, then indeed will I be solitary and alone," and Levi's death on April 5, 1895, left Ely Parker the last surviving member of his family.[9]

Some new faces appeared at police headquarters shortly after Parker's return. In May 1895, Frederick Dent Grant, the president's oldest son, and Theodore Roosevelt were appointed to the Board of Commissioners of the police department and soon moved into offices at police headquarters. Roosevelt was elected president of the board, and Grant became chairman of the Committee on Repairs and Supplies, the committee for which Parker worked. But Parker was not to see much of the new commissioners. His left side was still weak and interfered with his ability to walk. He went to Fairfield for two weeks, hoping to regain his strength and went back once a week during the summer, but there was no improvement. On August 27, he went to his office, but he felt and looked so ill that the commissioners granted him a leave of absence, not expecting to see him back again. He returned to Fairfield to the home of his friends Arthur and Josephine Brown, and there, on August 30, 1895, he died.[10]

He had said that he did not feel well and had retired early. When Minnie entered the room about nine o'clock, she found him dead—of Bright's disease, the medical examiner said. The next day Minnie telegraphed the news to Fred Grant in New York City. Grant told reporters that he had been thinking about General Parker on his way to the city the morning before. "I am superstitious," he said, "and when I heard of his death, I was not surprised." When Horace Porter heard the news he notified the members of the New York Commandery of the Loyal Legion of Parker's death and requested them to attend the funeral which was to be held in Fairfield on Wednesday, September 4.[11]

Both of Parker's worlds were present at his funeral. Fred Grant came from New York City, as did representatives of the Grand Army of the Republic, the Loyal Legion, the Society of Colonial Wars, and the New York City Police Department. But Harriet Converse also invited the Indians to come, and leading men and women of all the Iroquois tribes except the Mohawks were there. Parker's family was represented by Levi's daughter, Laura Doctor, and Nic's son, Frederick Ely Parker.

The services were held in the west parlor of Arthur Brown's home. A black broadcloth casket held Parker's body, which was dressed in full military uniform, including the medals of the military organizations to which he belonged. Among the many floral pieces was one forming a Christian cross in roses and another of roses in the form of a door, symbolizing Do-ne-ho-ga-wa's role as the keeper of the western door of the Iroquois longhouse. The full Episcopal service was read by Dr. W. Strother Jones of St. Paul's Episcopal Church, who was assisted by two other clergymen. Soloists sang "Lead, Kindly Light" and "Jesus, Lover of My Soul." The Indian men sat silently throughout; the women occasionally whispered among themselves, becoming quiet as the service began.

The coffin was carried out by representatives of the Grand Army, while members of the Loyal Legion and the Society of Colonial Wars served as honorary pallbearers. Four Indians then took their places, one at each wheel of the hearse, and walked silently beside it the two miles to Oak Lawn Cemetery. At the cemetery Harriet Converse removed from the casket the wampum she had placed there as a symbol of the horns of the deceased sachem, and replaced it with a small

The unveiling of the headstone marking the grave of Ely S. Parker in Forest Lawn Cemetery, Buffalo, New York, May 30, 1905. The stone was erected by the Buffalo Historical Society and Reno Post 44, Grand Army of the Republic, New York City. Samuel H. Beckwith, who was General Grant's cipher telegraph operator and a friend of Parker, is shown unveiling the stone. From Arthur C. Parker, *The Life of General Ely S. Parker.*

string of white wampum. The body was then interred with full military honors.[12]

The Indians were not pleased that Parker was buried so far from his Indian home, but they did not interfere with Minnie's plans to have him buried in Fairfield. The Buffalo Historical Society also wanted him buried in Buffalo and had offered a cemetery plot there while he was still living. The next year Minnie agreed to have the body moved, and on January 20, 1897, he was reburied in Forest Lawn Cemetery in Buffalo. The new grave was beside the graves of several other Indians and directly under the statue of his ancestor Red Jacket.

It was a fitting place for him. Forest Lawn Cemetery had been part of the old Granger farm where the Iroquois had once traded. The broken rainbow in Elizabeth Parker's dream which foretold the birth of a son who would become a white man as well as an Indian reached from the Tonawanda Reservation to the Granger farm. The last thing the dream interpreter told Elizabeth when she inquired about her dream was that "his sun will rise on Indian land and set on the white man's land. Yet the ancient land of his ancestors will fold him in death."[13]

Minnie, who had once enjoyed the splendor of Washington society, found her fortune at a low ebb after Parker's death. She was left with only a little furniture and clothing and no income at all. The pension of eight dollars a month she received as a veteran's widow was of little help to her. She put her husband's effects up for sale, his personal belongings, his library, and even the Red Jacket medal, which was eventually purchased by the Buffalo Historical Society. Then the Loyal Legion came to her assistance and paid her two thousand dollars for Parker's copy of the draft of Grant's terms of surrender, and Congress passed a special act entitling her to a larger pension of thirty dollars a month.

Less than two years after Parker's death, Minnie was married to James Tallmadge Van Rensselaer, a prominent attorney and a member of a well-known New York family. Their engagement "caused no end of a flutter of surprise in society," for at the age of fifty-five Van Rensselaer was thought a "hopeless bachelor." But two years after their marriage, he too died, and Minnie was once again a widow, though left in better circumstances.

Her daughter Maud was married to Arthur Bullard, a retiring member of one of the old families of Wayland, Massachusetts, and Minnie visited Maud and her husband there and later made her home with them. A resident of Wayland said that "she used to make frequent visits to her friends in New York and Boston. There was always a New Yorky aura about her in her dress and manner, yet she was much loved in Wayland, she was so friendly and vivacious." Another acquaintance said that Minnie "loved any event no matter how small and being limited to Wayland luncheons and teas must have seemed tame indeed." There, amid Wayland's quiet social affairs, Minnie lived to the age of eighty-two. She died in Wayland on March 27, 1932.[14]

Epilogue: The Measure of the Man

Aᴿᴛʜᴜʀ C. Pᴀʀᴋᴇʀ said in his biography that when James E. Kelly was working on his bust of General Parker, Kelly remarked:

"General Parker, in my estimation you are the most distinguished Indian who ever lived."

"That is not so," was the laconic reply. "Better and wiser red men lived before me and now live."

"Who are they?" asked the sculptor.

The Indian looked at him curiously and flashed back, "Can it be that you fail to recall Brant and Tecumseh, both military men, and a host of others?"

"Ah, General," said Mr. Kelly, as he worked on the plastic clay, "I see you have not caught my meaning. I do not intend to flatter you; I would not stoop to that—I mean that you are a man who has 'pierced the enemy's lines.' You have torn yourself from one environment and made yourself the master of another. In this you have done more for your people than any other Indian who ever lived. Had you remained with your people, and of your people alone, you might have been a Red Jacket, a Brant or a Tecumseh, but by going out and away from them you added to the honor that you already had and won equal, if not greater, honors among the white people. You proved what an Indian of capacity could be in the white man's world. The heroes you name did not. We have no way of measuring their capacity in our own standards. We do not even know exactly what they said; their speeches were all translated by interpreters. But we know what you have said as we know what you have done, and that measured by our own ideals."

"That may be true," answered the General to the sculptor, "but why should you test the capacity of the red man's mind in measures that may have an improper scale? Do you measure cloth with a balance or by the gallon?"

195

Abbreviations

APS	American Philosophical Society Library, Philadelphia, Pennsylvania
BECHS	Buffalo and Erie County Historical Society, Buffalo, New York
CHS	Chicago Historical Society, Chicago, Illinois
ESP	Ely Samuel Parker (1828–95)
HEHL	Henry E. Huntington Library, San Marino, California
HMC	Harriet Maxwell Converse (1836–1903)
HRS	Henry Rowe Schoolcraft (1793–1864)
ISHL	Illinois State Historical Library, Springfield, Illinois
LC	The Library of Congress, Washington, D.C.
LHM	Lewis Henry Morgan (1818–81)
NARS	National Archives and Records Service, Washington, D.C.
NL	The Newberry Library, Chicago, Illinois
NYHS	The New-York Historical Society, New York, New York
NYPL	The New York Public Library, New York, New York
NYSL	The New York State Library, Albany, New York
OIA	Office of Indian Affairs
OR	*The War of the Rebellion: A Compilation of the Official Records of the Union and Confederate Armies*
RG	Record Group (of documents in National Archives and Records Service, Washington, D.C.)
SHSW	The State Historical Society of Wisconsin, Madison, Wisconsin
URL	The University of Rochester Library, Rochester, New York
USG	Ulysses S. Grant (1822–85)

Notes

PREFACE

1. Miscellaneous notes of James E. Kelly, Kelly papers, NYHS; ESP to Thomas M. Howell, Jan. 31, 1891, in *Ontario County Times,* Jan. 4, 1893, clipping in Charles Milliken scrapbook, Ontario County Historical Society.

1 · A VISIT TO TONAWANDA

1. Morgan's meeting with Parker is described in "Copy of an Address Read by Schenandoah [Morgan] at the Monthly Council of the Cayugas April 17, 1844," LHM papers, URL.

2. N. H. Parker in Annual Report of the Commissioner of Indian Affairs (1857), p. 311.

3. Henry R. Schoolcraft, *Notes on the Iroquois,* pp. 3–19, 62–82, 191–200; Arthur C. Parker, *The Life of General Ely S. Parker,* p. 87.

4. Lewis Henry Morgan, *League of the Ho-de-no-sau-nee, or Iroquois,* pp. 54–103, 111–13. Morgan, however, refers to clans as "tribes," and tribes as "nations."

5. Parker, *Life of Ely Parker,* p. 85; ESP memorandum of Sept. 5, 1891, Arthur C. Parker papers, URL; Mrs. M. H. Barnard to A. C. Parker, Feb. 21, 1931, ESP papers, APS; William Parker pension file, NARS; *Spirit of the Times* (Batavia, N.Y.), May 28, 1864.

6. Parker, *Life of Ely Parker,* pp. 234–35; "Notes of a Visit to the Buffalo Creek and Tonawanda Reservations, etc., January 1846," LHM papers, URL.

7. LHM to Maj. Gen. [Benjamin F.] Butler, Dec. 14, 1863, military file of Isaac N. Parker, NARS.

8. Emily Edson Briggs, *The Olivia Letters,* p. 185. For Parker's white grandmother see "Notes of a Visit to the Buffalo Creek and Tonawanda Reservations, etc., January, 1846," LHM papers, URL. Ely Parker believed that his white grandmother was a daughter of the famous Indian captive, Frances Slocum, but since Frances Slocum was born in 1773, and William Parker was born about 1793, that could hardly be possible. See ESP's memorandum of Sept. 5, 1891, Arthur C. Parker papers, URL and Parker, *Life of Ely Parker,* pp. 317–20.

9. Charles J. Kappler, *Indian Affairs, Laws and Treaties* II:373–81, 397–401; *The Case of the Seneca Indians in the State of New York*, pp. 7, 14, 24–25, 51; Henry S. Manley, "Buying Buffalo from the Indians," *New York History*, Vol. 28, No. 3 (July 1947), pp. 313–29.

10. Schoolcraft, *Notes on the Iroquois*, pp. 227–32; William N. Fenton, *Parker on the Iroquois*, Book II; a translation by ESP of Jimmy Johnson's speech made Oct. 2–3, 1845, (HM PA38), HEHL; LHM to HRS, Oct. 7, 1845, HRS papers, LC; Isaac N. Hurd, "A Sketch Embracing the Doings and Facts Obtained at the Grand Council of the Iroquois . . . Oct. 1–3, 1845," LHM papers, URL.

2 · A WHITE MAN AS WELL AS AN INDIAN

1. Account by HMC in the *Buffalo Express*, Jan. 24, 1897, clipping in ESP papers, APS; Donehogawa [ESP] to Gayaneshaoh [HMC], Jan. 11, 1887, (HM PA67), HEHL.

2. The Seneca interpretation of dreams is discussed in Anthony F. C. Wallace, *The Death and Rebirth of the Seneca*, pp. 59–75.

3. Donehogawa [ESP] to "Dear Cousin" [HMC], Jan. 7, 1887, (HM PA66), HEHL. Even the year of Parker's birth is not certain, although it was probably 1828.

4. Fenton, *Parker on the Iroquois*, Book II, pp. 33–34 and note.

5. Parker, *Life of Ely Parker*, pp. 20, 233–34.

6. LHM, *League of the Iroquois*, p. 166; Fenton, *Parker on the Iroquois*, Book II, p. 38.

7. New York State Baptist Convention, *Annual Reports of the Tonawanda Indian Mission*, 1829, 1836–37; ESP to Edith L. Wilner, May 25, 1895, ESP papers, BECHS; Annual Report of the Commissioner of Indian Affairs (1843), pp. 362–63.

8. "Writings of General Parker," *Proceedings of the Buffalo Historical Society* VIII (1905): 528–31.

9. Parker, *Life of Ely Parker*, p. 235.

10. *The Lyndonville High School Annual*, Lyndonville, N.Y., No. 1 (June 1907); "Writings of General Parker," *Buffalo Historical Society* VIII (1905): 531; Isaac S. Signor, *Landmarks of Orleans County, New York*, pp. 193–95.

11. ESP, "Address at Yates Academy, Apr. 18, 1843," ESP papers, BECHS; LHM to Caroline Parker, July 30, 1847, LHM papers, URL.

12. Mrs. Louise Bacheldor in a clipping from the *Buffalo Express* (1915?), ESP papers, APS.

13. ESP to Nicholson Parker, Feb. 23, 1843, ESP papers, APS.

14. Caroline Parker to ESP, Oct. 29, 1843, and Minutes of Baptist Meeting, June 28, 1845, both in ESP papers, APS.

15. Mrs. Louise Bacheldor in a clipping from the *Buffalo Express* (1915?), ESP papers, APS.

16. U.S., Congress, Senate Doc. No. 156, 29th Congress, 2nd Session, pp. 2–4; Tonawanda chiefs to Silas Wright, Feb. 22, 1845, ESP papers, APS.

17. Tonawanda chiefs to secretary of war, Oct. 24, 1843, Records of the OIA, Letters Received, NARS (RG 75); I. Cook and T. Love to commissioner of

Indian affairs, Dec. 28, 1843, Records of the OIA, Letters Received, NARS (RG 75).

18. The People *ex rel.* Blacksmith v. P. L. Tracy, First Judge of Genesee, 1 Denio 617.

19. Appendix to *Annual Catalogue of Cayuga Academy, 1841–42;* Statement of ESP's expenses dated Mar. 28, 1846, ESP papers, APS.

20. ESP to Reuben Warren, Nov. 2 and Dec. 26, 1845, Warren papers, SHSW.

21. A composition read by ESP at Cayuga Academy, Nov. 18, 1845, ESP papers, APS.

22. LHM to HRS, Dec. 12, 1845, HRS papers, LC.

23. "A Report of a Seneca Council Held . . . upon the Tonawanda Reservation, Jan. 1–2, 1846," LHM papers, URL.

24. Charles T. Porter to HRS, Jan. 10, 1846, HRS papers, LC.

25. ESP to Reuben Warren, Jan. 27, 1846, Warren papers, SHSW.

26. Diary entry by ESP, Feb. 9, 1846, ESP papers, BECHS.

27. Sylvester Parsons to ESP, Mar. 9, 1846, ESP papers, APS; Benjamin F. Avery to William Medill, Oct. 15, 1846, Records of the OIA, Letters Received, NARS (RG 75).

3 · "HURRA FOR POLK!!"

1. Hurd, "A Sketch Embracing the Doings and Facts Obtained at the Grand Council of the Iroquois . . . Oct. 1–3, 1845," LHM papers, URL; ESP to Reuben Warren, Mar. 22, 1846, Warren papers, SHSW.

2. ESP to Reuben Warren, Mar. 22, 1846, Warren papers, SHSW; ESP to LHM, Mar. 21, 1846, LHM papers, URL.

3. ESP to Reuben Warren, Mar. 22, 1846, Warren papers, SHSW.

4. Milo Milton Quaife, ed., *The Diary of James K. Polk,* p. 302; U.S., Congress, Senate Doc. No. 273, 29th Congress, 1st Session; U.S., Congress, Senate Doc. No. 156, 29th Congress, 2nd Session, pp. 11–15.

5. ESP to LHM, Apr. 2, 1846, LHM papers, URL; U.S., Congress, Senate Doc. No. 156, 29th Congress, 2nd Session, pp. 4–5; printed petition in LHM papers, URL; *Spirit of the Times* (Batavia, N.Y.), Mar. 24 and 31, 1846.

6. Silas Wright to Tonawanda Chiefs, Apr. 18, 1846, ESP papers, APS; ESP to HRS, May 2, 1846, and reply of May 7, 1846, HRS papers, LC; ESP to Albert Gallatin, May 2, 1846, NYHS.

7. ESP to Reuben Warren, May 9, 1846, Warren papers, SHSW.

8. ESP to LHM, May 5, 1846, LHM papers, URL; ESP to Spencer H. Cone, June 8, 1846, ESP papers, APS; William Linn Brown to the Department of State, May 25, 1846, and Robert Campbell, Consul at Havana, to James Buchanan, May 25, 1846, NARS.

9. ESP to LHM, May 5, 1846, LHM papers, URL; Isaac Shanks, Isaac Doctor, and Nicholson Parker to ESP, May 19, 1846, ESP papers, APS.

10. Nicholson Parker to ESP, May 7, 1846, Tonawanda Chiefs to James K. Polk, May 7, 1846, and ESP to James K. Polk, May 18, 1846, all in Records of the OIA, Letters Received, NARS (RG 75); ESP to Reuben Warren, May 19,

1846, Warren papers, SHSW; ESP diary entries for May 18 and 21, 1846, ESP papers, APS.

11. ESP to Reuben Warren, May 19, 31 (with June 1), and June 15, 1846, Warren papers, SHSW; ESP to "Friend Davis," May 27, 1846, ESP papers, APS; *Daily National Intelligencer* (Washington, D.C.), Apr. 20, 1846.

12. ESP to Reuben Warren, June 25–26, 1846, Warren papers, SHSW; ESP to N. H. Parker, July 15, 1846, ESP papers, APS; Quaife, *Diary of James Polk,* pp. 301–302.

13. ESP to Reuben Warren, July 10 and 28, 1846, Warren papers, SHSW; ESP to Reuben Warren, July 12, 1846, ESP papers, BECHS.

14. Nicholson H. Parker to ESP, June 15, 1846, ESP papers, BECHS; ESP to Nicholson H. Parker, June 14 and 21, 1846, ESP papers, APS.

15. *Ithaca* [N.Y.] *Daily Chronicle,* Aug. 17, 1846 (clipping in ESP papers, BECHS).

16. ESP to Spencer H. Cone, June 8, 1846, ESP papers, APS; *Mental Elevator,* No. 13, Dec. 24, 1846, ESP papers, APS; Annual Report of the Commissioner of Indian Affairs (1846), pp. 215–16; U.S., Congress, Senate Doc. No. 156, 29th Congress, 2nd Session, p. 5; Tonawanda sachems and chiefs to William Medill, Sept. 18, 1846, Records of the OIA, Letters Received, NARS (RG 75).

4 · A LAWYER AND AN ENGINEER

1. ESP diary entries, Jan. 1–3, 5–9, 1847, ESP papers, APS; ESP to the chiefs at Tonawanda, Jan. 16, 1847, (HM PA52) HEHL.

2. Blacksmith and Johnson to ESP, Jan. 25, 1847, ESP papers, APS.

3. ESP to Reuben Warren, Jan. 29, Feb. 6, and Feb. 11, 1847, Warren papers, SHSW; *Daily National Intelligencer* (Washington, D.C.), Feb. 22, 1847; ESP to LHM, Feb. 13, 1847, LHM papers, URL.

4. U.S., Congress, Senate Doc. No. 156, 29th Congress, 2nd Session, pp. 1–2.

5. ESP to William Parker, Mar. 22, 1847, and newspaper clipping datelined Albany, Mar. 29 [1847], both in ESP papers, APS.

6. Statement of expenditures, Oct. 30, 1847, ESP papers, APS; *Spirit of the Times* (Batavia, N.Y.), Sept. 4, 1849.

7. W. W. Mosely to ESP, Nov. 12, 1847, ESP papers, APS; ESP to HRS, May 31, 1847, HRS papers, LC; Alfred B. Street to ESP, Nov. 5, 1847, ESP papers, NYSL; Alfred B. Street to ESP, Nov. 15, 1847, ESP papers, APS.

8. *Rochester Daily Advertiser,* Jan. 25, 1851; ESP to Reuben Warren, Nov. 11, 1847, Warren papers, SHSW.

9. "William Wirt's Advice to a Young Lawyer," quoted in *Success in Life: the Lawyer,* Mrs. L. C. Tuthill (New York: 1850) as printed in Carl Bode, ed., *Mid-Century America: Life in the 1850s,* pp. 48–50.

10. *The Post* (Ellicottville, N.Y.), June 1, 1910; ESP to "Friend Hannah" [Hannah L. Saxton], Mar. 21, 1850, letter owned by heirs of John W. Ellis of Ellicottville, N.Y.

11. Arthur C. Parker, "Ely S. Parker—Man and Mason," *Freemasons* 8 (2) (January–December, 1961):229–47.

12. Parker's Notes on the Road, Jan. 8–18, 1848, ESP papers, APS; ESP and Isaac Shanks to William Medill, Jan. 20, 1848, Records of the OIA, Letters Received, NARS (RG 75); ESP to HRS, Jan. 23, 1848, HRS papers, LC.

13. Parker's Notes on the Road Jan. 16–17, 1848, ESP papers, APS.

14. "Marking the Grave of Do-ne-ho-geh-weh," *Proceedings of the Buffalo Historical Society* VIII (1905):516.

15. *Spirit of the Times* (Batavia, N.Y.), June 20, 1848; Two indictments against Waldron, Mar. 13, 1848, and Minutes of Session, 1844–58, at Genesee County Court House, Batavia, N.Y.

16. William P. Angel to ESP, Feb. 20, 1848, Spencer Cone to ESP, Mar. 31, 1848, and ESP to treasurer of the state of North Carolina, Feb. 1, 1848, all in ESP papers, APS; ESP to William Medill, Sept. 25, 1848, and ESP to HRS, July 12, 1848, both in Records of the OIA, Letters Received, NARS (RG 75); H. M. Flagler to ESP, Nov. 28, 1848, ESP papers, URL.

17. See especially ESP to HRS, Apr. 10, 1848, and the undated note and descriptions following ESP's letter to HRS of May 8, 1848, (microfilm reel 38), HRS papers, LC.

18. LHM to ESP, Sept. 16, 1848, ESP papers, APS; *Declaration of the Seneca Nation of Indians, Changing Their Form of Government, and Adopting a Constitutional Charter*, Dec. 4, 1848.

19. ESP to HRS, July 10, 1848, HRS papers, LC; ESP to HRS, July 12, 1848, with enclosures, and ESP to P. E. Thomas, July 20, 1848, both in Records of the OIA, Letters Received, NARS (RG 75).

20. General rule adopted by the Supreme Court of Judicature, Aug. 16, 1806, 1 Johnson 528. For the story of Parker's rejection by the courts see Parker, *Life of Ely Parker*, p. 79, and A. H. Guernsey, "The Red Jacket Medal," *Harper's New Monthly Magazine*, XXXII (Feb. 1866):324–26.

21. LHM to ESP, Dec. 14 and 29, 1848, A. G. Rice to ESP, Apr. 30, 1849, and Reuben Warren to ESP, Feb. 21, 1849, all in ESP papers, APS; ESP to Benj. Wilcox, Sept. 10, 1860, ESP papers, URL.

22. Undated account by John H. Napier, ESP papers, APS.

23. *Spirit of the Times* (Batavia, N.Y.), Jan. 2 and Mar. 6, 1849; ESP to R. H. Shankland, Dec. 30, 1848, R. H. Shankland to William Medill, Jan. 5, 1849, and Millard Fillmore's endorsement of Mar. 8, 1849, on James Wadsworth's letter to William Medill, Mar. 4, 1849, all in Records of the OIA, Letters Received, NARS (RG 75).

24. The People *ex rel.* Waldron and others against Soper, County Judge of Genesee, 3 Selden 428; Memorial from chiefs at Tonawanda, Mar. 15, 1849, Records of the OIA, Letters Received, NARS (RG 75); Power of attorney granted to N. H. Parker by Tonawanda chiefs, Mar. 13, 1849, ESP papers, APS; N. H. Parker to ESP, Mar. 17, 1849, ESP papers, BECHS.

25. *Nunda* [N.Y.] *News*, Jan. 19, 1961, clipping owned by F. L. Casterline, Belmont, N.Y.

26. Tonawanda chiefs to OIA, Sept. 28, 1849, Records of the OIA, Letters Received, NARS (RG 75); LHM to ESP, Jan. 29, 1850, LHM papers, URL; ESP to HRS, Feb. 25, 1850, HRS papers, LC.

5 · GRAND SACHEM OF THE IROQUOIS

1. *Spirit of the Times* (Batavia, N.Y.), Dec. 3, 1850; ESP to Benj. Wilcox, Sept. 10, 1860, ESP papers, URL; New York (State) Engineer and Surveyor, *Annual Report on Canals* (1850). It is sometimes asserted that Ely Parker studied engineering at Rensselaer Polytechnic Institute in Troy, N.Y., but the school has no record of his attendance there. His name does not appear in the student sign-in book for the late 1840s and the early 1850s, nor does it appear in any list of the school's graduates. See also the doubt cast on the assertion in "Alumni Notes," *Polytechnic* XII (1) (Sept. 28, 1895):11.

2. LHM to ESP, Aug. 2, 1850, ESP papers, APS; "Expedition to Grand River, Canada, for Indian Relics, Oct. 28, 1850," LHM papers, URL; ESP, "The Cornplanter Tomahawk in the State Collections," *Fourth Annual Report of the Regents of the University* [of the State of New York] (1850), pp. 99–101.

3. LHM, *League of the Iroquois*, p. 313; undated lecture by ESP, ESP papers, NL.

4. LHM, *League of the Iroquois*, dedication; D. Webster to ESP, June 19, 1851, ESP papers, APS.

5. LHM to ESP, Jan. 29, 1850, LHM papers, URL; undated clipping with picture of ESP in the Rare Book Division, NYPL; *Rochester Daily Advertiser*, Mar. 11, 1852; ESP to Newton Parker, June 13, 1851, ESP papers, APS.

6. Spencer C. Parker (sic) to the secretary of the interior, Apr. 3, 1851, Records of the OIA, Letters Received, NARS (RG 75); New York State Assembly Act No. 374, Mar. 7, 1851, ESP papers, APS; Spencer Cone to ESP, July 31, 1851, ESP papers, APS.

7. *Spirit of the Times* (Batavia, N.Y.), Sept. 30, 1851; Fenton, *Parker on the Iroquois*, Book III, p. 38.

8. Parker, *Life of Ely Parker*, pp. 326–29; *New York Times*, Oct. 29, 1865.

9. Extract from the minutes of the New York State Canal Board, Oct. 20, 1851, ESP papers, APS; *Spirit of the Times* (Batavia, N.Y.), Nov. 18, 1851.

10. ESP to Millard Fillmore, Jan. 13, 1852, Fillmore papers, BECHS; typed copy of ESP to B. F. Hall, Oct. 14, 1852, ESP papers, APS; ESP to L. Lea, Nov. 27, 1852, ESP papers, APS; *Rochester Daily Union*, Jan. 24, 1853.

11. See ESP to R. J. McClelland, Apr. 30, 1853, where Parker signs himself "Principal Sachem of the Six Nations of Indians," and ESP to G. W. Manypenny, July 18, 1853, where he signs himself "Head Chief and Representative of the Six Nations." Both letters are in Records of the OIA, Letters Received, NARS (RG 75).

12. ESP to George W. Manypenny, July 18, 1853, and ESP to Marcus H. Johnson, June 11, 1855, both in Records of the OIA, Letters Received, NARS (RG 75).

13. Two letters of ESP to George W. Manypenny, both dated July 18, 1853, Records of the OIA, Letters Received, NARS (RG 75).

14. Blacksmith against Fellows and Kendle, 3 Selden 401; *Rochester Daily Advertiser*, Aug. 11, 1853.

15. "An Indian Craftsman," *The Masonic Review* 19 (1858):364; "The Chief of the Six Nations," *The New Age* 18 (1913):384.

16. Rochester Historical Society, *Publication Fund Series*, IV (1925):190.

17. *Daily Rochester Union*, Jan. 7, 1854, Jan. 8–10, 1855, and Jan. 9, 1856.

18. *Daily Rochester Union,* Aug. 10, 1854; *Rochester Daily Advertiser,* Aug. 23–27, 1853; "Camp at Syracuse, New York," Barnum's *Illustrated News,* Sept. 17, 1853, pp. 148–49; H. S. Fairchild to ESP, Aug. 25, 1854, ESP papers, APS.

19. ESP to F. Follett, Jan. 24, 1854, and ESP to Benj. Wilcox, Sept. 10, 1860, both in ESP papers, URL; *Daily Rochester Union,* June 25, July 11, and July 23, 1855.

20. *Daily Rochester Union,* Aug. 20, 1855; Caroline Parker to ESP, Feb. 15, 1855, and A. C. Johnson to ESP, Nov. 22, 1854, both in ESP papers, APS; Minnie Myrtle, *The Iroquois,* p. 17.

21. "An Indian Craftsman," *The Masonic Review* 19 (1858):364; ESP to Benj. Wilcox, Sept. 10, 1860, ESP papers, URL; "Marking the Grave of Do-ne-ho-geh-weh," *Buffalo Historical Society* VIII (1905):516.

22. ESP notebook memorandum, Sept. 12, 1856, ESP papers, URL; enclosures with ESP and N. H. Parker to Franklin Pierce, Oct. 17, 1856, Records of the OIA, Letters Received, NARS (RG 75).

23. George W. Manypenny to ESP, Sept. 29, 1856, and ESP and N. H. Parker to Franklin Pierce, Oct. 17, 1856, both in Records of the OIA, Letters Received, NARS (RG 75); ESP memorandum of conversation with Franklin Pierce, Oct. 21, 1856, ESP papers, APS.

24. *New York Times,* Jan. 30 and Feb. 4, 1858.

25. ESP to James Guthrie, Jan. 17, 1857, NARS (RG 121).

26. ESP to Benj. Wilcox, Sept. 10, 1860, ESP papers, URL; William F. Smith to ESP, Feb. 19, 1857, ESP papers, APS; Annual Report of the Light House Board (1857); James Guthrie to ESP, Mar. 4, 1857, NARS (RG 121).

27. *New York Herald,* Mar. 5, 1857; Fellows v. Blacksmith, 19 Howard 366.

28. ESP to William Parker, Mar. 8, 1857, ESP papers, APS.

6 · GALENA

1. *Galena Daily Courier,* Mar. 25, 1857; Stephen A. Douglas to Howell Cobb, Mar. 26, 1857, and reply of Mar. 27, 1857, NARS (RG 121).

2. *Galena Daily Courier,* Mar. 26, 1857. The *Buffalo Courier* item is quoted in *Daily Rochester Union,* Mar. 18, 1857.

3. N. T. Strong to William Clement Bryant, Feb. 9, Apr. 4, and Apr. 24, 1857, Bryant papers, BECHS; affidavit of Goodrich Greenblanket, Mar. 25, 1861, Records of the OIA, Letters Received, NARS (RG 75).

4. *Galena Daily Courier,* Apr. 8, 1857; ESP to Lewis H. Blair, June 9, 1857, ESP papers, APS.

5. ESP to Lewis H. Blair, June 9, 1857, ESP papers, APS.

6. Secretary of the interior to James Denver, May 26, 1857, Records of the OIA, Letters Received, NARS (RG 75).

7. ESP memoranda of June 24, 29, 30, and July 1857, ESP papers, URL.

8. B. B. Howard to N. Vedder, June 25, 1857, C. R. Starkweather to N. Vedder, June 25, 1857, and ESP to Howell Cobb, July 22, 1857, all in NARS (RG 121).

9. Frederick Follett to Lewis Cass, July 28, 1857, Follett to Howell Cobb, July 28, 1857, Richard H. Jackson to Howell Cobb, July 28 and Aug. 30, 1857, and E. B. Washburne to A. H. Bowman, July 28, 1857, all in NARS (RG·121).

10. [R. H. Jackson], *Politics and Its Corruptions in Northwestern Illinois,* printed pamphlet in ESP papers, APS.

11. Charles J. Kappler, *Indian Affairs, Laws and Treaties* II:579–82; copy of clipping from *New York Express,* Jan. 9, 1858, ESP papers, APS.

12. ESP to John Martindale, Jan. 25, 1858, ESP papers, URL; John Martindale to commissioner of Indian affairs, Dec. 17, 1859, Records of the OIA, Letters Received, NARS (RG 75).

13. *New York Times,* Jan. 30, 1858; *The Daily News* (Batavia, N.Y.), Jan. 3, 1882; N. H. Parker to ESP, May 17, 1860, ESP papers, APS; ESP to Benj. Wilcox, Sept. 10, 1860, ESP papers, URL.

14. New York *ex rel.* Cutler v. Dibble, 21 Howard 366.

15. *Weekly Northwestern Gazette* (Galena, Ill.), Sept. 28, 1858, and Sept. 20, 1859; *Galena Daily Advertiser,* Aug. 6 and 19, 1857; H. M. Flagler to ESP, Oct. 3, 1859, ESP papers, BECHS; ESP to M. B., Oct. 2, 1859, ESP papers, APS.

16. *Weekly Northwestern Gazette* (Galena, Ill.), June 28, 1859, and Nov. 27, 1861.

17. J. C. Smith to ESP, Mar. 4, 1865, CHS.

18. "The Indian Craftsman," *The Masonic Review* 23 (1) (1860):16–17. Parker was actually a grandson of Red Jacket's nephew, but being a member of the same clan as Red Jacket (the Wolf Clan) he was also a "clan grandson."

7 · CAPTAIN PARKER AND CAPTAIN GRANT

1. *Weekly Northwestern Gazette* (Galena, Ill.), June 28, July 19, and Aug. 9, 1859; *Galena Daily Advertiser,* July 8, 1859; Annual Report of the secretary of the treasury (1859), pp. 108–9, 115.

2. ESP to Howell Cobb, May 27, 1859, and Oct. 13, 1859, and Joseph C. Jennings to the president, Sept. 8, 1859, all in NARS (RG 121, Entry 26, Box 78); ESP to Chas. Hendrie, Oct. 26, 1859, ESP papers, APS; ESP to S. M. Clark, July 15, 1859, NARS (RG 121).

3. *Dubuque Daily Express and Herald,* Dec. 1, 1855; *Dubuque, Iowa, City Directory for 1860;* Parker, *Life of Ely Parker,* pp. 286–92. Parker's official travel is recorded in NARS (RG 217).

4. ESP, "The Character of Grant," in James Grant Wilson and Titus Munson Coan, eds., *Personal Recollections of the War of the Rebellion* I:344–45.

5. *Brooklyn Daily Eagle,* Sept. 25, 1892.

6. The barroom incident was related to the author by Cephas Hill at the Tonawanda Reservation on July 18, 1973. Hill had once owned a letter from ESP to his brother Nic which described the incident, but had sold it and lost track of its whereabouts. This letter, according to Hill, is also the basis for the incident Parker refers to in his *Life of Ely Parker,* p. 96.

7. ESP to James Harrison Wilson, Dec. 13, 1884, Wilson papers, LC.

8. ESP to S. M. Clark, Feb. 5, 1861, W. B. Franklin to S. P. Chase, Mar. 15 and 23, 1861, and S. P. Chase to W. B. Franklin, Mar. 26, 1861, all in NARS (RG 121).

9. ESP to S. M. Clark, Apr. 8, 1861, NARS (RG 121, Entry 26, Box 78).

10. *Dubuque Daily Times*, Apr. 10, 1861. For Red Jacket as Parker's grand-father, see chapter VI, note 18.

11. ESP, "The Character of Grant," in Wilson and Coan, *Personal Recollections*, p. 345.

12. ESP to F. J. Herron, May 1, 1861, NYHS.

13. Parker, *Life of Ely Parker*, pp. 99–100.

14. *Republican Advocate* (Batavia, N.Y.), Sept. 3, 1861; ESP to William P. Dole, Jan. 3, 1862, Records of the OIA, Letters Received, NARS (RG 75); pass issued to ESP by J. H. Martindale, Sept. 28, 1861, ESP papers, URL; "Writings of General Parker," *Buffalo Historical Society* VIII (1905):525.

15. "Writings of General Parker," *Buffalo Historical Society* VIII (1905):525; ESP to "the Honorable, The Senate & House of Representatives," etc., Jan. 20, 1862, NARS (RG 233); U.S., Congress, House Report No. 84, 37th Congress, 2nd Session.

16. *Republican Advocate* (Batavia, N.Y.), May 13 and Sept. 2, 1862; *Spirit of the Times* (Batavia, N.Y.), Sept. 6, 1862.

17. *Republican Advocate* (Batavia, N.Y.), June 10, 1862; ESP to J. R. Jones, Oct. 30, 1862, ESP papers, BECHS.

18. H. Perry Smith, *History of the City of Buffalo and Erie County* II:389; ESP to N. H. Parker, Feb. 23, 1862, ESP papers, APS; I. Newton Parker to Sarah Parker, Feb. 23 and Mar. 4, 1862, I. Newton Parker Correspondence, Buffalo Savings Bank: Roy W. Nagle Collection, BECHS.

19. War Department to John G. Sawyer, Aug. 28, 1890, NARS (RG 94); Orlando Allen to Wm. Wilkeson, Nov. 13, 1861, and Peter Wilson to General Scruggs, Nov. 11, 1861, both in Wilkeson papers, BECHS.

20. I. Newton Parker to Sarah Parker, Oct. 9, Nov. 12, and Dec. 28, 1861, and Jan. 13, 1862, I. Newton Parker Correspondence, Buffalo Savings Banks: Roy W. Nagle Collection, BECHS.

21. ESP to commissioner of Indian affairs, Mar. 5, 1862, and reply of Mar. 12, 1862, NARS (RG 75); State Historian of New York, *Second Annual Report, 1897*, pp. 9–10, 119–31; John Fisk to ESP, Apr. 4, 1862, ESP papers, BECHS.

22. Military record of Isaac N. Parker, NARS. An attempt was made in 1890 to list the New York Indians who had served in the Civil War. A probably incomplete list of 162 soldiers and sailors was compiled at that time (U.S., Congress, House Misc. Doc. No. 340, Part 15, 52nd Congress, 1st Session, p. 461).

23. Jno. E. Smith to L. Thomas, Apr. 2, 1863, and U. S. Grant to L. Thomas, June 25, 1863, both in NARS (RG 94).

24. "Writings of General Parker," *Buffalo Historical Society* VIII (1905):525–26; Parker, *Life of Ely Parker*, pp. 106–107, 237; *Republican Advocate* (Batavia, N.Y.), June 30, 1863.

8 · AN INDIAN AT HEADQUARTERS

1. ESP to Benj. Wilcox, Sept. 10, 1860, ESP papers, URL; "Marking the Grave of Do-ne-ho-geh-weh," *Buffalo Historical Society* VIII (1905):516.

2. ESP to N. H. Parker, Mar. 18, 1851, ESP papers, APS; miscellaneous notes of James E. Kelly, Kelly papers, NYHS; Parker, *Life of Ely Parker*, pp. 95–96.

3. *Brooklyn Daily Eagle*, Sept. 25, 1892; James E. Kelly manuscript notebook

at Appomattox Court House National Historical Park, Appomattox, Va.; miscella-neous notes of James E. Kelly, Kelly papers, NYHS; Myrtle, *The Iroquois*, p. 298; obituary of ESP in *Proceedings of the Grand Lodge of New York* (1896), p. 11.

4. Conversation with Bernard S. Van Rensselaer of Washington, D.C., June 19, 1973.

5. ESP to H. J. Ensign, July 29, 1863, in *Republican Advocate* (Batavia, N.Y.), Aug. 18, 1863.

6. ESP to H. J. Ensign, Nov. 10, 1863, in *Spirit of the Times* (Batavia, N.Y.), Nov. 28, 1863; ESP to N. H. Parker, Nov. 18, 1863, ESP papers, APS; General Order No. 45, 7th Div., 17th A. C., July 10, 1863, NARS (RG 393); Special Orders No. 256, Dept. of the Tennessee, Sept, 18, 1863, USG papers, LC.

7. Charles A. Dana, *Recollections of the Civil War*, pp. 81–86; James H. Wilson to S. H. Beckwith, Aug. 24, 1904, Bender collection, misc. correspondence of James H. Wilson, Wyoming State Archives and Historical Department.

8. James H. Wilson to S. H. Beckwith, Aug. 24, 1904, Bender collection, misc. correspondence of James H. Wilson, Wyoming State Archives and Historical De-partment; John Russell Young, *Around the World with General Grant* II:214–15; Frederic T. Locke, "Recollections of an Adjutant-General" in Wilson and Coan, *Personal Recollections* I:42–43.

9. Diary of William W. Smith, Nov. 3–Dec. 2, 1863, typed copy in LC, p. 23; ESP to N. H. Parker, Nov. 18, 1863, ESP papers, APS; James Harrison Wilson, *The Life of Charles A. Dana*, pp. 4–5; Horace Porter, *Campaigning with Grant*, pp. 358–59.

10. Diary of William W. Smith, LC, p. 24; ESP memorandum with clipping from the *New York Tribune*, Feb. 19, 1886, Arthur C. Parker papers, URL, and a similar memorandum dated Feb. 20, 1886, ESP papers, URL.

11. ESP to H. J. Ensign, Nov. 10, 1863 in *Spirit of the Times* (Batavia, N.Y.), Nov. 28, 1863; ESP to N. H. Parker, Nov. 18, 1863, and Jan. 25, 1864, ESP papers, APS; Wallace, *Death and Rebirth of the Seneca*, p. 13.

12. ESP to Caroline Parker, Nov. 21, 1863, and ESP to N. H. Parker, Jan. 25, 1864, both in ESP papers, APS.

13. ESP to Caroline Parker, Nov. 21, 1863, ESP papers, APS; ESP to H. J. Ensign, Nov. 10, 1863, in *Spirit of the Times* (Batavia, N.Y.), Nov. 28, 1863; ESP to N. H. Parker, Nov. 18, 1863, ESP papers, APS.

14. ESP to N. H. Parker, Jan. 25, 1864, ESP papers, APS; description of Grant from ESP to C. B. Rich, Dec. 25, 1863, in *Spirit of the Times* (Batavia, N.Y.), Feb. 20, 1864. The description is also printed in *New York Times*, Jan. 17, 1864.

15. ESP to Caroline Parker, Dec. 2, 1863, ESP papers, APS.

16. General Orders No. 9, Dec. 10, 1863, in *New York Times*, Jan. 5, 1864; miscellaneous notes of James E. Kelly, Kelly papers, NYHS.

17. ESP to N. H. Parker, Feb. 2, 1864, at Appomattox Court House National Historical Park, Appomattox, Va.

18. "Marking the Grave of Do-ne-ho-geh-weh," *Buffalo Historical Society* VIII (1905):515–18.

19. ESP to Reuben Warren, Jan. 7, 1847, Warren papers, SHSW; ESP to H. J. Ensign, Mar. 9, 1864, in *Spirit of the Times* (Batavia, N.Y.), Mar. 19, 1864; ESP to N. H. Parker, Feb. 2, 1864, at Appomattox Court House National His-torical Park, Appomattox, Va.; General Orders No. 1, Mar. 18, 1864, USG papers, LC.

9 · MILITARY SECRETARY

1. ESP to N. H. Parker, Oct. 7, 1863, and Apr. 27, 1864, ESP papers, APS; ESP to N. H. Parker, Apr. 8, 1864, typed copy in ESP papers, BECHS; ESP to J. E. Smith, Oct. 15, 1864, Bender collection, Wyoming State Archives and Historical Department.
2. ESP to E. B. Washburne, Apr. 12, 1864, Washburne papers, LC.
3. Parker, *Life of Ely Parker,* p. 111; miscellaneous notes of James E. Kelly, Kelly papers, NYHS; ESP to J. E. Smith, Apr. 18, 1864, ESP papers, BECHS; ESP, "The Character of Grant," in Wilson and Coan, *Personal Recollections* I:346.
4. *The Works of Walt Whitman* II:434; ESP to J. E. Smith, Apr. 18, 1864, ESP papers, BECHS.
5. Miscellaneous notes of James E. Kelly, Kelly papers, NYHS; Parker, *Life of Ely Parker,* pp. 111–12. Grant in his *Personal Memoirs* (II:210–11) gave credit to Comstock for realizing the mistake, but Parker insisted that Grant had forgotten how the incident occurred. Horace Porter's *Campaigning with Grant,* pp. 80–81, also gives the credit to Comstock.
6. Miscellaneous notes of James E. Kelly, Kelly papers, NYHS; ESP to "My dear friend," June 8, 1864, CHS; two drawings attributed to A. R. Waud in LC in which the officer at the left, although not identified, appears to be Parker.
7. The specimen of Parker's signature is from Special Orders No. 27, June 4, 1864, Benjamin F. Butler papers, LC; Parker, *Life of Ely Parker,* pp. 113–14.
8. James Harrison Wilson, *Under the Old Flag* I:399–400, 452–53; James H. Wilson to S. H. Beckwith, Aug. 24, 1904, Bender collection, misc. correspondence of James H. Wilson, Wyoming State Archives and Historical Department.
9. [R. H. Jackson], "Politics and Its Corruptions in Northwestern Illinois," p. 8, printed pamphlet in ESP papers, APS; Parker, *Life of Ely Parker,* p. 110; typescript, "Amos Webster on Grant," in Hamlin Garland papers, University of Southern California Library; Sylvanus Cadwallader to editor *San Diego Union,* Aug. 1903 (?), copy in ESP papers, APS.
10. ESP to W. R. Rowley, July 11, 1864, Rowley papers, ISHL; O. O. Howard and ESP, "Some Reminiscences of Grant," *McClure's Magazine* II (6) (May 1894):533; Horace Porter, *Campaigning with Grant,* p. 213.
11. Porter, *Campaigning with Grant,* pp. 207–8.
12. A. Emerson Babcock, *Isaiah Babcock, Sr. and His Descendants,* pp. 88, 91.
13. ESP to W. R. Rowley, July 8, 9, and 11, 1864, Rowley papers, ISHL.
14. USG to E. M. Stanton, Aug. 26, 1864, NARS (RG 94); General Orders No. 249, Aug. 30, 1864, OR, Series I, Vol. XLII, Part 2, p. 592; *New York Herald,* Sept. 7, 1864.
15. George K. Leet to W. R. Rowley, Sept. 7, 1864 (quoting a letter from Bowers), Rowley papers, ISHL; ESP to J. E. Smith, Oct. 15, 1864, Bender collection, Wyoming State Archives and Historical Department.
16. Manuscript notebook of James E. Kelly at Appomattox Court House National Historical Park, Appomattox, Va.; USG, *Personal Memoirs* I:233.
17. George K. Leet to W. R. Rowley, Sept. 18, 1864, Rowley papers, ISHL; miscellaneous notes of James E. Kelly, Kelly papers, NYHS; Parker, *Life of Ely*

Parker, p. 112; OR, Series I, Vol. XLII, Part 2, pp. 852–53, 856, 859, 865, 870–71, 898.

18. George K. Leet to W. R. Rowley, Nov. 1, 1864, Rowley papers, ISHL; ESP to N. H. Parker, Oct. 24, 1864, ESP papers, APS.

19. Annual Report of the Commissioner of Indian Affairs (1865), p. 680; I. Newton Parker to Sarah Parker, Dec. 1 and 2, 1862, Dec. 24, 1862, and Feb. 3, 1863, I. Newton Parker Correspondence, Buffalo Savings Bank: Roy W. Nagle Collection, BECHS; Newton Parker to Martha [Parker], Aug. 15, 1863, and Newton Parker to "My Dear Sister," June 26, 1864, both in ESP papers, APS; Sergeant Hudson to Asher Wright, June 14, 1864, Bryant papers, BECHS; LHM to Maj. Gen. [B. F.] Butler, Dec. 14, 1863, Isaac N. Parker military file, NARS.

20. State historian of New York, *Second Annual Report, 1897*, pp. 125–31; *New York Herald*, June 30, 1864.

21. *Spirit of the Times* (Batavia, N.Y.), Dec. 10, 1864; Joshua Cooke to Mrs. John Mountpleasant, published July 11, 1887, Arthur C. Parker papers, URL.

22. ESP to N. H. Parker, Nov. 19, 1864, ESP papers, APS; Parker, *Life of Ely Parker*, pp. 119–20; Porter, *Campaigning with Grant*, pp. 216–24, 406–10, 423–26; *New York Times*, July 14, 1886; David S. Sparks, ed., *Inside Lincoln's Army*, p. 487.

10 · ONE REAL AMERICAN

1. *General Ely S. Parker's Narrative* (1893); Sylvanus Cadwallader, *Three Years with Grant*, p. 323.

2. *General Ely S. Parker's Narrative* (1893); Porter, *Campaigning with Grant*, p. 481; *The Daily News* (Batavia, N.Y.) Oct. 8, 1892; Parker, *Life of Ely Parker*, pp. 133–34. See also Norman B. Wood, *Lives of Famous Indian Chiefs*, pp. 662–63.

3. *General Ely S. Parker's Narrative* (1893); James E. Kelly manuscript notebook at Appomattox Court House National Historical Park, Appomattox, Va.; miscellaneous notes of James E. Kelly, Kelly papers, NYHS; Parker, *Life of Ely Parker*, pp. 129–41.

4. Whitman quoted in Allan Nevins, "Where We Stand: Civil War Scholarship," *A Portion of That Field*, p. 18; *New York Express*, Apr. 18, 1865.

5. *Rochester Union and Advertiser*, May 26, 1865; *New York Herald*, May 24–25, 1865.

6. General Order No. 97, May 26, 1865, in ESP Staff Officer file, NARS (RG 94); Porter, *Campaigning with Grant*, pp. 9–10.

7. "Marking the Grave of Do-ne-ho-geh-weh," *Buffalo Historical Society* VIII (1905):517.

8. USG to E. M. Stanton, July 24, 1865, USG papers, LC; E. M. Stanton to James R. Doolittle, July 24 and 25, 1865, OR, Series I, Vol. XLVIII, Part 2, pp. 1117–18, 1122. The site of the meeting was twice changed before Fort Smith was selected.

9. *Galena Weekly Gazette*, Aug. 8, 1865; Jno. A. Rawlins to ESP, Aug. 8, 1865, USG papers, LC; ESP memorandum dated Mar. 15, 1886, Arthur C. Parker papers, URL.

10. Annual Report of the Commissioner of Indian Affairs (1865), pp. 202-3, 479–522.

11. ESP to J. E. Smith, Oct. 31, 1865, ESP papers, BECHS; *New York Herald,* Oct. 14 and 22, 1865; ESP to "Dear Brother" [N. H. Parker], Oct. 27, 1865, (HM PA92) HEHL.

12. *New York Times,* Nov. 21, 1865; John B. Ellis, *The Sights and Secrets of the National Capital,* pp. 323, 474; "Notes on the United States Since the War," *British Quarterly Review* XLII (July and Oct. 1865): 492–93.

13. A. H. Guernsey, "The Red Jacket Medal," *Harper's New Monthly Magazine* XXXII (Feb. 1866): 323–326.

14. T. S. Bowers to ESP, Jan. 7, 1866, USG papers, LC; ESP to T. S. Bowers, Jan. 18, 20, and 27, 1866, NARS (RG 159); excerpt from ESP's report of Jan. 27, 1866, included in a letter from E. M. Stanton to the president, Feb. 15, 1866, A. Johnson papers, LC.

15. D. N. Cooley to James Harlan, Feb. 22, 1866, and associated correspondence in NARS (RG 107); ESP to N. H. Parker, June 6, 1866, typed copy in ESP papers, BECHS.

16. ESP to Charles E. Mix, June 20, 1866, and ESP to Louis V. Bogy, Dec. 13 and 22, 1866, all in Records of the OIA, Letters Received, NARS (RG 75); ESP to N. H. Parker, June 6, 1866, typed copy in ESP papers, BECHS.

17. ESP to USG, Oct. 15, 1866, and E. M. Stanton to O. H. Browning, Oct. 15, 1866, both in NARS (RG 108); David William Smith, *Ely Samuel Parker,* pp. 55–58.

18. U.S., Congress, House Misc. Doc. No. 37, 39th Congress, 2nd Session.

19. *Ibid.;* Henry Wilson to ESP, Jan. 28, 1867, NL; Congressional Globe, 39th Congress, 2nd Session, p. 1677 (Feb..21, 1867); *Cleveland Leader,* Feb. 8, 1867.

11 · MINNIE

1. Adam Badeau to J. H. Wilson, Oct. 26, 1865, Badeau papers, Princeton University Library; ESP to J. E. Smith, Mar. 15, 1866, ESP papers, BECHS; *New York Herald,* Mar. 9, 1866; USG to E. M. Stanton, Mar. 21, 1866, USG papers, LC; promotions and brevets from ESP's military and pension files, NARS.

2. *Rochester Union and Advertiser,* Aug. 27, 1866; *New York Times,* Sept. 30, 1866; ESP to N. H. Parker, June 6, 1866, typed copy in ESP papers, BECHS.

3. *New York Herald,* Dec. 30, 1866, and Jan. 2 and 18, 1867.

4. Dee Brown, *Fort Phil Kearny: An American Saga,* pp. 215–16; James G. Randall, ed., "The Diary of Orville Hickman Browning," Vol. II, in *Collections of the Illinois State Historical Library* XXII (1933): 128; *New York Herald,* Jan. 31–Feb. 8, 1867.

5. ESP to J. A. Rawlins, Mar. 14, 1867, NARS (RG 108).

6. ESP to J. A. Rawlins, Apr. 1, 1867, NARS (RG 108).

7. *New York Herald,* Apr. 23–24, 26, and May 18, 1867.

8. Annual Report of the Commissioner of Indian Affairs (1867), pp. 2–3, 239–44; Hiram Martin Chittenden and Alfred Talbot Richardson, *Life, Letters and Travels of Father Pierre-Jean DeSmet SJ,* III:859–895.

9. Cornelius C. Cusick pension file, NARS; telegram from G. W. Black, Aug. 2, 1867, USG papers, LC; Henry M. Stanley, *My Early Travels and Adventures in America and Asia*, 1:154–58, 161.

10. Copied in the *Rochester Union and Advertiser*, Aug. 19, 1867.

11. ESP to J. E. Smith, Feb. 25, 1868, ESP papers, BECHS; H. McCulloch to ESP, Oct. 5 and 25, 1867, and H. McCulloch to USG, Oct. 1, 1867, all in NARS (RG 56). The latter letter with the War Department's endorsements is also in NARS (RG 94). *New York Herald*, Oct. 8 and Nov. 8, 1867.

12. Mrs. and Miss Sackett to A. Johnson, Sept. 17 [1866], A. Johnson papers, LC.

13. Newel Cheney, *History of the 9th Regiment, New York Cavalry*, pp. 195–96; Charles H. Weygant, *The Sacketts of America*, pp. 339–41.

14. It also appears that Anna Sackett was not Minnie's real mother. When Minnie remarried after Parker's death, she listed her parents as Thomas H. Orton and Sarah A. Penton. Mrs. Sackett's maiden name was Anna Sessilberg, although she had apparently been married prior to her marriage to William Sackett, for their marriage records list her variously as Mrs. Anna Amodier and Anna Modio. The Sacketts' marriage records are in the Church of the Epiphany, Washington, D.C. (Register II, p. 169), and in William Sackett's pension file in NARS. The certificate of Minnie Parker's second marriage is in ESP's pension file in NARS. See also Weygant, *The Sacketts of America*, pp. 242–43, 339–41.

15. Letter to the author from Mrs. Pierpoint Blair, Wayland, Mass., July 14, 1972; J. H. Wilson to S. H. Beckwith, Aug. 24, 1904, Bender collection, miscellaneous correspondence of J. H. Wilson, Wyoming State Archives and Historical Department; miscellaneous notes of James E. Kelly, Kelly papers, NYHS.

16. Horace Porter to J. H. Wilson, Dec. 18, 1867, Bender collection, Wyoming State Archives and Historical Department.

17. LHM, *League of the Iroquois*, pp. 251–52.

18. Horace Porter to J. H. Wilson, Dec. 18, 1867, Bender collection, Wyoming State Archives and Historical Department; W. R. Rowley to Adam Badeau, Dec. 30, 1867, Rowley papers, ISHL.

19. The account of Parker's marriage is taken fom the accounts in the following New York newspapers: *New York Times; New York Daily Tribune; New York Herald; Spirit of the Times* (Batavia); and from these Washington papers: *The Evening Star; The National Intelligencer; The National Republican; Daily Morning Chronicle;* and the *Evening Constitutional Union*.

20. J. A. Rawlins to ESP, Nov. 27, 1868, USG papers, LC; ESP to N. H. Parker, Mar. 25, 1868, ESP papers, APS; ESP to J. E. Smith, Feb. 25, 1868, ESP papers, BECHS.

21. Miscellaneous notes of James E. Kelly, Kelly papers, NYHS; ESP to Freddie, Frankie, Albert and Minnie, Oct. 1, 1868, ESP papers, APS.

22. *New York Times*, Mar. 5, 1869; Adam Badeau, *Grant in Peace*, pp. 160–61.

23. John M. Thayer to USG, Mar. 6, 1869, NARS (RG 48).

24. S. B. Treat to J. D. Cox, Apr. 10, 1869, and Asher Wright to S. B. Treat, Apr. 9, 1869, both in NARS (RG 48).

25. William Cox Cochran, *Political Experiences of Major-General Jacob Dolson Cox* II:1167, typewritten manuscript in Cox papers, LC; 14 U.S. Statutes at Large, 27; E. R. Hoar to J. D. Cox, Apr. 12, 1869, NARS (RG 60).

26. *New York Herald*, Apr. 14 and 17, 1869; Senate Executive Journal, Apr. 16, 1869. The record of Parker's appointment is in NARS (RG 48).

12 · COMMISSIONER OF INDIAN AFFAIRS

1. Annual Report of the Commissioner of Indian Affairs (1869), p. 484; Records of the OIA, Report Books, 19:98, NARS (RG 75); James D. Richardson, *A Compilation of the Messages and Papers of the Presidents* IX:3962.

2. Records of the OIA, Letters Sent, 98:245–46, NARS (RG 75); Annual Report of the Commissioner of Indian Affairs (1869), pp. 446, 485–86.

3. Walt Whitman, "An Indian Bureau Reminiscence," *The Works of Walt Whitman* II:425–27; Records of the OIA, Letters Sent, 93:385–86, and Report Books, 19:142 and 20:202, NARS (RG 75).

4. *Register of Officers and Agents, Civil, Military, and Naval, in the Service of the United States, on the Thirtieth September, 1869*, pp. 166–77; Annual Report of the Commissioner of Indian Affairs (1869), pp. 935–36; *New York Herald*, Aug. 26, 1869.

5. Charles Lewis Slattery, *Felix Reville Brunot*, p. 145.

6. Rayner Wickersham Kelsey, *Friends and the Indians, 1655–1917*, pp. 167–68.

7. ESP to N. H. Parker, May 25, 1869, ESP papers, APS; Records of the OIA, Letters Sent, 92:428, and Report Books, 19:132, NARS (RG 75).

8. *New York Herald*, Apr. 23 and 29, 1869.

9. *New York Herald*, June 8, 1869; Annual Report of the Commissioner of Indian Affairs (1869), p. 894; Records of the OIA, Report Books, 18:390–91, NARS (RG 75).

10. Records of the OIA, Report Books, 19:51, NARS (RG 75).

11. Richardson, *Messages and Papers of the Presidents* IX:3977–78; Annual Report of the Board of Indian Commissioners (1869), p. 492; Charles Morris, ed., *The Makers of Philadelphia*, p. 259; *New York Herald*, Jan. 17, 1870.

12. Records of the OIA, Letters Sent, 90:115–17, 123–24, NARS (RG 75); Jacob D. Cox to William Welsh, July 5, 1869, Cox papers, Oberlin College Archives.

13. *New York Herald*, July 13, 1869 and Dec. 30, 1870; *Report of Hon. ESP . . . on the Communication of William Welsh*, Edward E. Ayer collection, NL. See also Records of the OIA, Letters Sent, 93:181–82, NARS (RG 75).

14. *New York Herald*, Nov. 12, 1866, Sept. 6–7 and Nov. 16, 1869; *New York Times*, Nov. 22, 1869; Will of John A. Rawlins, Sept. 5, 1869, Office Register of Wills, Washington, D.C.; James Harrison Wilson, *The Life of John A. Rawlins*, pp. 375, 502–7; ESP to J. C. Smith, Feb. 15, 1887, ISHL.

15. Hamilton Gay Howard, *Civil War Echoes*, pp. 120–22; *New York Herald*, Feb. 21, 1870; Briggs, *The Olivia Letters*, p. 185.

16. Howard and ESP, "Some Reminiscences of Grant," *McClure's Magazine* II (6) (May 1894): 535; Porter, *Campaigning with Grant*, p. 83.

17. Annual Report of the Commissioner of Indian Affairs (1869), p. 449; Records of the OIA, Letters Sent, 92:285 and 93:208, NARS (RG 75); Annual Report of the Commissioner of Indian Affairs (1870), pp. 467–68; Robert J. Ege, *Tell Baker to Strike Them Hard!*, pp. 45–46, 119.

18. Records of the OIA, Letters Sent, 95:179, and Report Books, 19:312, NARS (RG 75).

19. *New York Herald,* May 25–26, 1870; *New York Times,* June 10, 1870.

20. Annual Report of the Board of Indian Commissioners (1870), pp. 38–42; *New York Times,* June 10, 1870.

21. *New York Times,* June 12 and 14, 1870.

22. Records of the OIA, Report Books, 20:137–38, NARS (RG 75); *Report of Hon. ESP . . . on the Communication of William Welsh,* Edward E. Ayer collection, NL; U.S., Congress, House Report No. 39, 41st Congress, 3rd Session, p. iv.

23. *New York Herald,* Aug. 18, Oct. 29, Nov. 1, and Dec. 9, 1870; P. J. DeSmet to Paul and Augusta DeSmet, Oct. 22, 1870, DeSmet papers, Washington State University Library.

24. U.S., Congress, House Report No. 39, 41st Congress, 3rd Session, pp. 22, 34; P. J. DeSmet to Paul and Augusta DeSmet, Oct. 22, 1870, DeSmet papers, Washington State University Library; *New York Herald* and *New York Times,* Dec. 19, 1870; Annual Report of the Board of Indian Commissioners (1870), pp. 25–27, 121–22.

13 · ON TRIAL

1. U.S., Congress, House Report No. 39, 41st Congress, 3rd Session, pp. 111–22.

2. E. P. Smith to George Whipple, Dec. 15, 1870, American Missionary Association Archives, Amistad Research Center, Tulane University, New Orleans, Louisiana.

3. *Report of Hon. ESP . . . on the Communication of William Welsh,* Edward E. Ayer collection, NL; *New York Herald,* Jan. 5, 1871.

4. E. E. Cady to W. R. Rowley, Jan. 21, 1871, Rowley papers, ISHL; U.S., Congress, House Report No. 39, 41st Congress, 3rd Session, p. 69.

5. U.S., Congress, House Report No. 39, 41st Congress, 3rd Session, pp. 18–34, 94–95, 240–41.

6. *Ibid.,* pp. 31, 76.

7. *Ibid.,* pp. 58–63.

8. Norton P. Chipman, *Argument of N. P. Chipman on Behalf of Hon. E. S. Parker, Commissioner of Indian Affairs;* William Welsh et al., *Taopi and His Friends or the Indians' Wrongs and Rights,* p. 75.

9. *New York Herald,* Feb. 9, 21–22, 1871.

10. U.S., Congress, House Report No. 39, 41st Congress, 3rd Session, pp. i–vii, 32–33.

11. Records of the OIA, Report Books, 20:391–92, and Letters Sent, 101:186–87, NARS (RG 75); ESP to USG, June 29, 1871, The Rutherford B. Hayes Library, Fremont, Ohio; *New York Herald,* June 30, 1871.

12. *New York Times,* July 18, 1871; USG to George H. Stuart, July 22, 1871, Stuart papers, LC, quoted in Robert Winston Mardock, *The Reformers and the American Indian,* p. 106.

13. W. Welsh to LHM, Mar. 20, 1873, LHM papers, URL; *New York Times,* Aug. 13, 1875; William Welsh to Jacob D. Cox, Sept. 13 and 21, 1871, Cox papers, Oberlin College Archives.

14. Annual Report of the Commissioner of Indian Affairs (1869), p. 448, and (1870), p. 467; "Writings of General Parker," *Buffalo Historical Society* VIII (1905):532.

15. *Erie Daily Republican,* Feb. 1, 1871, *Troy Daily Times,* Apr. 12, 1871, *Portland Daily Press,* Mar. 6. 1871, and *Philadelphia Post,* Mar. 27, 1871, all clippings in USG papers, LC.

16. *The Chronicle* (Southport, Conn.), Dec. 13, 1900; *The Bridgeport* (Conn.) *Sunday Post,* Nov. 14, 1937.

17. Elizabeth V. H. Banks, *This Is Fairfield, 1639–1940,* p. 114.

18. *The Bridgeport* (Conn.) *Sunday Post,* Nov. 14, 1937.

19. *New York Times,* June 28, 1873; D. Sherman to commissioner of Indian affairs, May 1, 1872, Records of the OIA, Letters Received, NARS (RG 75); *The Bridgeport* (Conn.) *Sunday Post,* Nov. 14, 1937; ESP to J. Q. Smith, Mar. 27, 1876, Records of the OIA, Letters Received, NARS (RG 75).

20. *New York Times,* Sept. 1, 1895; Parker, *Life of Ely Parker,* p. 160; 1876 newspaper clipping containing address by D. Sherman before the Indians of Cattaraugus and Allegany reservations and Teachers' Institute of the Indian schools, Records of the OIA, Letters Received, NARS (RG 75); Clarence F. Birdseye et al., eds., *Annotated Consolidated Laws of the State of New York* II:2396.

21. "Writings of General Parker," *Buffalo Historical Society* VIII (1905):535; *New York Daily Tribune,* July 12, 1893; *New York Times,* Oct. 1, 1876.

14 · MULBERRY STREET

1. Undated newspaper clipping headed "Extra," and containing ESP'S obituary, ESP papers, APS.

2. *New York Times,* Jan. 15 and May 9, 1892, and Sept. 1, 25–26, and Oct. 21–22, 28, 1895; *New York Tribune,* Sept. 25–26 and Oct. 21–22, 28, 1895.

3. Records of St. Paul's Episcopal Church, Fairfield, Conn., II:52.

4. Everett R. Turnbull, *The Rise and Progress of Freemasonry in Illinois, 1783–1952,* pp. 250–52.

5. ESP to A. H. Markland, Jan. 27, 1886, Aaron J. Cooke papers, William L. Clements Library, University of Michigan; incomplete letter ESP to J. E. Smith, March 15 and April 6–7, 1886 (HM EG Box 45), HEHL.

6. ESP to J. C. Smith, Feb. 15, 1887, ISHL; ESP, "The Character of Grant," in Wilson and Coan, *Personal Recollections* I:347–48; miscellaneous notes of James E. Kelly, Kelly papers, NYHS; ESP's copy of the draft terms of surrender, NYHS; ESP to A. H. Markland, Apr. 10, 1885, ESP papers, APS.

7. ESP to F. D. Grant, Apr. 5, 1888, USG papers, LC; incomplete letter ESP to J. E. Smith, March 15 and April 6–7, 1886 (HM EG Box 45), HEHL.

8. Thomas Kilby Smith to Walter George Smith, June 1, 1886, (HM KS-188), HEHL.

9. Clinton B. Fisk to E. A. Hayt, Aug. 22, 1878, and ESP to E. A. Hayt, Aug. 23, 1878, Records of the OIA, Letters Received, NARS (RG 75); N. H. Parker to LHM, Nov. 28, 1875, LHM papers, URL; ESP to HMC, Oct. 2, 1886, (HM PA63), HEHL; Parker, *Life of Ely Parker,* p. 117; notes of former Genesee County historian, Charlotte Read, Genesee County Holland Land Office Museum, Batavia, N.Y.

10. William N. Fenton, "Harriet Maxwell Converse," *Notable American Women* I:375–77; Lawrence E. Eyres, "Harriet Maxwell Converse," *The Chemung Historical Journal* III (2) (Dec. 1957):379–83; miscellaneous notes of James E. Kelly, Kelly papers, NYHS; The Wolf [ESP] to The Wandering Snipe [HMC], July 10, 1894, ESP papers, APS.

11. ESP to Gayaneshaoh [HMC], Dec. 24, 1885, Arthur C. Parker papers, URL.

12. The Wolf [ESP] to My beloved Snipe [HMC], July 6, 1893, (HM PA89), HEHL.

13. Parker, *Life of Ely Parker,* pp. 164–67; Donehogawa [ESP] to Gayaneshaoh [HMC], Dec. 7, 1886, and Jan. 11, 1887, (HM PA65 and 67), HEHL.

14. ESP to Cousin Gayaneshaoh [HMC], undated letter in Edward E. Ayer collection, NL; The Wolf [ESP] to The Snipe [HMC], Oct. 4, 1887, (HM PA72), HEHL; ESP to W. C. Bryant, Dec. 19, 1889, NYSL; Records of the OIA, Report Books, 20:51, NARS (RG 75).

15. Plea of ESP against the removal of Red Jacket's remains, Apr. 19, 1852, ESP papers, APS; "Obsequies of Red Jacket at Buffalo, Oct. 9, 1884," *Transactions of the Buffalo Historical Society* III (1885).

16. Parker, *Life of Ely Parker,* pp. 212–13; "Red Jacket, or Sagoyewatha, 1751–1830, Chief of the Senecas," *Magazine of American History* XXIII (6) (June, 1890):494–96; Frank H. Severance, "Work of the Buffalo Historical Society," *Magazine of American History* XXIII (5) (May 1890): 412; minutes of the Red Jacket Monument Committee, 1890–91, BECHS.

17. James E. Kelly manuscript notebook at Appomattox Court House National Historical Park, Appomattox, Va.; miscellaneous notes of James E. Kelly, Kelly papers, NYHS; *Art and Sculpture of James Edward Kelly, 1855–1933;* ESP to J. E. Kelly, Feb. 13, 1894, letter owned by Paul C. Richards, Bridgewater, Mass.

18. Miscellaneous notes of James E. Kelly, and ESP to J. E. Kelly, Nov. 4, 1891, Kelly papers, NYHS.

19. *The Bridgeport* (Conn.) *Sunday Post,* Nov. 14, 1937; *San Diego Union,* July 20, 1893, clipping in Sylvanus Cadwallader papers, LC; "Writings of General Parker," *Buffalo Historical Society* VIII (1905):534–35; Noah T. Clarke, *The Wampum Belt Collection of the New York State Museum,* pp. 102–3, 120.

20. Jacob A. Riis, *The Making of an American,* pp. 243–44.

15 · THE BROKEN RAINBOW

1. ESP, "Address by General Ely S. Parker, U. S. V.," *Final Report of the Battlefield of Gettysburg* I:321–25; *New York Daily Tribune,* Sept. 25, 1891; *New York Times,* Sept. 24–25, 1891.

2. ESP to Caroline Parker, Oct. 26, 1883, Arthur C. Parker papers, URL; The Wolf [ESP] to The SS [HMC], Mar. 8, 1890, Arthur C. Parker papers, URL; J. H. Salisbury to HMC, Mar. 8, 1890, and The Wolf [ESP] to The SS [HMC], Mar. 24, 1890, both in ESP papers, APS; Smith statement in Lloyd Lewis's notes from James E. Kelly's notebook, Lewis papers, USG Association, Carbondale, Ill.

3. Isaac T. Parker to D. Sherman, Nov. 11, 1873, Records of the OIA, Letters Received, NARS (RG 75); *The Daily News* (Batavia, N.Y.), Mar. 21 and May 27, 1892; *New York Times*, Jan. 21, 1888, and Mar. 21, 1892; 1876 newspaper clipping containing an address of D. Sherman, and clipping from *Chautauqua Farmer*, Sept. 4, 1878, both in Records of the OIA, Letters Received, NARS (RG 75); clipping entitled "A Remarkable Woman," Arthur C. Parker papers, URL.

4. D. Sherman to commissioner of Indian affairs, Oct. 5, 1877, Records of the OIA, Letters Received, NARS (RG 75); L. M. Wright to W. C. Bryant, Sept. 15, 1877, Bryant papers, BECHS; *The Daily News* (Batavia, N.Y.), Mar. 21 and May 27, 1892; Parker, *Life of Ely Parker*, pp. 194–95.

5. ESP to Caroline Parker, July 14, 1884, ESP papers, BECHS; *New York Tribune*, Dec. 20, 1896; *The Bridgeport* (Conn.) *Sunday Post*, Nov. 14, 1937.

6. Conversation with Bernard S. Van Rensselaer of Washington, D.C., June 19, 1973.

7. *New York Daily Tribune*, July 12, 1893; miscellaneous documents in ESP pension file, NARS; Minnie Parker to W. C. Bryant, July 24 [1893], Bryant papers, BECHS.

8. *New York Times*, Jan. 1, 1881; The Wolf [ESP] to The SS [HMC], Mar. 8, 1890, Arthur C. Parker papers, URL; *New York Daily Tribune*, Dec. 13 and 17, 1893; affidavits in ESP pension file, NARS.

9. The Wolf [ESP] to The Wandering Snipe [HMC], July 10, 1894, ESP papers, APS; *Rochester Daily Union and Advertiser*, Oct. 10, 1894; *The Chronicle* (Southport, Conn.), Oct. 11, 1894; *The Daily News* (Batavia, N.Y.), Mar. 29 and Apr. 8, 1895; ESP to James E. Kelly, May 24, 1892, typed copy in Kelly papers, NYHS.

10. *New York Times*, May 7 and June 12, 1895; ESP to "My Dear Niece," Aug. 6, 1895, ESP papers, URL; *New York Herald*, Sept. 1, 1895.

11. ESP death record, Town of Fairfield, Conn.; *The Chronicle* (Southport, Conn.), Sept. 5, 1895; *Brooklyn Daily Eagle*, Aug. 31, 1895; *New York Times*, Sept. 1 and 4, 1895.

12. *Bridgeport* (Conn.) *Evening Post*, Sept. 4, 1895; *The Bridgeport* (Conn.) *Standard*, Sept. 4, 1895; *The Daily News* (Batavia, N.Y.) Sept. 7, 1895; *The Chronicle* (Southport, Conn.), Sept. 5, 1895.

13. Minnie Parker to W. C. Bryant, July 25 [no year], Bryant papers, BECHS; two clippings from the *Buffalo Express* (?) dated Jan. 20 and 24, 1897, ESP papers, APS; "Burial of Do-ne-ho-ga-wa," *36th Annual Report of the Board of Managers of the Buffalo Historical Society*, pp. 33–36.

14. Miscellaneous documents in ESP pension file, NARS; James Grant Wilson, "Grant's Historic Utterances," *The Outlook* 55 (14) (Apr. 3, 1897):890; *The Daily News* (Batavia, N.Y.), May 24, 1897; *New York Times*, July 16, 1897; *New York Tribune*, Dec. 20, 1896, and Aug. 30, 1899; letters to the author from Mrs. Pierpoint Blair (July 14, 1972) and Isabel W. Wight (Nov. 17, 1977, and January 11, 1978), both of Wayland, Mass.; Minnie Van Rensselaer death record, Town of Wayland, Mass.

Bibliography

MANUSCRIPTS

THE MOST IMPORTANT collections of Ely S. Parker's papers are in the following institutions:

American Philosophical Society Library, Philadelphia, Pennsylvania.
Buffalo and Erie County Historical Society, Buffalo, New York.
Henry E. Huntington Library, San Marino, California.
The Newberry Library, Chicago, Illinois.
The New York State Library, Albany, New York.
The University of Rochester Library, Rochester, New York.
The State Historical Society of Wisconsin, Madison, Wisconsin (in the Reuben B. Warren papers).

Smaller groups of Parker's papers, or single items, are in these institutions:

Appomattox Court House National Historical Park, Appomattox, Virginia.
Chicago Historical Society, Chicago, Illinois.
Genesee County Holland Land Office Museum, Batavia, New York.
The Historical Society of Pennsylvania, Philadelphia, Pennsylvania.
Illinois State Historical Library, Springfield, Illinois.
Museum of the American Indian (Library, Heye Foundation), Bronx, New York.
The New-York Historical Society, New York, New York.
The New York Public Library, New York, New York.
The Rutherford B. Hayes Library, Fremont, Ohio.
Six Nations Indian Museum, Onchiota, New York.
State University College, Oswego, New York.
The War Library and Museum of the Military Order of the Loyal Legion of the United States, Philadelphia, Pennsylvania.

216

A few of Parker's papers are owned by the following individuals:
  Heirs of John W. Ellis, Ellicottville, New York (one letter).
  Robin Lallmang Pascua, Alexandria, Virginia (three record books of the
    Tonawanda Senecas written in part by Parker).
  Paul C. Richards, Bridgewater, Massachusetts (two letters).

Additional letters written by Parker as commissioner of Indian affairs are to
be found in various institutions. They have not been included here because
Parker's correspondence as commissioner is available in its entirety in the
National Archives and Records Service, Washington D.C. (Record Group
75).

The National Archives and Records Service also contains many other
papers by and relating to Ely S. Parker. The most important of these are in
the following record groups:
  RG   48   Records of the Office of the Secretary of the Interior, Ap-
            pointments Division.
  RG   75   Records of the Office (or Bureau) of Indian Affairs.
  RG   94   Records of the Adjutant General's Office.
  RG 107   Records of the Office of the Secretary of War.
  RG 108   Records of the Headquarters of the Army.
  RG 121   Records of the Public Building Service.
  RG 217   Records of the U.S. General Accounting Office.

The papers in Parker's personal military and pension files in the National
Archives and Records Service also contain significant materials. The military
and pension files of the following persons were also consulted: Harrison
Alexander; Samuel H. Beckwith; Cornelius C. Cusick; Isaac Newton Parker;
William Parker; and William Sackett.

Finally, the following manuscript collections also contain materials by or
relating to Ely S. Parker:
  American Missionary Association Archives, Amistad Research Center,
    Tulane University, New Orleans, Louisiana (microfilm).
  Adam Badeau papers, Princeton University Library, Princeton, New
    Jersey.
  Mrs. Walter Bender collection, Historical Research and Publications
    Division, Wyoming State Archives and Historical Department,
    Cheyenne, Wyoming.
  William Clement Bryant papers, Buffalo and Erie County Historical
    Society, Buffalo, New York.

William Clement Bryant papers, Columbia University Libraries, New York, New York.

Sylvanus Cadwallader papers, The Library of Congress, Washington, D.C.

Records of the Church of the Epiphany (Episcopal), Washington, D.C.

George S. Conover scrapbook, Buffalo and Erie County Historical Society, Buffalo, New York.

Aaron J. Cooke collection, William L. Clements Library, The University of Michigan, Ann Arbor, Michigan.

Jacob D. Cox papers, The Library of Congress, Washington, D.C.

Jacob D. Cox papers, Oberlin College Archives, Oberlin, Ohio.

Charles A. Dana papers, The Library of Congress, Washington, D.C.

Pierre-Jean DeSmet collection, Washington State University, Pullman, Washington.

James William Eldridge collection, Henry E. Huntington Library, San Marino, California.

Millard Fillmore papers, Buffalo and Erie County Historical Society, Buffalo, New York.

Hamlin Garland papers, University of Southern California Library, Los Angeles, California.

Ulysses S. Grant papers, The Library of Congress, Washington, D.C. (microfilm).

George H. Harris papers, Rochester Public Library, Rochester, New York.

Andrew Johnson papers, The Library of Congress, Washington, D.C. (microfilm).

James E. Kelly manuscript notebook, Appomattox Court House National Historical Park, Appomattox, Virginia.

James E. Kelly papers, The New-York Historical Society, New York, New York.

Robert E. Lee Headquarters papers, Virginia Historical Society, Richmond, Virginia.

Lloyd Lewis papers, The Ulysses S. Grant Association, Morris Library, Southern Illinois University, Carbondale, Illinois.

Charles Milliken scrapbook, Ontario County Historical Society, Canandaigua, New York.

Lewis Henry Morgan papers, The New-York Historical Society, New York, New York.

Lewis Henry Morgan papers, The University of Rochester Library, Rochester, New York.

William P. Palmer collection, Western Reserve Historical Society, Cleveland, Ohio.

Arthur C. Parker papers, The University of Rochester Library, Rochester, New York.

I. Newton Parker Correspondence, Buffalo Savings Bank: Roy W. Nagle

Collection, Buffalo and Erie County Historical Society, Buffalo, New York.

Maris Bryant Pierce letters, Dartmouth College, Hanover, New Hampshire.

Horace Porter papers, The Library of Congress, Washington, D.C.

John A. Rawlins papers, The Houghton Library, Harvard University, Cambridge, Massachusetts.

Red Jacket Monument Committee Minutes, 1890–91, Buffalo and Erie County Historical Society, Buffalo, New York.

Robert E. Lee Memorial Foundation, Stratford, Virginia.

William R. Rowley papers, Illinois State Historical Library, Springfield, Illinois.

Henry Rowe Schoolcraft papers, The Library of Congress, Washington, D.C. (microfilm).

Records of St. Paul's Episcopal Church, Fairfield, Connecticut.

John Corson Smith folder, Chicago Historical Society, Chicago, Illinois.

Thomas Kilby Smith collection, Henry E. Huntington Library, San Marino, California.

William W. Smith diary, The Library of Congress, Washington. D.C.

George Hay Stuart papers, The Library of Congress, Washington, D.C.

Town of Fairfield, death records, Fairfield, Connecticut.

Town of Wayland, death records, Wayland, Massachusetts.

Reuben B. Warren papers, The State Historical Society of Wisconsin, Madison, Wisconsin.

Elihu B. Washburne papers, The Library of Congress, Washington, D.C.

William Wilkeson papers (letters concerning Indian volunteers), Buffalo and Erie County Historical Society, Buffalo, New York.

James Harrison Wilson papers, The Library of Congress, Washington, D.C.

NEWSPAPERS

The following newspapers were used in this study. Some additional newspaper clippings not included here are to be found in various manuscript collections as indicated in the notes.

Batavia, New York: *The Daily News,* 1878–98; *Republican Advocate,* 1861–65; *Spirit of the Times,* 1846, 1848–52, 1861–67.

Bridgeport, Connecticut: *Bridgeport Evening Post,* August 31 and September 4, 1895; *Morning Union,* January 22, 1897; *The Bridgeport Daily Standard,* October 24, 1871; September 4, 1895; *The Bridgeport Sunday Post,* November 14, 1937.

Brooklyn, New York: *Brooklyn Daily Eagle,* September 25, 1892, August 31, 1895.

Buffalo, New York: *Buffalo Commercial Advertiser and Journal,* September 29 and October 15, 1884, November 14, 1888, March 23, 1892, February 5, 1903.

Cleveland, Ohio: *Cleveland Leader,* February 8, 1867.

Detroit, Michigan: *Detroit Daily Free Press,* February 28–April 7, 1857.

Dubuque, Iowa: *Dubuque Daily Times,* June 25–September 20, 1859, January 1–June 30, 1861; *Dubuque Daily Express and Herald,* December 1, 1855, February 2, 1858–June 30, 1859; *Dubuque Herald,* 1860–61, May 1, 1885; *Telegraph-Herald,* August 17, 1947.

Ellicottville, New York: *The Post,* June 1, 1910.

Galena, Illinois: *Galena Daily Advertiser,* July 8, 1857–February 16, 1860; *Galena Daily Courier,* January 1–June 8, 1857; *Galena Weekly Gazette,* May–October, 1865; *Weekly Northwestern Gazette,* January 1, 1857–April 30, 1861.

Hartford, Connecticut: *The Hartford Daily Courant,* September 2, 1895.

New York, New York: *New York Express,* April 18, 1865; *New York Herald,* March and July 1857, May, 1864–June, 1868, April, 1869–September, 1871; *New York Sun,* September 1, 1895; *New York Times,* 1851–99; *New York Tribune,* December, 1867, 1875–99.

Norfolk, Virginia: *The Southern Argus,* January–June, 1856, January 1–March 11, 1857.

Nunda, New York: *Nunda News,* January 19, 1961.

Rochester, New York: *Rochester Daily Advertiser,* 1850–53; *Rochester Daily Democrat,* July 23, July 26, and August 15, 1851; *Daily Rochester Union* [and Advertiser], 1853–94; *Frederick Douglass' Paper,* December 23, 1853–June 29, 1855.

Southport, Connecticut: *Southport Chronicle,* 1867–71, 1891–95, January 25, 1897; December 13, 1900; *Fairfield Advertiser,* 1884–90; *Pequot Record,* July 1–5, 1890; *Southport Times,* 1879–81.

Washington, D.C.: *Daily Morning Chronicle,* December 1867; *Daily National Intelligencer,* 1846–48; *Evening Constitutional Union,* December 1867; *The Evening Star,* December 1867; *The National Intelligencer,* December 1867; *The National Republican,* December 1867; *National Tribune,* November 6, 1884–December 31, 1885, September 5, 1895.

UNITED STATES PUBLIC DOCUMENTS

Annual Reports of the Board of Indian Commissioners, 1869–71.

Annual Reports of the Commissioner of Indian Affairs, 1838–71.

Annual Reports of the Lighthouse Board (Treasury Department), 1855 and 1857.

Annual Reports of the Secretary of the Treasury, 1855–63.

Congressional Globe, 39th Congress, 2nd Session.

Heitman, Francis B. *Historical Register and Dictionary of the United States Army*. Two volumes. Washington: Government Printing Office, 1903.

Kappler, Charles J., ed. *Indian Affairs: Laws and Treaties*. Five volumes. Washington: Government Printing Office, 1903–41.

Register of Officers and Agents, Civil, Military, and Naval, in the Service of the United States, on the Thirtieth September, 1869. Washington: Government Printing Office, 1870.

U.S., Congress, House Report No. 84, 37th Congress, 2nd Session, Report of the Committee on the Judiciary on the Memorial of Ely S. Parker Praying Congress to Grant him Citizenship.

———, House Misc. Doc. No. 37, 39th Congress, 2nd Session. Transmitting a Report by Col. Parker on Affairs Between the United States and the Various Indian Tribes.

———, House Report No. 39, 41st Congress, 3rd Session. Investigation into Indian Affairs, 1871.

———, House Misc. Doc. No. 340, Part 15, 52nd Congress, 1st Session. Report on Indians Taxed and Indians Not Taxed in the United States (Except Alaska) at the Eleventh Census, 1890.

———, House Report No. 725, 54th Congress, 1st Session, Committee on Invalid Pensions Report on Pension for Minnie Parker.

———, Senate Doc. No. 273, 29th Congress, 1st Session. Message from the President of the United States, Communicating a Petition of the Tonawanda Band of Seneca Indians, Praying that Steps May be Taken to Abrogate the Treaties of 1838 and 1842.

———, Senate Doc. No. 156, 29th Congress, 2nd Session. Report on Memorial from Citizens of New York [regarding exemption of the Tonawanda Band of the Seneca Tribe from the operation of the Treaty of May 20, 1842].

———, Senate Ex. Doc. No. 13, 40th Congress, 1st Session. Report on Indian Hostilities (the massacre at Fort Phil Kearny).

———, Senate Executive Journal, 41st Congress, Special Session. (Journals of the 41st to the 51st Congress, 1869–91, vols. 17–27.)

———, Senate Report No. 1356, 54th Congress, 2nd Session. Committee on Pensions Report on Pension for Minnie Parker.

United States Statutes at Large, Vol. 14.

The War of the Rebellion: A Compilation of the Official Records of the Union and Confederate Armies. 128 volumes. Washington: Government Printing Office, 1880–1901.

COURT CASES INVOLVING THE TONAWANDA SENECAS

Blacksmith against Fellows and Kendle, 3 Selden 401.
Fellows v. Blacksmith, 19 Howard 366.

New York *ex rel.* Cutler v. Dibble, 21 Howard 366.

The People *ex rel.* Blacksmith v. P. L. Tracy, First Judge of Genesee, 1 Denio 617.

The People *ex rel.* Waldron and others against Soper, County Judge of Genesee, 3 Selden 428.

The People v. Ichabod Waldron, Genesee County [New York] Court and General Sessions, June 12, 1848.

WORKS RELATING DIRECTLY TO ELY S. PARKER

"Alumni Notes." *Polytechnic* XII (1) (Sept. 28, 1895):11.

Armstrong, William H. "Red Jacket's Medal: An American Badge of Nobility." *Niagara Frontier* 21 (2) (Summer 1974):26–36.

Brown, D. Alexander. "One Real American." *American History Illustrated* IV (7) (November 1969):12–21.

Brown, Dee. *Bury My Heart at Wounded Knee: An Indian History of the American West*. New York: Bantam Books, 1972. (Chapter 8, "The Rise and Fall of Donehogawa.")

"Burial of Do-ne-ho-ga-wa." *Thirty-sixth Annual Report of the Board of Managers of the Buffalo Historical Society for the Year 1897*. Buffalo, N.Y.: Buffalo Historical Society, 1898, pp. 33–36.

Case, James R. "Ely Samuel Parker—1828–1895." *Knight Templar*, May 1977, pp. 7–8.

"The Chief of the Six Nations." *New Age* 18 (1913):382–85.

Denslow, William R. *Freemasonry and the American Indian*, 1956. (Originally published in *Transactions of the Missouri Lodge of Research* 13.)

Denslow, William R. *Ten Thousand Famous Freemasons* IV. Reprinted from the *Transactions of the Missouri Lodge of Research* for the Educational Bureau of the Royal Arch Mason Magazine (Trenton, Mo., 1959), p. 309.

"Ely Samuel Parker: From Sachem to Brigadier General." *New York State and the Civil War* I (4) (Oct. 1961): 1–5.

Felton, Harold W. *Ely S. Parker: Spokesman for the Senecas*. New York: Dodd, Mead and Co., 1973. (A juvenile book based on Arthur C. Parker's *Life of General Ely S. Parker*.)

FitzSimons, Neal. "Do-Ne-Ho-Geh-Weh: Seneca Sachem and Civil Engineer." *Civil Engineering* 43 (6) (June 1973): 98.

Furman, McDonald. "A Remarkable History: Some Account of the Federal Officer Who Engrossed General Grant's Terms of Surrender at Appomattox." *Education* XV (7) (Mar. 1895): 420–22.

Gertz, Elmer. "Three Galena Generals," *Journal of the Illinois State Historical Society* Vol. L (1) (Spring 1957): 24–35.

Guernsey, A. H. "The Red Jacket Medal." *Harper's New Monthly Magazine* XXXII (Feb. 1866):323–26.

Hewitt, J. N. B. Review of *The Life of General Ely S. Parker, Last Grand Sachem of the Iroquois and General Grant's Military Secretary* by Arthur C. Parker. *The American Historical Review* XXV (4) (July 1920):732–34.

Hodge, Frederick Webb. *Handbook of American Indians North of Mexico,* Part II. (Smithsonian Institution, Bureau of American Ethnology, Bulletin 30.) Washington: Government Printing Office, 1912.

"An Indian Craftsman." *The Masonic Review* 19 (1858):363–65.

"The Indian Craftsman." *The Masonic Review* 23, (1) (1860):16–17.

"Marking the Grave of Do-ne-ho-geh-weh." *Proceedings of the Buffalo Historical Society* VIII (1905):511–20.

Parker, Arthur C. "Ely S. Parker, Last Grand Sachem." *American Indian* 1 (Winter 1944):11–15.

———. "Ely S. Parker—Man and Mason." *Freemasons.* New York (State) Grand Lodge. American Lodge of Research, *Transactions* 8 (2) (Jan.–Dec., 1961):229–47. (Pages 248–57 of this same issue also include some "Notes on 'Ely S. Parker–Man and Mason'" by Temple R. Hollcroft.)

———. *The Life of General Ely S. Parker, Last Grand Sachem of the Iroquois and General Grant's Military Secretary* XXIII. Buffalo, N.Y.: Publications of the Buffalo Historical Society, 1919.

Parker, Augustus G., ed., *Parker in America, 1630–1910.* Buffalo, N.Y.: Niagara Frontier Publishing Co., 1911.

Parker, Ely S. Obituary in *Proceedings of the Grand Lodge of New York* (1896):10–11.

"Recent Deaths." *Army and Navy Journal,* Sept. 7, 1895, p. 6.

"Red Jacket and Ely Parker." Buffalo Historical Society *Museum Notes* I (1) (Apr.–May 1930):6–7.

Smith, David William. *Ely Samuel Parker, 1828–1895: Military Secretary, Indian Commissioner and Commissioner of Indian Affairs.* Unpublished master's thesis at Southern Illinois University at Carbondale, Ill., June 1973.

[Smith, John C.]. "Honorary Veteran General Ely S. Parker." *Masonic Veterans Association of Illinois* (1896):99–102.

"Some Distinguished Soldiers." *Army and Navy Journal,* Dec. 7, 1895. p. 235.

Yeuell, Donovan. "Ely Samuel Parker." *Dictionary of American Biography* VII Pt. 2. New York: Charles Scribner's Sons, 1934.

THE PUBLISHED WRITINGS OF ELY S. PARKER

Additional Reasons for Purchasing the Indian Mound and Other Territory Adjacent to the State Experimental Station. Geneva, N.Y., 1888.

"Address by General Ely S. Parker, U. S. V." *Final Report of the Battlefield of Gettysburg* I:321–25. New York Monuments Commission for the Battlefields of Gettysburg and Chattanooga. Albany: J. B. Lyon Co., 1900.

"The Character of Grant." *Personal Recollections of the War of the Rebellion,* ed. James Grant Wilson and Titus Munson Coan, vol. I:344–48. New York: New York Commandery of the Loyal Legion of the United States, 1891.

"The Cornplanter Tomahawk in the State Collection." *Fourth Annual Report of the Regents of the University* [of the State of New York]" (1850). Senate Doc. No. 30, pp. 99–101.

General Ely S. Parker's Narrative [of the Surrender at Appomattox Court House]. Printed as a souvenir of the Ulysses S. Grant Birthday Celebration, New York City, Apr. 27, 1893.

Report of Hon. E. S. Parker, Commissioner of Indian Affairs, to the Hon. Secretary of the Interior, on the Communication of William Welsh, Esq., Relative to the Management of Indian Affairs. Washington: Joseph L. Pearson, 1870 [actually 1871].

(With O. O. Howard). "Some Reminiscences of Grant." *McClure's Magazine* II (6) (May 1894):532–35.

"Writings of General Parker," *Proceedings of the Buffalo Historical Society* VIII (1905):520–36.

GENERAL

Abel, Annie Heloise. *The American Indian Under Reconstruction.* Cleveland: Arthur H. Clarke, 1925.

American Journal of Numismatics: "Red Jacket's Medal." XX (2) (Oct. 1885):25–26; "The Red Jacket Medal." XXV (4) (Apr. 1891):102; "Red Jacket Medals." XXI (3) (Jan. 1897):84–85.

Annual Catalogue of Cayuga Academy, 1841–42.

Annual Register of Officers and Members of the Society of Colonial Wars. New York, Jan. 1895.

Art and Sculpture of James Edward Kelly, 1855–1933, Book One. New York: Robert Bruce, 1934.

Babcock, A. Emerson. *Isaiah Babcock, Sr. and His Descendants.* New York: Eaton and Mains, 1903.

Badeau, Adam. *Grant in Peace, From Appomattox to Mount McGregor: A Personal Memoir,* 1887. Reprinted by Books for Libraries Press, Freeport, N.Y., 1971.

Bale, Florence Gratiot. *Historic Galena: Yesterday and Today.* Galena, Ill.: Harbin and Harbin, 1939.

Banks, Elizabeth V. H. *This is Fairfield, 1639–1940.* New Haven: Walker-Rackliff, 1960.

Belden, Bauman L. *Indian Peace Medals Issued in the United States*. New York: American Numismatic Society, 1927.

Birdseye, Clarence F., et al., eds., *Annotated Consolidated Laws of the State of New York as Amended to January 1, 1910* II. New York: Banks Law Publishing, 1909.

Bode, Carl. *Midcentury America: Life in the 1850s*. Carbondale and Edwardsville, Ill.: Southern Illinois University Press, 1972.

Briggs, Emily Edson. *The Olivia Letters: Being Some History of Washington City for Forty Years as Told by the Letters of a Newspaper Correspondent*. New York: Neale, 1906.

Brown, Dee. *Fort Phil Kearny: An American Saga*. New York: G. P. Putnam's Sons, 1962.

Cadwallader, Sylvanus. *Three Years with Grant*. Edited by Benjamin P. Thomas. New York: Alfred A. Knopf, 1956.

"Camp at Syracuse, New York." Barnum's *Illustrated News*, Sept. 17, 1853, pp. 148–49.

The Case of the Seneca Indians in the State of New York. Philadelphia: Merrihew and Thompson, 1840.

Catton, Bruce. *Grant Takes Command*. Boston: Little, Brown, 1969.

Cauble, Frank P. *The Proceedings Connected with the Surrender of the Army of Northern Virginia, April, 1865*. Appomattox Court House National Historical Park, 1962 (reproduced by National Technical Information Service, Springfield, Va.).

Cheney, Newel. *History of the Ninth Regiment, New York Volunteer Cavalry*. Jamestown, N.Y.: Martin Merz and Son, 1901.

Chipman, Norton P. *Argument of N. P. Chipman on Behalf of Hon. E. S. Parker, Commissioner of Indian Affairs*. Washington: Powell, Ginck, 1871.

Chittenden, Hiram, and Richardson, Alfred Talbot. *Life, Letters and Travels of Father Pierre-Jean DeSmet S. J.* Four volumes. New York: Francis P. Harper, 1905.

Clarke, Noah T. *The Wampum Belt Collection of the New York State Museum*. Albany: The University of the State of New York, 1931.

Dana, Charles A. *Recollections of the Civil War*. With a new introduction by Paul M. Angle. New York: Collier Books, 1963.

Declaration of the Seneca Nation of Indians, Changing Their Form of Government, and Adopting a Constitutional Charter. Dec. 4, 1848.

Dubuque, Iowa, City Directory for 1860.

Dunlap, Lloyd A. "The Grant-Lee Surrender Correspondence." *Manuscripts* XXI (2) (Spring 1969):79–91.

Ege, Robert J. *Tell Baker to Strike Them Hard!* Bellevue, Nebr.: Old Army Press, 1970.

Ellis, John B. *The Sights and Secrets of the National Capital*. Chicago: Jones, Junkin, 1869.

Eyres, Lawrence E. "Harriet Maxwell Converse." *The Chemung Historical Journal* III (2) (Dec. 1957):379–83.

Fenton, William N. "Harriet Maxwell Converse." *Notable American Women, 1607–1950: A Biographical Dictionary* I:375–77. Cambridge, Mass.: Harvard University Press, 1971.

————, ed. *Parker on the Iroquois.* Syracuse, N.Y.: Syracuse University Press, 1968.

Forsyth, George A., "The Closing Scene at Appomattox Court House." *Harper's New Monthly Magazine* XCVI (575) (Apr. 1898): 700–11.

Fritz, Henry E. *The Movement for Indian Assimilation, 1860–1890.* Philadelphia: University of Pennsylvania Press, 1963.

"Galena and Its Lead Mines." *Harper's New Monthly Magazine* XXXII (192) (May 1866): 681–96.

Grant, Ulysses S. *Personal Memoirs of Ulysses S. Grant.* Two volumes. New York: Charles L. Webster, 1886.

The History of Jo Daviess County, Illinois. Chicago: H. F. Kett, 1878.

Holton, Gladys Reid. *The Genesee Valley Canal.* Brockport, N.Y.: Stylus Graphics, 1971.

Howard, Hamilton Gay. *Civil War Echoes: Character Sketches and State Secrets by a United States Senator's Son and Secretary.* Washington: Howard, 1907.

Johnson, Elias. *Legends, Traditions and Laws, of the Iroquois, or Six Nations, and History of the Tuscarora Indians.* Lockport, N.Y.: Union Printing and Publishing, 1881.

Kelsey, Rayner Wickersham. *Friends and the Indians, 1655–1917.* Philadelphia: The Associated Executive Committee of Friends on Indian Affairs, 1917.

Lewis, Lloyd. *Captain Sam Grant.* Boston: Little, Brown, 1950.

Loubat, J. F. *The Medallic History of the United States of America, 1776–1876.* Two volumes. New York: Published by the Author, 1878.

The Lyndonville High School Annual. Lyndonville, New York, No. 1, June 1907.

Manley, Henry S. "Buying Buffalo From the Indians." *New York History* XXVIII (3) (July 1947):313–29.

Mardock, Robert Winston. *The Reformers and the American Indian.* Columbia, Mo.: University of Missouri Press, 1971.

Marshall, Charles. "The Last Days of Lee's Army." *The Century Magazine* LXIII (6) (Apr. 1902):932–35.

Morgan, Lewis Henry. *League of the Ho-de-no-sau-nee, or Iroquois.* Secaucus, N.J.: Citadel, 1972. (Reprint of the original 1851 edition.)

Morris, Charles, ed. *The Makers of Philadelphia.* Philadelphia, 1894.

Myrtle, Minnie. *The Iroquois, or the Bright Side of Indian Character.* New York: Appleton, 1859.

Nevins, Allan. "Where We Stand: Civil War Scholarship." *A Portion of That Field.* Urbana, Ill.: University of Illinois Press, 1967.

New York State Baptist Convention, *Annual Reports of the Tonawanda Indian Mission*, 1829, 1836–37.

New York (State) Engineer and Surveyor. *Annual Report on Canals*, 1850–55.

"Notes on the United States Since the War." *The British Quarterly Review* XLII (July and Oct. 1865):433–97.

"Obsequies of Red Jacket at Buffalo, October 9th, 1884." *Transactions of the Buffalo Historical Society* III (1885).

Phisterer, Frederick. *New York in the War of the Rebellion, 1861 to 1865*. Third edition. Six volumes. Albany: J. B. Lyon Co., State Printers, 1912.

Porter, Horace. *Campaigning with Grant*, ed. Wayne C. Temple. New York: Bonanza Books by arrangement with Indiana University Press, 1961.

Prucha, Francis Paul. *Indian Peace Medals in American History*. Madison: The State Historical Society of Wisconsin, 1971.

Quaife, Milo Milton, ed. *The Diary of James K. Polk During His Presidency, 1845 to 1849*. Chicago: A. C. McClurg, 1910.

Rahill, Peter J. *The Catholic Indian Missions and Grant's Peace Policy, 1870–1884*. The Catholic University of America, Studies in American Church History, vol. 41. Washington: Catholic University of America Press, 1953.

Randall, James G., ed. *The Diary of Orville Hickman Browning* II. (Collections of the Illinois State Historical Library, Vol. XXII.) Springfield, Ill.: Illinois State Historical Library, 1933.

"The Recent Changes in the Indian Bureau." *The Nation*, Aug. 17, 1871, pp. 100–01.

"Red Jacket, or Sagoyewatha, 1751–1830, Chief of the Senecas." *Magazine of American History* XXIII (6) (June 1890):494–96.

Register of the Military Order of the Loyal Legion of the United States. Boston: Commandery of the State of Massachusetts, 1906.

Resek, Carl. *Lewis Henry Morgan: American Scholar*. Chicago: University of Chicago Press, 1960.

Richardson, James D. *A Compilation of the Messages and Papers of the Presidents, Prepared Under the Direction of the Joint Committee on Printing, of the House and Senate, Pursuant to an Act of the Fifty-second Congress of the United States* IX. New York: Bureau of National Literature, 1897.

Richardson, James F. *The New York Police: Colonial Times to 1901*. New York: Oxford University Press, 1970.

Riis, Jacob A. *The Making of an American*. New York: The Macmillan Co. New edition, published Oct. 1924.

Rochester Historical Society. *Publication Fund Series* IV (1925).

Rushmore, Elsie Mitchell. *The Indian Policy During Grant's Administrations*. Jamaica Queensborough, N.Y.: Marion, 1914.

Schoolcraft, Henry R. *Notes on the Iroquois or Contributions to the*

Statistics, Aboriginal History, Antiquities and General Ethnology of Western New York. New York Senate Doc. No. 24. New York: Bartlett and Welford, 1846.

Seaver, James E. *Life of Mary Jemison: Deh-he-wa-mis.* Fourth edition. New York and Auburn: Miller, Orton and Mulligan. Rochester: D. M. Dewey, 1856.

"The Senecas in the War of 1812." *Proceedings of the New York State Historical Association* XV (1916):78–90.

Severance, Frank H. "Work of the Buffalo Historical Society." *Magazine of American History* XXIII (5) (May 1890):411–12.

Signor, Isaac S. *Landmarks of Orleans County, New York.* Syracuse, N.Y.: D. Mason, 1894.

Slattery, Charles Lewis. *Felix Reville Brunot.* New York: Longmans, Green, 1901.

Smith, H. Perry. *History of the City of Buffalo and Erie County* II, Syracuse, N.Y.: D. Mason, 1884.

Sparks, David S., ed. *Inside Lincoln's Army: The Diary of Marsena Rudolph Patrick, Provost Marshall General, Army of the Potomac.* New York: Thomas Yoseloff, 1964.

Stanley, Henry M. *My Early Travels and Adventures in America and Asia* I. Second edition. London: Sampson Low, Marston, 1895.

State Historian of New York. *Second Annual Report, 1897.* Albany: Wynkoop Hallenbeck Crawford, State Printers.

Stone, William L. *The Life and Times of Sa-go-ye-wat-ha, or Red Jacket.* Albany, N.Y.: J. Munsell, 1866.

Tatum, Lawrie. *Our Red Brothers and the Peace Policy of President Ulysses S. Grant.* Lincoln, Nebr.: University of Nebraska Press, 1970.

Trumble, Alfred. "An American Artist." *The Catholic World* LVIII (343) (Oct. 1893):65–80.

Turnbull, Everett R. *The Rise and Progress of Freemasonry in Illinois, 1783–1952.* Grand Lodge of Illinois, 1952.

Wallace, Anthony F. C. *The Death and Rebirth of the Seneca.* New York: Vintage, 1972.

Waltmann, Henry G., "Circumstantial Reformer: President Grant and the Indian Problem." *Arizona and the West* XIII (4) (Winter 1971):323–42.

Welsh, William, et al. *Taopi and His Friends or the Indians' Wrongs and Rights.* Philadelphia: Claxton, Remsen and Haffelfinger, 1869.

Weygant, Charles H. *The Sacketts of America: Their Ancestors and Descendants, 1630–1907.* Newburgh, N.Y., 1907.

Whitford, Noble E. *History of the Canal System of the State of New York Together with Brief Histories of the Canals of the United States and Canada.* Albany, N.Y.: Brandow, 1906.

Whitman, Walt. *The Works of Walt Whitman, the Deathbed Edition.* Two volumes. New York: Funk and Wagnalls, 1968.

Wilson, Edmund. *Apologies to the Iroquois.* New York: Vintage, 1960.

Wilson, James Grant, and Coan, Titus Munson, eds. *Personal Recollections of the War of the Rebellion: Addresses Delivered Before the New York Commandery of the Loyal Legion of the United States, 1883–91.* Four volumes. New York: Published by the Commandery, 1891.

Wilson, James Harrison, *The Life of Charles A. Dana.* New York: Harper and Brothers, 1907.

———. *The Life of John A. Rawlins.* New York: Neale, 1916.

———. *Under the Old Flag.* Two volumes. New York: Appleton, 1912.

Wood, Norman B. *Lives of Famous Indian Chiefs.* Chicago: L. W. Walter, 1906.

Young, John Russell. *Around the World with General Grant.* Two volumes. New York: American News, 1879.

Index